Crisis of Empire
Britain and America in the Eighteenth Century

Jeremy Black

continuum

Continuum UK, The Tower Building, 11 York Road, London SE1 7NX
Continuum US, 80 Maiden Lane, Suite 704, New York, NY 10038

www.continuumbooks.com

First published 2008
Paperback edition 2010

British Library Cataloguing-in-Publication Data
A catalogue record for this book is available from the British Library.

ISBN: PB: 978-1-4411-0445-8

Typeset by Pindar NZ, Auckland, New Zealand
Printed and bound in India by Replika Press Pvt Ltd

CRISIS OF EMPIRE

Contents

Preface   vii

Introduction: Seventeenth-Century Background   1

1 The Growth of British North America, 1700–38   23

2 Imperial Rivalries, 1739–53   51

3 The Defeat of France, 1754–60   69

4 Gathering Crisis, 1760–74   89

5 Civil War, 1775–8   123

6 France and America Win, 1778–83   155

7 After the Revolution   173

8 Conclusions   183

   Notes   185
   Selected Further Reading   205
   Index   209

For Virginia friends

Preface

Britain and the USA help define much of world history in recent centuries, and the relationship between the two is crucial to this history. This book focuses on a key period of this relationship, one that moulded the character both of the British Empire and of the USA, and thus of this relationship. The rise and crises of empires will always fascinate the observer because in their fate we see much of human history. Certainly, the struggle of and for empire in the eighteenth century was key to the fate of North America and, more generally, to that of the West Indies and the North Atlantic. British victory followed by the American Revolution helped define and delimit the modern world. At the European level, the players were Britain, France and Spain, each eager for predominance and for advantages such as trade, land and prestige. Within North America, there were the local agents of these powers but also their subjects, who had interests and views of their own. There were also the Native Americans who were more than simply the passive victims of European expansion. Instead, they interacted with the Europeans and helped shape the image of the American interior.

This book focuses on the relationship between Britain and the 13 colonies that were to be the basis for the United States of America. Yet in doing so there is an awareness of wider resonances, within North America and further afield. As far as the 13 colonies are concerned, there is a determined effort to see developments not simply in terms of the colonists, but also to give due weight to both Native and African Americans. This reflects current interests, but is also an important context for the relationship under discussion. Indeed, Queen Elizabeth II captured some of this in her speech to a Special Joint Session of the General Assembly of Virginia at Richmond on 4 May 2007:

> When I visited fifty years ago, we celebrated the 350th anniversary [of the foundation of Jamestown in 1607] largely from the perspective of those settlers, in terms of the exploration of new worlds, the spread of values and of the English language, and the sacrifice of those early pioneers.
>
> These remain great attributes, and we still appreciate their impact today. But 50 years on, we are now in a position to reflect more candidly on the Jamestown legacy.
>
> Human progress rarely comes without cost. And those early years in Jamestown, when three great civilizations came together for the first time, Western European, Native American and African, released a train of events which continues to have a profound

social impact, not only in the United States, but also in the United Kingdom and Europe
… It is right that we continue to reassess the meaning of historical events in the changing
context of the present, not least in this, the 200th anniversary, in the United Kingdom,
of the Act of Parliament to abolish the trans-Atlantic slave trade.

The title of this book echoes one by Ian Christie, and, in so doing, I reflect on
his scholarship and support: Ian was one of my referees. I have also benefited
greatly from the comments of Robin Baird-Smith, Guy Chet, Bill Gibson, Kent
Hackmann, Richard Middleton, Andrew O'Shaughnessy, Julie Sweet and Neil
York on an earlier draft, and of Jeremy Gregory and Elizabeth Mancke on a
section of the draft. Rick Schneid provided helpful advice. A particular memory
of Anglo–American links during the writing of this book came from a pleasant
day spent at Wroxton Abbey, lecturing on Lord North, George III, and the War
of American Independence, for the 50th anniversary meeting of the Banbury
Historical Society. Wroxton was a seat of the Norths, and Lord North was MP for
Banbury. As a reminder of the multiple nature of Anglo–American links, Wroxton
is now the British campus of an American university. I have also benefited from
lecturing at the Robert H. Smith International Center for Jefferson Studies at
Brigham Young University, and the Lexington Historical Society.

It has been a great pleasure to visit the USA repeatedly since the mid-1960s, in
some cases up to seven times every year. I have benefited enormously from the
opportunities offered by lecture invitations, and from the hospitality of American
friends. Visiting and revisiting in good company many of the places mentioned
in this book has been a cause of particular pleasure. In the period when I was
writing this book in 2007–8, places visited included Boston, Concord, Newport,
Lexington, New Haven, Pensacola, Philadelphia and Worcester.

In dedicating this book to Virginia friends, I am thanking not only them
but also many others. I have been fortunate to visit Virginia many times since
1988, not least in order to lecture in Charlottesville, Fairfax, Fredericksburg,
Harrisonburg, Lexington, Norfolk, Richmond, Williamsburg and Yorktown. It
is a particular pleasure to remember the hospitality of Porter Blakemore, Frank
Hamilton, Brenda Laclair and Bill Marshall, and the enjoyment of vistas from
the sparkling waters of the James River at spring fullness to the smoky light of
autumn evenings in Bath County.

Introduction: Seventeenth-Century Background

'Have we some strange Indian with the great tool come to court, the women so besiege us?' The porter's question in Shakespeare's play *Henry VIII* (1613)[1] reflected the strength of English curiosity about the outside world soon after the foundation of a colony called Virginia. Compared to Portugal and Spain, the English came late to imperial power across the oceans, but, from the late fifteenth century, they were interested in what was eventually to be seen as North America. Fishing expeditions from Bristol, England's leading Atlantic port, may have reached Newfoundland's bountiful offshore Grand Banks, if not North America, in the 1480s or 1490s. The first precise information, however, relates to the Italian John Cabot who sailed west from Bristol in the ship *Matthew* in 1497, hoping to reach the wealth of Asia reported by Marco Polo and others who had travelled east, not west, from Europe. Cabot arrived, instead, probably in Newfoundland, his 'new found' land.

Newfoundland was to be a major source of wealth for England, but of fish, and not the bullion the Spaniards obtained from their conquests of Mexico and Peru. The fisheries eventually led large numbers of ships and men to cross the Atlantic and return each year. This resulted in two important foundations for future English activity: first, knowledge about Atlantic navigation, specifically the currents, winds and coastlines of the North Atlantic, and, secondly, a sense that sailing across the Atlantic was normal. With their deep-sea range, the Newfoundland fisheries were seen as particularly important to the strategic strength of the country, indeed as a 'nursery' of sailors, for both war and peace. Newfoundland, nevertheless, was on the Atlantic margin of the Americas, and there was scant need for significant permanent settlements there. Humphrey Gilbert claimed Newfoundland for Elizabeth I of England in 1583, but he perished at sea before he could return to England to make good on his claim, and subsequently it proved hard to transform a scattering of fishing stations into a settlement colony.

Ambitions for gain and expansion also led to English interest in lands farther south. A breakdown in relations with Spain was important in the situation. As tension rose in the 1570s, privateering attacks on Spanish trade and settlements in the New World became more common. War followed, from 1585 to 1604, the key issue being Elizabeth's support for the eventually successful Protestant Dutch rebels against the rule of Philip II of Spain.

War with Spain provided an opportunity for colonization. Efforts were made
to establish a colony on the American mainland, naming it Virginia in honour
of Elizabeth. In 1585, 108 colonists were landed on Roanoke Island, in what is
now North Carolina, but they found it difficult to feed themselves, had tense
relations with the Native American population, and were taken off the following
year. Another attempt was made in 1587, but when a relief ship arrived in 1590,
it found the village deserted: disease, starvation or Native Americans may have
wiped out the colonists. Nevertheless, the positive impression created by Thomas
Hariot's *A Brief and True Report of the New Found Land of Virginia* (1588) and
other reports encouraged fresh efforts to establish a colony, as did the sense that
England was missing out on the opportunities won by Spain.[2]

It was not until a base was established by the Virginia Company at Jamestown
in the Chesapeake in 1607 that a permanent English colony was founded on
the eastern seaboard. Spain regarded this colony as an invasion of its rights and
protested about its foundation, but, although the defences at Jamestown were
prepared to resist Spanish attack, it did not come. Virginia was too distant from
the centres of Spanish power, the closest of which was at St Augustine on the
Atlantic coast of Florida.

At Jamestown, there were heavy initial losses of settlers, but largely owing to
the impact of disease in an unfamiliar environment.[3] Nevertheless, the colony
expanded as a result of the continued arrival of new settlers from England,
without which it would have foundered, and of the willingness to put an
emphasis on growing food. Prospects from tobacco cultivation encouraged the
expansion of settlement, which concerned the Native Americans. Cutting down
woodland hit the Native American economy, while they were angered by the
settlers' failure to trade with them on acceptable terms.[4] After much bloodshed,
nearby Native American resistance was overcome in 1622–4 and 1644.

Yet, no gold or silver was found in Virginia, nor was it possible to trade with
the Spanish colonies in order to obtain sugar and tobacco that could be profitably
sold in England, as Spain was determined to exclude foreign traders. The bankrupt Virginia Company failed in 1624, an important indicator of the problems
posed by settlement in North America. The company's charter was revoked and
control over Virginia went to the Crown, being exercised by a royal governor.

The second English colony on Chesapeake Bay was Maryland, which was chartered in 1632. The royal charter, issued by Charles I to Cecil, 2nd Lord Baltimore,
gave the proprietor considerable powers that owed something to the model
of medieval palatine powers such as those of the Prince Bishops of Durham.
The selection of Maryland reflected the recently deceased George, 1st Lord
Baltimore's disillusionment with the climate and prospects of Newfoundland
and the opposition by Virginia to his establishing himself in that colony. The new
colony was seen as a place of refuge for English Catholics, and the first settlement

was established in 1634. The following year, however, reflecting the challenges to authority on the frontiers of Empire, Leonard Calvert, Maryland's Governor and the brother of the 2nd Lord, had to overcome opposition from the English traders based on Kent Island on the eastern side of the Chesapeake.

Given the constitutional issues that were to divide the Empire in the 1770s, and the frequently reiterated claim by present-day Americans, such as President George W. Bush in his speech during the 400th anniversary commemoration of the foundation of Jamestown,[5] it is important to note that liberty was not the key theme in the foundation of English North America. Indeed, in Virginia and elsewhere, the use of the (more authoritarian) Roman law derivatives in the conceptualization of the imperial sovereignty of the English Crown provided a central coherence in terms of the Crown's legal rights to newfound lands. Far from being uniquely liberal, this legal framework matched those of other European states. It ensured that the English colonies were united in a 'central, imperial and legal authority',[6] a framework that was eventually to prove insufficiently flexible to confront the challenges that were to face the Empire.

Meanwhile, another strand in English North America was developing in a very different fashion. In colder waters than those off Virginia, a settlement created in 1602 by Bartholomew Gosnold, on an island near what he had named Cape Cod, suffered because of Gosnold's failure to develop trading contacts with the Native Americans and, in the face of the latter's hostility, it had to be abandoned.[7] Moreover, a trading base on the Sagadahoc River on the Kennebec River in modern Maine, founded on behalf of the Plymouth Company in 1607, was abandoned the following year.

In 1620, however, the Pilgrim Fathers, a group of Protestant nonconformist separatists, sailed from Plymouth in England on the *Mayflower*. They made a landing at Cape Cod, and established a settlement at what they termed Plymouth on the west side of Cape Cod. The settlers were a mix of so-called saints and strangers, essentially a 40/60 split, with the former mostly nonconformists who had taken refuge in Leiden (in the Netherlands) and the latter recruited by Thomas Weston and the Merchant Adventurers who put up much of the money and handled the negotiations. This colony never had a charter from the Crown, and only the shakiest of agreements with the Virginia Company, which lay claim to the continent from the St Croix River on the Bay of Fundy to Cape Fear (North Carolina), and with the Council for New England. The Plymouth settlement, nevertheless, began the development of a colony in New England, a term first used in 1614 by Captain John Smith, when he described the coastline east and north of the Hudson River, and popularized by his *Description of New England* (1616).

The settlers sought to create a godly agrarian world, and believed that their righteousness made them more entitled to the land than the Native Americans;

although it was not only Protestant nonconformist settlers who saw Native Americans as savages.[8] Repeating the situation after the Spaniards had arrived in the Americas, the New England settlers were helped greatly by the impact on the Native Americans of smallpox, or what was probably smallpox, in 1616–18 and 1634. These epidemics proved devastating for the Algonquians, Abenaki and others. Alongside the losses in numbers, disease brought a psychic crisis, with a sense of powerlessness and of weakness in the face of the magic of the English settlers.

The separatists were followed by other settlers who, although not separatists, were also zealous for a godly commonwealth. As a result, they were increasingly uncomfortable with the High Church activism in England championed by William Laud, Bishop of London from 1628 to 1633 and Archbishop of Canterbury from 1633 to 1645. These more mainstream Protestants, sponsored by the Massachusetts Bay Company established in 1629, founded Boston in 1630. Thanks to settlement in the 1630s, when, due to ecclesiastical pressure in England for conformity, migration to the American colonies was far greater than in the 1620s, this colony expanded rapidly. New settlements included Concord (1635) and Exeter (1638).

The Native Americans were unable to confront the growth of the English presence successfully, while the settlers' brutal defeat of the Pequots in a brief war in 1637 confirmed the Puritans' position and their conviction of divine support. This was important to the character of New England, but so also was a suspicion of the authority of the Crown. A longstanding tension over the legitimacy and nature of secular power was to be important to this key strand in British America.

Settlement spread, for example, in the Connecticut River Valley from 1634. Hartford was founded there in 1636, followed by New Haven in 1638. The spread of settlement in part arose from religious division. Connecticut and Rhode Island were established as breakaway settlements from Massachusetts in response to differences over Church government. Rhode Island was founded in 1636 by Roger Williams who had been expelled from Massachusetts for preaching religious toleration. This reflected the extent to which the anti-authoritarian character of the New England ethos had a fissiparous quality. Furthermore, religion provided both a site of control, not least moral control, and a cause of divisiveness. At the same time, entrepreneurial factors, including land speculation, played an important role in the English settlement of New England.[9]

With this spread, a new landscape of English townships, agrarian control, flora and fauna, including rats and bees, was created.[10] Trees, crucially, were replaced by worked land, with the wood transformed into products such as barrels and masts. By 1642, there were over 15,000 English settlers in New England, and by 1650 nearly 23,000; although more settlers went to the Chesapeake and the West

Indies than to New England. Indeed, but for the differential impact of disease on mortality rates, the West Indies would have dominated English settlement in the New World, whereas the mortality rates in the Chesapeake were comparable to those of London.

The rate of migration in part reflected the severe economic problems of early seventeenth-century Europe. The population rise of the previous century had led to pauperism and, for much of the population, there was scant prospect of advancement. This encouraged emigration, although there were important variations. Whereas those who went to Virginia and the West Indies were frequently young single men, families headed by older men dominated the emigration to New England, a pattern that was to be repeated during the following century.

An emphasis on spreading inland settlement can lead to an underrating of the role of ports, especially Boston, and the continued transoceanic links with England. Ships brought immigrants, products, money and news, and their likely arrival was the focus of continual discussion and concern in the colonies. On the English side, the ports, particularly Bristol, were, in turn, important in spreading news and opinions about North America.[11]

In contrast to New England, the bleaker environment of eastern Canada proved unpropitious for Sir William Alexander of Menstrie, who, in 1621, was granted a charter giving him and his heirs a claim to a New Scotland in what are now the Maritime Provinces of Canada. The charter was renewed by Charles I in 1625, but it proved impossible to establish a successful settlement on the south shore of the Bay of Fundy. Alexander's son, also William, established a colony at Port Royal in the Bay of Fundy in 1628, but, like Québec, which had been captured from France in 1629, it was handed over to France in 1632 as part of the peace agreement at the close of the unsuccessful war. The French had already captured the settlement established in 1629 at Port aux Balemes in Cape Breton. Although in 1633 he gained the title Viscount Canada, Alexander died bankrupt in 1640, and it was the French who founded a settlement at Port Royal that lasted.[12] It was not only French enmity that was the problem. Mild maritime influences lessened the impact of the harsh continental climate, but the growing season became shorter with higher latitudes, and this reduced the appeal of settlement.

At the same time as the English in a state-sanctioned fashion, were founding settlements in North America, other European powers were doing the same. Québec was established by the French in 1608, and New Amsterdam (later New York) and Albany by the Dutch in 1614 and 1624 respectively. In the Delaware Valley, the Swedes founded Fort Christina in 1638.

The spread of settlement affected the Native American population. One result of the greater commercial opportunities the Europeans provided for them was an increase in warfare between the tribes, as they sought to control contact with the Europeans, and the goods they offered, and because there was an inherent changeability in relations between tribes. European involvement in the warfare resulted in problems, because the Native Americans were well attuned to fighting in the unmapped hinterland,[13] and their general lack of fixed battle positions made it difficult for the Europeans to devise clear tactical goals in combat, and also ensured there was no role for European volley fire, which was only effective on open ground. Furthermore, as experts with bows and arrows, the eastern Native American peoples were readily able to make the transition to muskets, which were easier to aim, and the bullets of which, unlike arrows, were less likely to be deflected by brush and could not be dodged. These factors combined to reduce the advantage in military technology the settlers might have possessed. In the Pequot War of 1637, the overwhelming superiority in firearms of the English helped bring them victory in the Connecticut River valley, but also the fact that their enemy was not supported by other tribes, especially the Narragansetts.

From the 1640s, a decade in which the Virginia and Maryland assemblies were prohibiting the arming of slaves by their masters, the spread of firearms among Native Americans made them even more effective opponents of European colonists.[14] The French originally refused to supply firearms, but, after an initial prohibition, the Dutch began trading them, and, as warfare increased in scope, restrictions on the supply of firearms decreased. In the early 1640s, the French began to sell muskets to baptized Native American allies to strengthen them against the Mohawks, who themselves traded freely for Dutch muskets after agreements in 1643 and 1648. By 1648, the Mohawks had amassed at least 800 muskets. Moreover, the Swedes provided the Susquehannock of the Delaware Valley with cannon, and they used them against both Iroquois and the English. However, this transfer of artillery was unusual and, without cannon, the Native Americans could make little impact on European forts. Warfare between the tribes and their dependence for weapons, alcohol and the sale of furs on the Europeans greatly weakened the Native Americans.

The Europeans were also weakened by disputes between them, but less so than the Native Americans. The mid-century English/British civil wars of 1638 to 1652 were less of a threat to the English Empire than might have been expected due to the extent to which France, Spain and the Dutch were also heavily involved in foreign war and internal turmoil. Nevertheless, the crisis affected the colonies as well as the British Isles. In 1638, in an important act of defiance of imperial authority, Massachusetts refused an order to submit its charter for scrutiny and slighted the condemnation of the charter by the Privy Council. Charles I was considering a forceful response when the crisis of authority in Scotland that led to the outbreak of civil war there gathered pace.

The civil wars disrupted trans-Atlantic links, affecting not only patterns and practices of authority, but also trade, finance, migration and social links. Civil war also constituted a severe psychic storm, both for many individuals and collectively. Aside from trans-Atlantic disruption, there was conflict within the colonies, and in some, for example Maryland in 1645–7, a chaotic breakdown in authority.

Although the Civil Wars weakened the English Empire, they resulted, in England, in a more assertive, republican, government that was in a position to mobilize and assert power. Indeed, by 1650, the English navy had become the largest in the world, a development that was to be continued by the subsequent Cromwellian regime. One of the roles of the fleet was to ensure in 1652 that, in the aftermath of the Civil Wars, Virginia, and, following its example, Maryland, submitted; they had refused to do so in 1650–1.

The new government also sought to develop the colonies in synergy with England. The Navigation Acts of 1650 and 1651 excluded other powers from the trade of the English colonies. War with the Dutch followed in 1652–4, and recorded a marked increase in English naval strength. The English republican empire reknit trans-Atlantic links, although they were different to those under the Stuarts. For example, there was a small Puritan re-emigration, from New England back to England, mainly of gentry and a few ministers.

In 1660, monarchy was restored in the British Isles and in the English colonies, in the person of Charles II, who reigned until 1685. The protectionist legislation of the 1650s was reprised in the Navigation Act of 1660 and the Staple Act of 1663. Colonies were intended by government to help the metropole and were treated accordingly. Any idea of them as communities, let alone separate communities, did not arise in London. Indeed, it was a minority view even for many of those directly involved in Empire. The latter included those who saw themselves as long-term settlers, but also young men who went to the colonies to make money, intending, as many did, to return.

America was not only an investment at the personal level. In addition, a sense of imperial commercial identity developed, and was reflected by the prohibition of exports direct from the colonies to foreign markets, and, instead, the requirement that they be exported to England or one of its colonies. Until the Navigation Act of 1660, 85 per cent of the sugar and 42 per cent of tobacco from the colonies of Bermuda, Virginia and Maryland had been shipped directly to continental European markets.[15]

Conflict also resumed with the Dutch. In 1664, at time of peace, an English squadron under Colonel Richard Nicholls easily captured New Amsterdam, the poorly fortified key centre in Dutch North America, and renamed it New York in honour of Charles II's brother, James, Duke of York, later James II. He had been given the lands between the Connecticut and Delaware rivers in a charter from his brother. The English claimed that they were simply asserting Charles' rights, and that they were not breaching the peace, but control over New Amsterdam was also seen as a way to enforce English protectionist legislation.[16] War formally broke out in 1665. The Treaty of Breda of 1667 that ended the conflict confirmed English possession of New York.

During the Third Anglo-Dutch War (1672–4), the Dutch easily recaptured New York in 1673, but, at the end of the war, the town was returned to England by the Peace of Westminster. Thereafter, the English/British Crown remained in power there for just over a century.

North America was also an increasingly important area of migration. By 1700, there were about 210,000 Europeans in English North America. In part, this expansion in numbers reflected the conquest of New Netherland which had, in the 1650s, already acquired the New Sweden established from 1638 in the Delaware Valley. New Netherland was a conquest organized by the English as two colonies, New York and New Jersey.

In addition, there was a burst of English colonization, with the establishment and settlement of new colonies: Carolina (1663), Delaware (1664) and Pennsylvania (1681). Philadelphia was founded the following year. Alongside this, there was a reorganization of existing colonies. Connecticut, founded in 1636, and New Haven (1638) became the colony of Connecticut in 1662; Plymouth (1620) and Massachusetts Bay (1630) followed as the Commonwealth of Massachusetts in 1691, and New Hampshire separated from Massachusetts in 1680.

The new colonies expanded the range of political experiments that English North America represented. Pennsylvania was given by Charles II to William Penn as what was in effect the biggest private estate in the world, but, as such, it provided Penn with the opportunity to try out his views on preserving virtue through public policy and public policy by virtue.[17] Pennsylvania was to be a Quaker refuge, but the potential radicalism this entailed was contained by insisting that Pennsylvania's laws had to be monitored by the Privy Council. James, Duke of York resisted granting a representative assembly to New York, which had not had one under the Dutch, but got one in 1683.

Virginia and Maryland meanwhile expanded as a result of the continued arrival of new settlers, and as tobacco became their major crop. These colonies centred on Chesapeake Bay, with its bountiful waters, mild climate and the extensive waterways which meant that plantations had ready access to trade. Indeed, in the seventeenth century, both colonies clung to the Bay, although the low population density of free settlers (as opposed to their slaves and indentured servants) ensured a more dispersed settlement pattern than that in New England.

Tobacco's limited capital requirements and high profitability encouraged settlers (more than went to New England) and investment; and, because it was an export crop, the links with England were underlined. The needs and difficulties of tobacco cultivation and trade, however, created serious problems for farmers, contributing to Bacon's Rebellion (see p. 14), and these problems ensured particular sensitivity to labour availability and cost. The demand for labour and the long terms of service exacted in return for providing transportation to Virginia led to dealing in servants, and the hiring of servants or indentured labour was harsher and more degrading than in England. This was a key aspect of the social politics of seventeenth-century Virginia.[18]

Prior to the 1680s, savings in the costs of the production and marketing of tobacco were important in expanding the market and thus encouraging the growth of Virginia and Maryland. Then there were about three decades of stagnation at a time of rising labour prices, followed, during the eighteenth century, by increased demand, albeit also with rising production costs. Moreover, to complicate the general pattern, booms and busts created serious problems for producers. Alongside this, there was a shifting regional pattern in production.[19]

Booms and busts contributed to social and economic differentiation among the settlers, with the wealthy and those with plentiful credit better able to cope with busts and to profit from booms. This differentiation had political consequences within Virginia, while many of the poor whites moved to other colonies or to the frontier of settlement within Virginia. Furthermore, there were gradations within those who were not poor. The larger planters, for example, tended to maintain their commitment to tobacco, whereas those with less capital diversified into other crops. Everyone planted crops other than tobacco to feed themselves and provide self-sufficiency.

At the same time, the volatility of the colonial economy also affected prominent individuals and families. This encouraged land speculation as well as other attempts to use the colonial system to their own profit. All this contributed to a semi-feudal aspect of North American society. Indeed, rather than seeing this solely with reference to the terms on which colonial grants were made, semi-feudal proprietorship was more widely expressed. This parallels the re-feudalization seen in parts of the Mediterranean, especially southern Italy, and the spread of serfdom in Eastern Europe. There, a determination and ability to control labour in an area where, unlike Western Europe, it was in short supply, as well as to contain labour costs and to profit from the opportunity to export to Western Europe, led to the spread of serfdom. The attitudes and powers of landlords in Eastern Europe were crucial to this spread. Even when serfdom was not at issue, peasants found that they were put under serious pressure due to landlord demands, taxation, debts and market insecurity.

Considering North America alongside the Mediterranean and Eastern Europe is pertinent not only for the slaves of the former (although slaves had no rights, unlike serfs), but also for many of the poor whites, and, in particular, takes note of the different courses resulting from the social politics of English North America. There were, however, contrasts between North America and Eastern Europe, not least that in North America indentured servants were freed on the completion of their service. Moreover, in North America, social differentiation among the free whites was linked not only to control over labour but also to the opportunities for the acquisition of land provided by the open frontier. The prominent were best placed to use political connections in order to acquire land that they could then sell to new settlers or use for members of their family.

The number of English emigrants to North America far outnumbered those to South Asia and West Africa, neither of which attracted settlers, and this emigration greatly accentuated the impact of migration earlier in the century, increasing the number and percentage of non-Native Americans in the English New World. The pace of settlement was higher in the English than in the French North American colonies, because the opportunities in the English colonies were as much a matter of governmental attitude as of agricultural and urban possibilities, although the latter were each less in the French colonies. The English were particularly tolerant of Protestant religious groups outside the established Churches, although the position in individual colonies varied: in Virginia in 1643, Puritan nonconformity was banned, whereas, six years later, Lord Baltimore, the Catholic proprietor of Maryland, had the Assembly enact a law of toleration. Hitherto, the Church of England had been the sole established religion there.

The overall contrast with French religious intolerance helped ensure that, by 1700, despite Britain's population being only about a quarter of that of France, the number of French inhabitants in Canada had risen only to about 10,000. Indeed, many of the Huguenots (Protestants) who fled France after the revocation of the Edict of Nantes (which had given them the right to follow their faith) in 1685 found shelter in England, and some then went to the English colonies, as they could not do to their French counterparts. Moreover, whereas much of the French Catholic population was ready to migrate within France, in contrast, in Britain, not only was there a high degree of internal migration, but there was also a greater willingness to emigrate to, or act as an entrepreneur in, distant areas. Compared with France and Spain, the population, on average, lived closer to the sea, a consequence of Britain's island nature, while London and Bristol, which were central points in the English migration system, also acted as key centres for trans-Atlantic emigration. Thus, the latter was not separate to domestic migration, but, instead, part of the same process.

At the individual level, emigration followed the possibilities created by trade and other contacts. Voluntary emigration, indeed, was a cumulative process, as it made particular use of networks of family, friends and other contacts, especially neighbourhood and religious groups. This provided the collective solidarity that helped individuals overcome the multiple hardships and anxieties of migration and settlement. Voluntary settlement was also encouraged by sponsors, especially the proprietors of colonies, who helped shape the development of particular colonies, giving them a distinctive character that was lacking in the individual English counties. All these factors combined to provide a mass of information about work and settlement in America, although it was difficult to distinguish fact from rumour as Empire always attracted projectors (a lasting feature of American public culture) and flourished on rumour.[20]

Migrants arrived in existing settlements where some settled, finding employment. Others helped push forward the frontier of settlement, taking advantage of the new land made available by victories over Native Americans or expansion at their expense. Earlier territorial claims were given a degree of substance by this advance, although only up to a point. In 1663, Charles II, for example, had granted to eight supporters the proprietorship of a colony from the Atlantic to the Pacific called Carolina.

The reach to the Pacific made sense in terms of works such as John Ferrar's *The Map of Virginia* (1651), which enhanced the appeal of Virginia by suggesting that the New Albion in modern California 'discovered' by Francis Drake on the Pacific and claimed by him for Elizabeth I in 1579 was close by on the other side of the Appalachians. The map proclaimed that it could be reached in ten days' march 'from the head of the James River, over those hills and through the rich adjacent vallies beautified with as profitable rivers, which necessarily must run into the peaceful Indian Sea, maybe discovered to the exceeding benefit of Great Britain'.

Alongside such improbable hopes, knowledge of the interior increased. To the north, the search for the furs that could be lucratively exported to European markets took English and French travellers well beyond their bases on Hudson Bay and on the Great Lakes. The most far-flung journey in the late seventeenth century was that of Henry Kelsey, a member of the Hudson's Bay Company at Fort York. In 1690, he joined a group of Crees on their journey home from trading at the Bay, and, by his return in 1692, had crossed the Saskatchewan River and become the first white man to reach the great grasslands of western Canada. Like other overland journeys, Kelsey's was dependent on the support and knowledge of Native Americans. This symbiotic character was to be downplayed in subsequent discussion of exploration in terms of discovery by Europeans.

The creation of the colony of Carolina, which freed the area from dependence on the colony of Virginia, as well as denying Native American interests, indicated the extent to which English territorial claims bore no relation to the frontier of settlement. The assertion of such claims rested in part on a conviction that the apparent Native American inability or unwillingness to settle and develop land, left America free for imperial acquisition and improvement, and that what was not cultivated was free for settlement.[21] Moreover, the Native American view that the sovereignty of their tribal units could be incorporated into the English political system, clashed with the English perception of Native Americans as subjects and with the colonists' determination to control them.[22]

These beliefs were self-serving, but the sense of the land, especially uncultivated land, as free for English settlement stemmed from a powerful conviction of human responsibility to make the best use of the gifts and opportunities given by God, a religious conviction that helped condition moral, judicial and social assumptions within England and her American colonies. Applied in the latter, in a Christian context that was determined by English norms, these attitudes provided ready guidelines by which most commentators considered Native American mores and practices inadequate, and a similar stance was adopted towards those mores judged, generally unfairly, as inherent to slave society. Thus religion helped provide a sense of providential protection of a new nation, as well as a ranking of peoples and a justification for settlement that prefigured the Social Darwinism seen in the late nineteenth-century heyday of imperialism. This justification also greatly affected the subsequent history of the colonial period, although the recent 400th anniversary of the settlement of Jamestown indicates how attitudes have changed, with a more positive account of the Native Americans now prominent.[23]

English policy toward the Native Americans was inconsistent, and conflict with them was not continuous, not least due to the low density of population, but, where it occurred, the Native Americans were under considerable pressure. In King Philip's War in New England in 1675–6, the settlers were outmatched in forest combat by Native Americans who had adopted firearms, until the settlers began to copy their enemy's tactics and also to make good use of Native American allies. The Native Americans opposed to the settlers suffered from Mohawk hostility, and from disease, starvation, lack of ammunition and relentless settler pressure.[24] The defeated Native Americans became bonded labourers to settlers.[25]

Further south, settler dominance took a different form, with a move towards the use of slaves in the Chesapeake labour system in the decades around 1700. White indentured workers were difficult to retain in the face of the opportunities offered by rapidly spreading English settlement. Demographics also proved a key element in encouraging slavery, namely the fall in the birth rate in England in the 1640s. This affected Chesapeake planters in the early 1660s, with both fewer young men entering the Virginian labour market from England and a rise in real wages in Virginia.[26] Moreover, the English-settler population of the Chesapeake did not grow through natural increase until toward the close of the century. Unlike land, free labour was expensive. These difficulties encouraged the move towards the use of slaves.

An alternative labour source, that of the Native Americans, was hit hard by European diseases, which cut numbers. Furthermore, the Native Americans resisted control. Nevertheless, there was a slave trade in Native Americans, and captured Native Americans were used as slaves: some were sent from Connecticut to Barbados after King Philip's War in 1675–6, while Tuscaroras defeated in Carolina in 1715 were enslaved; but their numbers were inadequate. Seizing them often depended on assistance from allied Native Americans, with the Creeks selling Choctaws and Apalachees to Carolina in the 1700s.[27] African workers were regarded as more effective and industrious than the Native Americans, and commanded higher prices. Under coercion, and disoriented by the experience of seizure and shipment, African slaves proved more controllable than whites and Native Americans, and it was more difficult for the Africans to flee.[28]

The development of slavery interacted with white racism, which contributed to the culture of English North America, although, as with New England Puritanism, there was a strong regional dimension, with slavery concentrated in the Chesapeake and further south. In Virginia, economic advantage and coercive power were linked to a belief that Africans were inherently inferior – an attitude that drew on what was seen as 'their God-given characteristics and the circumstances of their arrival in America'.[29] Poor whites seemed less of a problem when slaves could fill the role of bottom of the heap. The distinction was made readily apparent in law, with punishments made harsher for slaves.

The establishment of Carolina in 1670 led to a strengthening of the slave econo-my of the English Atlantic. The new colony was closely linked to the English West Indies, not least through the port of Charles Town or Charlestown.[30] Carolina provided opportunities for younger sons from the crowded islands, particularly Barbados. The settlers from these islands brought African slaves with them, ensuring that a sizeable African labour force soon developed in the new colony.[31] Carolina became a key exporter of colonial goods, including, from the 1690s, rice; the cultivation of both rice and indigo required large numbers of slaves.[32]

Nevertheless, by 1700, only 23,000 Africans had arrived in English North America, and most of the labour needs were still met by white servants. The crossing distance (and therefore time) to North America, a key index of the profit-ability of the slave trade, was also greater than that from Africa to the Portuguese colony of Brazil, which was the leading slave society in the Americas.

The development of Carolina, following on from the earlier growth of the Chesapeake tobacco trade, greatly helped the New England and Middle Colonies by providing them with a ready economic function. Whatever the impression created by later agrarian commentators, the settlers producing food for their own consumption was not sufficient, as it would not enable the import of essentials from England. Instead, these imports were financed, with profit to the English economy, and the costs of government were met, by taking part in a wider system of economic exchange. In particular, food was shipped to the plantation economies of the South and the West Indies. Aside from the direct role in the slave trade, as well as the presence of slaves in New England and the Middle Colonies, this ensured a close link to the developing economics of the world of slavery. There might be relatively few slaves in North America, compared with the numbers that were to come, but there were large numbers already in the West Indies and they had to be fed. There was also an export from New England and the Middle Colonies of fish, timber (masts) and, eventually, wheat to England.

The politics of the homeland were important in the development of English colonies, and their history in the seventeenth century reflected the instability of England. In both, this was an era of rapid change that challenged existing ideas and institutions, and ensured that developments occurred against a background of instability and crisis. Rather than thinking primarily in terms of a tension between colonial autonomy and English authority, differing political positions spanned the Atlantic. As a result, under Charles II (r. 1660–85), the formal authority of the Crown over the government of Massachusetts was increased, culminating in the nullification of its 1629 charter in 1684; while, conversely, opposition to greater royal authority was seen on both sides of the Atlantic.

This was a period of conflict within the colonies, reflecting both issues of authority and rival interests. In 1676, Bacon's Rebellion occurred among part of the settler population in Virginia. As with problems in some colonies the following century, contention over policy toward Native Americans was linked to questions of control over military force and indeed of who was running the colony. Many of the colonists supported Nathaniel Bacon, a landowner who pressed for firm action against Native Americans and for a rejection of what was seen as the governor's ineffective policy toward them. Virginia was a colony where, since the 1620s, attitudes towards the Native Americans had been distant and, frequently, hostile. The governor, Sir William Berkeley, a wealthy landowner who represented elite interests, was unable to hold Jamestown, and the rebellion only collapsed after Bacon died in October. Bacon's Rebellion indicated the dangers that activism from outside the circles of power posed to public order and elite control, as the unpredictable Bacon both had Jamestown burned down and began recruiting indentured servants and slaves into his army.

The role of the Crown as the ultimate arbiter of control and guarantee of the social hierarchy was seen when Charles II replaced Berkeley with Sir Hubert Jeffreys whom he sent with over 1,000 troops, the first regulars to be stationed in Virginia. Regulars ensured that there was no dependence on militia. The dispatch of this force at a time of international crisis in Europe indicated the importance placed on Virginia.[33] There was a parallel 'Huy and Crye' rebellion in Maryland in 1676, directed against the autocratic and pro-Catholic policies of the proprietor, Lord Baltimore.

As in the British Isles, religion played a role in much of the politics of the period. For example, due in part to a shared Protestantism, there was only limited difficulty when (Dutch) New Netherland became (English-ruled) New York in the 1660s and 1670s, although ethnic divisions were to play a role in New York politics and there were tensions, including Leisler's Rebellion, in the crisis of authority caused by the Glorious Revolution of 1688–9.[34] In the 1670s, the Church of England hoped to establish a diocese in Virginia, even drawing up a deed of appointment of a bishop, but the problems of financing a bishop and establishing his authority were insurmountable.

From his accession in 1685, the attempt by James II of England (and VII of Scotland) to impose autocracy clashed, in both the British Isles and the colonies, with the corporate ideal of government. It also accentuated Protestant suspicions of the intentions of an openly Catholic monarch. In New York, which became a royal colony with his accession, the representative assembly, first convened in 1683, and the Charter of Liberties and Privileges issued at the same time, were both dissolved. James also created a Dominion of New England (1686–9) that sought to give force to royal edicts and to overcome colonial autonomy. As a result, the Navigation Acts, which had been ignored by a number of the colonies, were enforced.

Supported by a company of regular troops in Boston, the Governor, Sir Edmund Andros, who came from an aristocratic and military background, imposed taxes in 1687, despite complaints about taxation without representation, and also challenged the position of Congregationalism by, instead, favouring religious toleration. Opposition was suppressed with fines and imprisonment, while town meetings were banned. In 1688, the Dominion was extended to include New York and New Jersey. Instead of elected legislative assemblies, it had one Crown-appointed council.

At the same time, there were distinctive elements in the American response to the King. For example, the overthrow of James, in the Glorious Revolution of 1688–9, was popular with colonial elites, not only because it promised to roll back Stuart autocracy, but also because it provided legitimation for America's evolving politics.[35] As an aspect of the Glorious Revolution, Andros was overthrown (and imprisoned) in April 1689 when the news reached the New World, leading to a militia rising in Massachusetts. The Dominion disintegrated as colonists restored the governments replaced by James. The unpopularity of the Dominion of New England left a difficult legacy for subsequent attempts to create a colonial military union. The authority of the Calverts in Maryland was also overthrown by a 'Protestant Association,' which led to the replacement of proprietary by royal government.[36]

Although James's overthrow can be seen as looking toward a later displacement of royal governors in 1775, in fact it was not a forerunner to the 1775 Revolution. Instead, the American assemblies were working with the new regime in England against the old, and James's overthrow helped strengthen the community of sentiment that spanned the Atlantic. Subsequent defeats in Britain for Jacobitism (attempts at the restoration of the Stuart male line) in 1716 and 1746 played the same role. News of those risings were closely followed in America, and they were important events in political consciousness there, not least through sustaining a sense of Catholic challenge.

As such, these episodes serve as a reminder that the dissolution of the trans-Atlantic link should not be seen as becoming steadily more probable. Indeed, they fit the overarching assumption in the book that the crisis of empire was a product of eighteenth-century dynamics, rather than of longstanding simmering resentments and growing estrangement reaching back to the early colonial period.

This is an important issue as many scholars present a story of growing estrangement over the seventeenth and eighteenth centuries, finally erupting in 1775 and gaining lasting political form the following century. In contrast, this study seeks to demonstrate the building blocks as well as the contingencies of Anglicization. Alongside the complex inner workings of the Empire, its societies, values and economies, which helped express and strengthen it, there were contingencies. They took two forms. External stimuli, conflict with the Bourbons and Native Americans, drew metropole and colonies closer, as they were later to do for Britain and the USA, whereas the absence of such pressures led to distance and tension, and even conflict, between them. Secondly, there were contingencies in the shape of political challenges within the Empire, such as those posed by the policies of James II and, subsequently, Jacobite plans.

Indeed, had Jacobitism been successful in the British Isles, there might well have been a conflict with some of the colonies. This counterfactual (what-if) is valuable as it underlines the role of political contingency in the subsequent development of English North America and of the Anglo-American relationship. The mid-century civil wars had ended with Royalist supporters in the New World brought to heel. The situation might have been different after 1689 had a Stuart England sought to reimpose control in North America, not least if the Dutch under William III of Orange were willing to continue the war with James II by sending aid to these colonists. However, the Dutch would have been heavily committed to war on the continent with Louis XIV of France, which would have left James, if successful in England, able to turn on rebellious colonies.

In the event, the Glorious Revolution was followed in both the British Isles and the colonies by the implementation of a new order. This included a measure of religious toleration, as well as an extension of government based on the Westminster Parliament, and new colonial charters. That of Massachusetts was issued in 1691: it established a royal governor and a representative assembly.

Due to the Union of 1707, the Westminster Parliament also included Scotland, so that British, rather than English, became an appropriate description of the Empire. Yet there was no such inclusion of Ireland or the New World colonies.

Indeed, the Glorious Revolution ensured that Parliament shared more actively in the regulation of colonial affairs, but this took place without constitutional (as opposed to practical) limitations on this imperial prerogative to match those in Britain. Moreover, there was an unwillingness to concede that colonial subjects shared in the ancient rights and privileges of Englishmen, while the royal prerogative was presented as limiting the authority of colonial assemblies.[37] This was unwelcome from the colonial perspective and became more significant in the run-up to the American Revolution.

More specifically, government in London sought to revive ideas seen under James II, not least by having Andros serve as Governor of Virginia from 1693 to 1698. In order to make administration more effective and, in particular, to encourage a united military response at a time of serious problems in the war with France and its Native American allies, the government wanted a unified military command in New York and New England. It also sought the allocation by assemblies of permanent revenues for the support of royal officials. Both measures were unwelcome in the colonies, and Massachusetts and South Carolina were particularly marked in their opposition. The first measure was abandoned in 1701 and the second had failed in all colonies bar Virginia by 1702. In the 1690s, Connecticut successfully saw off pressure to provide military support.

Colonial proprietors also saw their position circumscribed as a result of the disruption attendant upon the Glorious Revolution. William Penn's position was weakened and the resulting Charter of Privileges for Pennsylvania and Delaware of 1701 left power with an elected assembly, the guidance for which was provided by the rights of the freeborn subjects of England.

Nevertheless, the extension of British government in the colonies was evident in the revised Navigation Act of 1696, which authorized colonial Vice-Admiralty courts, and with the creation in 1700 of a General Post Office that had branches in the colonies. The American Post Office Act followed in 1711.

Furthermore, the spread of a measure of religious toleration (markedly so in contrast with the French and Spanish Empires) led to pressure on colonial assemblies to copy the Toleration Act of 1689. It also led to the Naturalization Act of 1740 which offered the rights of British subjects to foreign Protestants and Jews in the colonies. This helped make them more attractive places to live and work. Religious toleration of Protestants interacted with church establishments which showed great vitality toward the close of the seventeenth century, with the Congregationalists in New England, and the Anglicans in Virginia, Maryland, the Carolinas and New York, establishing numerous congregations. These, in turn, underlined the links of colony and church.

At the same time, toleration went only so far. This was vividly demonstrated by the Salem witch trials of 1692 in Massachusetts. These trials, which led to 20 executions, indicated the nature and extent of psychological tensions that could burst to the fore. They also underlined that the range of victims in American society was not restricted to Native or African Americans. The instability of New England politics contributed to the crisis, as did the pressure of a rising population on the local economy, but materialist interpretations can only go so far, and it is important to understand the powerful, foreboding and disruptive sense of the living presence of evil.[38]

Parliamentary assertiveness added a dimension to the relations between Crown and colonies, one indeed that was to be important until their breakdown in the mid-1770s. In other respects, this relationship between Crown and colonies had been modified in favour of cooperation, not only by the reaction to James II but also because war with France (1689–97, 1702–13) put a premium on colonial assistance in the war effort. The contiguity or proximity of English colonies with French possessions was particularly important in this respect: colonial military assistance was both necessary and possible, although, as a less welcome consequence for the colonists, the pressure of war was to lead to a more active imperial grip in colonies deemed of strategic importance.

In the Nine Years' War with France (1689–97), 'English' activity in North America was almost entirely locally generated. There was scant direction or assistance from England itself. William III, the new King, was focused on the war in Europe where he was under heavy pressure from France.

Instead, maritime attacks by the New England colonies played a key role. In May 1690, in response to French/Native American raids, an expedition of seven ships and 446 men under Sir William Phips, sent by the Court of Massachusetts, successfully captured an unprepared and poorly defended Port Royal in Acadia (now Nova Scotia). An oath of allegiance to the English Crown was administered, although it had scant meaning as far as the Acadians were concerned.

That July, an expedition of 32 New England ships and 2,200 troops directed at Québec, the capital of New France, failed owing to adverse winds, a firm defence, a shortage of ammunition, low morale and an epidemic of smallpox. An advance north from Albany fell victim to poor logistics and morale. Failure also resulted in a marked increase in dissension, and in a shattering of confidence which helped lead Massachusetts and Plymouth to accept the reimposition of direct royal rule with the Massachusetts charter in 1691. The expense of preparations against Canada in 1709–11 similarly led to a change in the fiscal system in Connecticut.

Nevertheless, the expeditionary warfare was important to the development of governmental sophistication, as, in order to finance these expeditions, Massachusetts issued paper bonds against future revenue. Looked at differently, but equally accurately, this was a desparate measure that left the colony with heavy debts.

Phips visited England in 1691, and pressed on William III the need to continue the attack on Canada and the value of its fur and fisheries. Nevertheless, despite plans, no more attacks on Québec were launched because it was peripheral to the concerns of English government, politicians and public opinion. They remained more focused on Europe and, within the New World, on the West Indies. In 1692, Phips himself became the first governor of Massachusetts under its new charter. As such, he was in charge at the time of the Salem witch trials which owed something to anxiety about a conflation between Satanism and the French and Native American enemies who seemed so powerful and threatening at the time. Phips himself died in London in 1695 whither he had travelled in order to defend his conduct from critics. This was a journey that indicated the continued importance of trans-Atlantic governmental links.[39]

The story, however, was not only of England and France. In spite of the ravages of disease, especially smallpox which had hit hard in the 1630s, the Iroquois confederacy further west was able to function as a North American great power, if that term is not anachronistic for a context in which all the players were dwarfed by the environment and also only able to deploy limited strength. Nevertheless, the Iroquois were a more or less equal contender with England and France in the military struggles of the region, which made the Covenant Chain, or alliance linking the Iroquois and New York, of considerable importance. Indeed, the Iroquois were more of a threat than the English to the core of the French colony, ensuring that their peace agreement with both France and England in 1701 posed a challenge for the English colonies.[40]

There was a military technology dimension. In New England, Native Americans acquired the ability to cast bullets and make gunflints, although they were unable to make gunpowder or guns. Some Native American tribes learned to employ European fortification devices such as bastions as early as the 1670s, and by 1675 they were using flintlocks. Trained from at least the age of 12, able to march at least 30 miles, experts at marksmanship and firing from cover, and reliant on merit for military leadership, the Native Americans were formidable foes.

The military balance in the region was not to shift significantly in favour of the Europeans until the following century, by which time the Native Americans were greatly outnumbered. Furthermore, European fortresses were important because their garrisons could resist and even harass raiding parties (whereas Native American palisaded villages were more vulnerable to capture[41]), but the fortresses did not guarantee control. In addition, the British sent few regulars to North America until the 1750s. Moreover, the European ability to travel by sea became less valuable militarily once they moved away from coastal regions. Instead, success in frontier warfare depended in part on Native American assistance or on adaptation to the Native American way of war, as in the case of King Philip's War (1675–6), when the colonists moved in loose order and adapted to the available cover.

Disunity among the Native Americans was also very important, and encouraged alliance with Europeans. In the Pequot War of 1637, the English were supported by the Narragansetts, while, in 1675, in a battle known as the Great Swamp Fight, Pequot warriors, in turn, helped the English against the Narragansetts. 'King Philip', the English term for Metacom, the Sachem of the Pokanokets, was killed in 1676 by a Native American in an ambush arranged by Benjamin Church, the head of a force of English and allied Native Americans.

More generally, some Native Americans converted to Christianity, and the converts, though few, tended to support the Europeans. Traditional cultural and religious beliefs and imperatives were lost with conversion. This was part of a process more widely seen with European expansion, as with that of Spain in what became Latin America. On the other hand, many Native Americans were not receptive to missionaries, whereas many Europeans captured by Native Americans showed a surprising willingness to remain.

The power balance between Native American and colonist was shifted less by weaponry than by demography. The Europeans came to North America to colonize rather than to trade, and they came in increasing numbers. In contrast, Native American numbers did not grow. Moreover, although themselves in flux as new settlers, Anglo-French immigrants had settled ideas of government and social organization. This could lead to a weakening lack of flexibility on their part in response to local circumstances, but could also be a strength. It was the rising number of settlers, and the ability, thanks to advantages of mobility, logistical support and reinforcement, to concentrate forces at points of conflict, that proved crucial to European success. This was more important than the specifications of their weapons.

War, in turn, had demographic consequences. About 7,900 of the 11,600 Native Americans living in southern New England on the eve of King Philip's War died through battle, disease or exposure, or were removed by being sold as slaves or becoming permanent refugees.[42] Thus, the possibility of future resistance was lessened. Cultural attitudes might also have played a role. It has been argued that the Europeans were willing to lose a large proportion of their troops in order to win, and that this gave them an advantage against Native American societies where the population had less extensive notions of the acceptable social limits of casualties,[43] although there is need for caution in lumping together what were often very different Native American defensive strategies. At any rate, by 1700, English penetration of the interior was limited, certainly very much so in comparison to that of Spain in Mexico, but important inroads had been made.

Comparison with other European New World colonies is instructive, but, in terms of English policy and the options open to English landowners, merchants and migrants, it is also necessary to consider the English New World alongside English enterprise elsewhere. Here the key comparison is not with South Asia or

West Africa, not least because English imperialism in both was fundamentally a matter of trading enclaves, but, instead, with Ireland.[44]

Indeed, Ireland, with its seventeenth-century history of expropriation, settlement, commercial control and involvement in Anglo-French conflict, offered many parallels with the North American colonies. There were also key differences, not least the Parliament in Dublin that covered all of Ireland, the existence and role of the established Church, and the disaffection of the (majority) Catholics and Presbyterians, excluded from power and subject to civil disabilities. Ireland, nevertheless, was continually in the background of American history as an example of imperial government.

The Glorious Revolution was a reminder that the course of developments was far from inevitable. The seventeenth century indeed closed in the English world with a difficult decade of demographic blows, economic troubles, fiscal turmoil, military setbacks and political unease. How English North America would fare in the future remained very unclear.

1

The Growth of British North America, 1700–38

At Kensington Palace in London, on 1 August 1734, Tomochichi, a representative of the Lower Creeks, was received by George II. This meeting registered the pace of British expansion as it stemmed from the chartering, in 1732, of the colony of Georgia, named after George, and the attempt to secure its future, in the face of hostile Native American and Spanish interests, by alliance with the most powerful local tribe. Tomochichi came to London with James Oglethorpe, the key figure in the foundation of the colony. The occasion was reported in the press.

Each sought to act in an appropriate manner, but this was made difficult by a lack of understanding of the priorities of the other. Symbolism thus came to the fore. Tomochichi presented George with 'feathers of the eagle, which is the swiftest of birds, and who flieth all round our nations. These feathers are a sign of peace in our land, and have been carried from town to town there, and we have brought them over to leave with you, O Great King, as a sign of everlasting peace.'

The reciprocal gift-giving of Native American society, however, was not taken so far in Europe (nor by colonists), and George, who was anyway noted for meanness, did not present a gift. He did, nevertheless, lend Tomochichi and his retinue one of his coaches. They toured the Court and were impressed by the size of the palace.[1] Despite having the colony named after him, George did not have much interest in Georgia, let alone Native Americans. Yet this colony played a role in the deterioration of relations with Spain that led to the outbreak of war between the two powers in 1739.

Britain, not England, is the focus from the early eighteenth century. Parliamentary Union with Scotland in 1707 ended its exclusion from what had been an English Empire,[2] as the protectionist Navigation Acts now encompassed Scotland. This was to be very important to the dynamic of British commercial and colonial expansion, not least to trade, migration, religion and warfare. Economic motives, indeed, were important in winning support for Union, especially in Glasgow,[3] which, with Liverpool, was to take over from Bristol the role of key port to the British Atlantic. Glasgow was to be particularly significant in the handling of tobacco from the Chesapeake, and by 1758 was Britain's foremost tobacco port. Not only Atlantic Scotland was affected, for, by mid-century, Aberdeen had an important export trade in sailcloth and coarse linen to North America.[4]

Migration from Scotland to North America became far more important than hitherto, Scotsmen gained official positions, Robert Dinwiddie becoming Lieutenant Governor in Virginia in 1751, while Scottish regiments were to play a major role in the British Army in North America. The religious dimension was also significant, with Presbyterianism in North America receiving a powerful lift from the Scottish link, while later episcopal orders reached America via Scottish episcopalians.

The early eighteenth century was a period of only modest growth in the British population, particularly until the mid-1740s, but, nevertheless, that of British North America rose appreciably. By 1740, French-ruled Canada had only about 56,000 inhabitants, whereas British North America had nearly a million people of European background. This rise was to help define a set of colonies that were able to transform their origins so as to encompass, in addition, a major expansion into the interior. Without this growth, moreover, it would have proved more difficult to defeat the Native Americans and control the African American slaves. Political and economic possibilities were therefore in part dependent on labour flows which have to be considered alongside capital flows.

Neither Louisiana nor New France, the St Lawrence valley, were as promising for settlement as many of the British colonies, especially for grain cultivation, but the element of opportunity was as much set by the more liberal attitude of successive British governments to the composition of the migrant populations. The British were especially tolerant of religious groups outside the established churches. This was noted by anxious French envoys, Charles, Count of Guerchy commenting in 1763 and 1764 on emigration to North America by French Protestants (Huguenots) travelling via Britain.[5] New France (Canada for the sake of clarity) contained some Protestant and Jewish merchants, but it was overwhelmingly Catholic, and Huguenots were not supposed to settle there.[6]

The French proprietary companies that administered Louisiana from 1717 until it reverted to Crown control in 1731 sought to encourage immigration, which was seen as crucial to prosperity, and there was both voluntary and forced immigration: the first slaves reached Louisiana in 1719. Voluntary immigration, however, proved largely unsuccessful as far as French settlers were concerned, although there was an important German immigration.[7] By 1763, there were only about 4,000 whites and 5,000 blacks in the colony.

Canada was also a disappointment for settlers, with only about 11,370 French people settling there between 1608 and 1759.[8] Indeed few people left France for Canada each year, and most of the indentured labourers who were sent to work in Canada went back to France at the close of their service.[9] The climate was discouraging as was the shortage of readily cultivable land. There was no frontier of agricultural settlement comparable to that in the Middle Colonies in British North America. Moreover, neither Canada nor Louisiana had positive connotations in the minds of the French people. The colonies were associated with indentured labour, hostile environments and savage Native Americans. At least the relatively limited amount of settlement helped ease French relations with Native Americans who knew that their lands were not desired as they were by the more numerous British settlers. This encouraged the Abenakis of northern New England to ally with France rather than Britain.

British settlement spread geographically both westward and into the gaps between the coastal enclaves, although such a concept neglects the role of earlier settlement by Native Americans, and should properly be rephrased colonial settlement. Much of this settlement entailed the clearing of the indigenous woodland. As a consequence, the axe was a key tool of early America, although, as it was not used as a weapon, it was robbed of some of its potential symbolic value. The American axe, with its tapering and flat head, proved particularly effective. This was then combined with the use of criss-cross fences constructed of split rails without nails, so that what had been woodland was now controlled space. The demand for land took precedence over trade in relations with Native Americans.

Control was not only expressed at the level of the individual settler.[10] In response to the increasing possibilities and to the need for a different governmental structure, Carolina was divided into two colonies, North and South Carolina, in 1713. New Jersey had been constituted as a royal colony in 1702. New towns included Baltimore (1728), Richmond (1730) and Georgetown (1735). These new towns had an impact on the urban hierarchy of North America and a more significant consequence on relations within particular colonies. Thus, within Maryland, the rise of Baltimore had an impact on Annapolis, while, in Virginia, that of Richmond represented an inland move of the centre of gravity. Williamsburg, the colony's capital, remained important, but it also was more marginal to the colony itself, although its location on the Chesapeake also underlined its significance as an intermediary between colony and homeland.

The poverty of some settlers did not discourage others from migrating, because wage rates were higher in the New World than in the British Isles. Moreover, an Act of Parliament of 1697, which allowed people to seek work outside their own parish if they carried a certificate, made the poor more mobile. This encouraged the migration of indentured servants to America.

Emigration to the British colonies from outside the British Isles affected both the general character of the colonies and specific locations, and was part of a general process by which international migration was commonplace in Europe. As a result, in looking at flows to America, it is important to consider alternative possibilities for emigration and how they changed. The balance of relative advantage was a key issue, but this balance has to be understood in multiple dimensions, including that of religious opportunity.

Germans, especially from the Rhineland, were particularly concentrated in Pennsylvania, where a Lutheran Church organization developed from the 1720s. Other German Protestant groups in Pennsylvania included Moravians. Indeed, the Moravian mission at Gnadenhütten was destroyed by Native Americans in November 1755. A group of Moravians also tried to settle in Georgia, but they would not serve in the militia because they were pacifists, and, therefore, were forced to leave. Germans were also found in other colonies. In North Carolina in 1710, a group of German (Palatine) and Swiss immigrants established the estuarine town of New Bern, which was so successful that it became the capital of the colony in 1770. By then, maybe as much as 30 per cent of North Carolina's population was of German descent.[11] This immigration was of particular importance given the frontier character of the colony in this period. Many of these Germans had come from the Rhineland, where, in the Palatinate, there had been severe persecution of Protestants in the 1700s and 1710s.

To such Protestants, British rule represented freedom, and, especially, the key freedom of religious liberty, but the intertwining of religious dissent with migration helped ensure that a unified religious mission in British North America was not plausible, and also posed serious issues for any church establishment. Virginia maintained its opposition to non-Anglican churches, while New England was dominated by the Congregationalists, but elsewhere there was a measure of ecclesiastical pluralism.

Religious refugees were not always viewed with favour, but were particularly encouraged in Georgia, a new colony, chartered in 1732, with its capital, Savannah, founded in 1733. Religious freedom in Georgia, however, did not include Jews or Catholics, and the charter founding the colony allowed for freedom of conscience, except for papists.

Savannah, at once port, capital, centre of population, and, crucially, military base, enabled the fledgling colony to anchor the British presence between South Carolina and Spanish-ruled Florida. From the Spanish perspective, Georgia was an unwelcome southward extension of British power and pretensions. Many of these refugees came from the Archbishopric of Salzburg, which indicated the importance of colonization in the British Empire for ordinary people far distant from the Atlantic coast. Such refugees were also seen as a way to anchor the British presence in South Carolina, not least in the face of rising slave numbers. Thus, Swiss were settled at Purrysburg in 1732.

There was also a Jewish immigration, such that Jews were a small but important section of many urban centres including New York, Philadelphia and Charleston. The Georgia Trustees ordered James Oglethorpe, their member in Georgia, to send away a shipload of Jews who arrived in Savannah, but he did not because they had a much-needed doctor on board.

Immigration from outside the British Isles interacted with the European ethnic variation dating from seventeenth-century settlement, not least as a result of varied political control. This variation was captured by travellers, such as the Swedish naturalist Peter Kalm who toured there in 1748–51. He noted the variations arising from Dutch, German and Swedish settlement in the Middle Colonies of Delaware, New Jersey, New York and Pennsylvania.[12] German migration to Philadelphia via the Netherlands rose appreciably from 1727 and remained high until cut short by the outbreak of war between Britain and France in the mid-1750s. By 1750 a majority of the colony's whites were not of English descent. In order to redeem the cost of their passage, most Germans arriving in the New World were redemptioners, indentured servants bound to work off the debt they had incurred. Alongside hardship came opportunity: the Germans greatly enriched agricultural practice in Pennsylvania and further afield. Compared to their English counterparts, they made more use of manure and took greater note of contours when ploughing, and their barns were also better for animal husbandry.

A different European ethnic variety could be seen in the Carolinas and Georgia for the reasons already given. Such variations underlined the extent to which kinship could not serve as the basis for political identity and agency at the level of an individual colony, however important it might be for the dynamics of local societies.

Yet in both the Middle Colonies and the South there was also an Anglicization. This reflected not so much the pressure of authority as the values of consensus. This Anglicization was longer-lasting in the Middle Colonies, and indeed had helped lead in New York to Leisler's Rebellion at the time of the Glorious Revolution. After the rebellion's failure, angry Dutch settlers had moved to New Jersey and to inland New York. Their opposition to clerical authority, and to the attempt to make the Church of England the established church in New York City, was to provide the seedbed for a positive response to the Great Awakening of religious renewal, although that movement also led to an important measure of Anglicization.[13] Anglicization was also a product of the fall in German migration from the mid-1750s, a fall that reflected both war in North America and the appeal of emigration from Germany to Eastern Europe.[14]

Coercion within the British Empire also played a major role in increasing settlement, with convicts, slaves and indentured servants all important. The dispatch of convicts to provide a labour force was a pointed instance of how colonies were supposed to accommodate what was seen as surplus population, and, again, Britain was acting in accordance with a general European practice. After the War of the Spanish Succession (1702–13), demobilization among British soldiers and sailors released large numbers of fit men trained to violence into a labour market that could not cope. In response, concern about rising crime led to the Transportation Act of 1718. For the first time, this allowed for transportation, not only as part of the pardoning process in the case of capital offences, but as a penalty for a wide range of non-capital crimes. This range included grand larceny, the theft of property between a shilling (five new pence, about £10 in 2008 values) and £2 (about £200 in 2008 values).

Parliament went on to pass another 16 Acts between 1720 and 1763 that established transportation as a penalty for crimes from perjury to poaching. As a result, as many as 50,000 convicts were transported from the British Isles to North America in 1718–75. The shipboard mortality rate was about 14 per cent, a number comparable with the experience of Africans sent as slaves: infectious disease in the crowded conditions was, again, the major problem. The majority of the convicts went to Virginia and Maryland, with most of the rest being sent to Pennsylvania. Very few were sent to New England.[15] Georgia was in part founded to help debtors who were convicts.

Contrasts in the destination of convicts reflected, and also accentuated, the contrasting social character and political culture of the colonies, especially the lesser role of social distinction and control in New England. Conversely, the Chesapeake colonies saw more explicit social differentiation among the white population, and also a greater degree of social control by the elite. In making such statements, it is important not to neglect social tensions within the New England colonies. An emphasis on town meetings can lead to a downplaying of coercive possibilities that had been fully recorded in 1692 in the trials and convictions in Salem, Massachusetts on the charge of witchcraft.

All too often, there is a tendency to emphasize variations in the group under discussion and to neglect those among others, but this is misleading. In what was a rapidly changing *mélange* of human societies – white, African American and Native American – these variations registered, as well as moulded, the complex interplay of existing circumstances with new opportunities and problems. This underlines the extent to which pre-Revolutionary America was not a static society, nor one in which what became proto-Revolutionary sentiments were the sole source of change and instability.

Alongside slaves, the use of convicts testified to the widespread belief among the propertied that coercion was the only way to deal with the labour needs of settlement colonies. In this view, coercion made possible the diligent and purposeful supervision required for the proper improvement of the colonies, and, possibly, of both slaves and convicts. Forced labour as compulsory improvement, in practice put the emphasis on labour, not improvement. It is not clear, however, that forced labour, which was most common in the Upper South, was welcomed by the colonists. Benjamin Franklin was to condemn the practice and to suggest that America should send its rattlesnakes to Britain in return.

Britain was also increasingly prominent in the Atlantic slave trade, and was the leading state in that trade from the 1710s.[16] Most slaves transported by the British were sent to the West Indies, but many also went to British North America. The number of slaves there rose from about 20,000 in 1700 to over 300,000 by 1763. This was a rate of increase that was faster than that of the white population, high as that of the latter was. Moreover, the higher death rate among slaves, which owed much to their harsh working conditions, was such that the aggregate number underplays that of those who directly experienced slavery in North America.

The rise in the number of slaves reflected the regional dynamic of Southern export agriculture. This was particularly so as South Carolina and, later, Georgia were developed as plantation economies, supplementing those on the Chesapeake. In South Carolina and, eventually, Georgia, rice became an additional plantation crop, which was a product of the particular opportunities of the tidewater environment. The profitability of plantation crops helped offset the initial costs of production, while the wealth brought by and represented in slaves was such that per capita wealth among whites was highest in the South. This encouraged white immigration.

In contrast, there were comparatively few immigrants to New England after 1640. Indeed, its demographic structure was closer to parts of Canada settled by European farmers than to the South. Yet as a reminder of the need to keep class, or at least social difference, in the equation alongside region, most Southern landowners owned few slaves, and indeed many had none. This was particularly true of the Piedmont, but was also true of the more prosperous coastal regions. In both, however, political power was linked to social prominence.

Slavery had been banned by the Trustees of the new colony of Georgia in 1735. This was not out of hostility to slavery (Oglethorpe indeed served on the board of the Royal African Company which ran the slave stations), as out of a desire to base the colony on small-scale agrarian activity, rather than on aristocratic plantations. The Trustees wanted to create a colony of virtuous small farmers, a theme later to be associated with Thomas Jefferson, President from 1801 to 1809, and also to focus on wine or silk production; although neither of the latter worked out very well. Defensive considerations also played a role, and the law was entitled 'An Act for rendering the Colony of Georgia more defensible by prohibiting the importation and use of Black Slaves or Negroes into the same'. It was feared that a slave population would pose major problems of control, which argued a lack of confidence in the ability to contain slaves.

The colonists, however, opposed the banning of slavery from the outset, not least because they had to watch their South Carolina neighbours getting rich using cheap labour, while they could barely eke out a living in an environment where cultivation was arduous. The Malcontents, the leading political faction in Georgia that opposed the Trustees, published several pamphlets calling for legalization of the slave trade, but they were initially unsuccessful.

Whatever the situation in Georgia, the slave trade was integral to the commercial economy and the shipping of the British Atlantic. The slave trade was also crucial to entrepreneurial circles in Britain, and to the financial world there; while it exerted a range of influences elsewhere in Britain, particularly, but not exclusively, in the ports. London dominated the slave trade until the 1710s, when it was replaced by Bristol; the developing port of Liverpool took the leading position from the 1740s. The regulatory framework that had maintained London's dominance had been dismantled in 1698, when the African trade was freed from the control of the monopolistic Royal African Company, legalizing the position of private traders. The role of smaller ports, such as Barnstaple, Bideford, Dartmouth, Exeter, Lancaster, Plymouth, Poole, Portsmouth, Topsham and Whitehaven, helped spread the impact of the slave trade on the economy, although several, including Devon's ports, played only a minor role, and many merchants and ships were involved in the trade on only a temporary basis.

The impact on the British economy was not limited to the supply of slaves. The provision of food and other products to the slave plantations was also important. For example, in his *Tour of Scotland 1769* (1771), Thomas Pennant recorded of the inland English town of Keswick, that trade had encouraged local industry, which was chiefly 'engaged in manufactures of ... a coarse sort of woollen cloth called cottons sent to Glasgow, and from thence to Virginia for the use of the Negroes ... the manufactures employ great quantities of wool from Scotland and Durham'. Thus, agriculture, industry and commerce across a wide swathe of Britain were linked in the service of this trade.

The colonial contribution included the shipment of food for slaves: of salt cod from Newfoundland to Charleston, and of food from the mainland colonies to the British West Indies, where the slave population was far larger than in North America. This export of food encouraged transport developments within the colonies, such as the Great Philadelphia Wagon Road. The colonial contribution also included slaving from the ports of Newport, Bristol and Providence in Rhode Island. Based on molasses from the West Indies, Rhode Island produced rum that could be exported in return for slaves.[17] Moreover, the farms around Narragansett Bay in Rhode Island were some of the largest in New England and the place where slaves for agricultural labour were most viable.

This was a reminder of the multiple links and dynamics that were important in the British Atlantic, creating and reflecting entrepreneurial opportunities. Although government, often at the behest of lobbies, sought through legislation to control this energy, in practice the commercial drives proved difficult to contain. The development of multiple links between North America and the West Indies was particularly significant in this sphere.

Regional variations in plantation economies had important consequences for slave society. Owing to the varied demands of tobacco and rice cultivation, and to related economic and social characteristics, slaves in the Chesapeake were more affected by white life, living as they did on relatively small farms, and in close proximity to the owners. From the 1720s the slave workforce could reproduce itself, and this ensured that it became fast-growing. In contrast, in the rice lands of South Carolina, there were fewer, but larger, plantations, and the percentage of slaves in the population was greater. Moreover, the higher death rates in these tidewater rice lands ensured that, although, by the 1750s, the slave workforce could reproduce itself, the proportion of African slaves to American-born slaves was higher in South Carolina than in the Chesapeake. As a consequence, slaves in South Carolina were more autonomous and more influenced by African culture and material life, and relations between slaves and whites remained more antipathetical than where they lived in close proximity, although it is not easy to assess slave attitudes.[18] As a result, slavery in South Carolina was more similar to that in the West Indies than to slavery in Virginia, although mortality rates and natural reproduction ensured that, in some respects, it came to have more in common with the situation in Virginia.

As a reminder of the variety of circumstances, some slaves were owned by free African Americans (including a large community on the eastern shore of Virginia), and other slaves were owned by Native Americans. To underline the complexity, slave society also demonstrated the effectiveness of white-imposed hierarchies. For example, certain plantations, including on the islands off the coast of South Carolina, were left to the oversight of black slaves. Looked at differently, this was an aspect of the Africanization of part of colonial America, an Africanization that was an integral part of slave society.

Alongside the emphasis on plantations and the colonies from Virginia south, it is important to note the extent of slavery in New England and the Middle Colonies. Legal throughout these colonies, slavery was important both as a source of service in households, as well as of labour outside the household,[19] Cities such as New York (where there was a slave revolt in 1712, and a conspiracy in 1741), Boston and Philadelphia therefore contained significant populations of slaves, although there were also free African Americans.

As with Native Americans, relations between whites and slaves involved negotiation and compromise, but coercion was more pronounced and the whip was a key indicator of the risk of punishment. This was both a pragmatic tool of control and a product of a desire to prove mastery over slaves.[20] The prevalence of slavery was such that the standard images of slave life in terms of plantation work have to be supplemented by others that were far more varied.

At the same time, discussion of slaves in terms of economic use risks under-rating the extent to which slavery, as well as earlier enslavement, were harsh processes. Slave workers generally slept in poor, unsanitary and unheated accommodation, and their food was deficient in calories and nutrients. Most of their work was tedious, and there were few prospects of betterment. Masters needed a modus vivendi in which better work was obtained through reasonable conditions, but slaves were scarcely equal in this relationship.

The continued import of slaves helped limit the impact of those African Americans who gained their freedom. These were indeed a small minority, not least in those colonies where there were many African Americans, so that in the 1770s they were about 2 per cent of the African Americans in Virginia, and fewer than 1 per cent of those in South Carolina.[21] Yet these free African Americans further complicated attempts to ensure a racial segregation of tasks, attempts linked to anxieties about the number of African Americans and their potential threat to socio-racial assumptions and boundaries.[22]

There was particular concern to limit the chances of African Americans developing links with Native Americans, not least by being employed in trade with them and thus learning languages and making contacts. This, for example, was banned by South Carolina. The possibility of such an alliance was a particular concern in the South, and, indeed, runaway slaves did not only seek refuge with the Native Americans, they also sought to stir them up against the colonists. Fear encouraged colonists to press Native Americans to return runaways. There was a provision in the British–Creek treaty of 1733 establishing Georgia that offered rewards to Creeks who returned slaves, the reward depending on whether the slaves were alive or dead. There were other similar treaties, all of which showed the colonists' attempts to foster hostility between African and Native Americans.

Slaves were owned by law and held by force, but in America the major problem for many settlers was set by relations with Native Americans. Conflict with the French interacted with tension and warfare with Native Americans. The latter largely arose from the settler land hunger that the demographic growth of the British colonies exacerbated. Yet the conflict with the French that provided another context for war with Native Americans was set by European power politics.

During the War of Spanish Succession (1702–13), France and Spain were allies, although on the whole the British took the initiative during this conflict. This was helped by the degree to which the French navy proved particularly neglectful of the New World, while the Spanish navy was very weak. This ensured that French and Spanish capability there became largely a matter of activity on land.[23]

It was easy to present French competition as impressive and threatening. In 1699, for example, Pierre Le Moyne, Sieur d'Iberville, founded Fort Maurepas on Biloxi Bay on the Gulf of Mexico, Mobile following in 1702, and New Orleans in 1718.[24] An English warship encountered in 1699 on the lower Mississippi at English Bend was intimidated into departing. French intentions were certainly impressive. Fort Maurepas, which was founded to guard access to the Mississippi, had four bastions constructed of logs, three of them mounted with cannon. The following year, more artillery arrived and Fort Mississippi was constructed.

Yet the commitment of French resources was slight, not least in comparison with the deployment of forces in Europe. Fort Mississippi had only a 15-man garrison with a small cannon on an elevated bank, had no real fortifications, and was abandoned in 1706–7. Fort Maurepas had 12 cannon and 12 swivel guns by the end of 1700, but was also abandoned. The entire garrison of disease-ridden Louisiana was no more than 45 in 1706. It suffered from the absence of a hospital and of fresh meat, and from insufficient swords, cartridge boxes, nails, guns and powder, from demoralization and desertion, and its survival rested on acceptance by the native population. In 1710, the woodwork at Fort Louis in Mobile was so rotten with humidity-caused decay that the cannon could not be supported.

Further north, the French in 1715 sent a garrison of only 20 to Michilimackinac, and planned one of only ten for Detroit. Four years later, the French force that captured the Texan mission of San Miguel de los Adaes from Spain was only seven-strong; the opposition, a single soldier unaware that the two powers were at war. Pierre Petit de Coulange established the French post on the Arkansas River in 1732 with only 12 soldiers.[25] Yet to the British the situation was more threatening, and the emphasis was on the forts rather than their limited strength.

In 1702, Governor James Moore of Carolina invaded Florida at the head of 500 to 600 Carolina volunteers and 300 to 600 Native American allies, an invasion at least partly motivated by the quest for the slaves.[26] The fortress of St Augustine, however, successfully resisted attack. It was too strong to storm, Moore's cannon were inadequate, and warships from the key Spanish colony of Cuba relieved the garrison, forcing Moore to retreat precipitously, without his cannon or eight of his 14 ships.[27] This failure exhausted the resources of the Carolina government and indicated the importance of command of the sea.

In 1704, Moore, with a largely Native American army (mostly Creeks and with rebel Apalachee support), ravaged Western Florida, attacking the Spanish missions among the Apalachees near Tallahassee: having defeated a Spanish-Apalachee counterattack, he returned with over 1,000 slaves. Charleston, in turn, repelled a Franco–Spanish attack in 1706, the Carolina militia defeating the attackers, and, thereafter, the British and their Native allies resumed the pressure on Florida, raiding Pensacola in 1707 and 1708, and advancing as far as Mobile in 1709.

As part of a continuing process of attacking the Spanish missions, the British had very much gained the initiative; but this was dependent on Creek support, particularly in applying pressure on West Florida. Indeed, thanks to the Creeks, the Spanish mission system contracted.[28] Thomas Nairne, South Carolina's Indian agent, travelled among the Creeks and Chickasaws in 1708 in an attempt to secure their support against France and Spain, not least by using the fur and slave trades.

Further north, the Iroquois tried to maintain neutrality, but the French pressed on the New England settlements, largely by arming the Abenakis of modern-day Vermont and launching raids from 1703. A destructive one against Deerfield in 1704, in which 56 people were killed and 109 captured, was particularly notable, but it also indicated the challenge facing raiders: 48 French-Canadian militia and 200 Native Americans had to march nearly 600 miles in the depth of the winter.[29] In December 1703, Colonel Joseph Dudley, the Governor of Massachusetts, had reported to John Churchill, 1st Duke of Marlborough, the leading British general:

> The first year by frequent visits and a free trade with the Indians I kept them at peace, but the French Jesuits amongst them have about six months past persuaded them to break all oaths and promises, and the first three days of their irruption, they destroyed one hundred and fifty poor people in the out and scattered parts of the Province of Maine next to them, but since I have not have had any great damage, but am at a great cost of about two thousand pounds per month to maintain forces upon the frontiers, and cruising sloops upon the coast to prevent their supply of themselves and depredations upon us, which they do in small parties.

Dudley complained that hostile Native Americans took shelter in 'impassable places whither it is impossible to march after them, and carry our necessary provisions being desert grounds where neither carriage nor horse can pass'. In 1706, however, he was more optimistic:

> I have ever since [the initial raids] had so good intelligence of their marches that I have met them everywhere and disappointed them so as I have not lost one village ... keep me in continual hurry marching of small parties all along the frontiers.[30]

In 1708, there was another Native American attack: on Haverhill near Boston. Aside from the destruction inflicted during the raids, there was a more general disruption to colonial society in New England.

In turn, the New Englanders struck at French bases, but they were happier mounting amphibious attacks than engaging in frontier warfare. The latter was a harsher course where the settlers had to face Native Americans, the rigours of the terrain, and their opponents' effective transport system, which was based on birchbark canoes. In 1704, a 550-strong Massachusetts force attacked the coastal settlement of Castine in modern Maine, but decided that Port Royal, the leading French base in Acadia, was too formidable an objective. Port Royal was attacked in 1707, but, although the New England (largely Massachusetts) army was over 1,000 strong and greatly outnumbered the defending force, the attack miscarried badly in the face of a vigorous defence.

This and other operations encouraged the development of the colonial manufacture of guns, which provided a market for the greatly expanding iron industry.

At the same time, the colonists' need for gunpowder and other *matériel,* such as lead for musket balls and flints for the flintlock muskets, encouraged dependence on Britain and indeed on government in the shape of the Board of Ordnance.

Failure at Port Royal increased pressure for the use of regular troops, although that was delayed by the demands of the European theatre, which consistently received greater priority as Britain was under heavy pressure both in the Low Countries and in Spain, while in 1708 the French attempted an invasion of Scotland on behalf of the Jacobite pretender to the throne. As a result of these pressures, there was no support, as originally promised, from regulars for an invasion of Canada in 1709. A colonial force was prepared at Albany and marched to Lake Champlain, but it was wracked by disease and did not advance further due to the cancellation of the expedition planned for the St Lawrence.[31] This led to complaints, but the promise of 4,000 regulars, although unfulfilled, was an important indication of British governmental interest, while the willingness of New York to send troops to join the Albany force was a significant development in provincial cooperation.

The following year, 400 British marines joined with 1,500 militia, mostly from Massachusetts but with units from Connecticut, Rhode Island and New Hampshire, to capture Port Royal: the garrison was less than 100 strong. The British bombardment of the fort (which was in a poor state) was key. Instead of burning down the settlement, and then departing with their loot, the captors left a garrison in Port Royal, which was an important indication of a determination to retain control: the military commitment also entailed a financial one.[32] Port Royal was renamed Annapolis Royal, and Acadia Nova Scotia.

In 1711, a bolder initiative was launched, an attack on Canada's capital, Québec. This was the largest expedition hitherto to North America. Preparations, however, were hasty and the government relied too much upon their own over-optimistic assumptions of logistical support from New England. The arrival of eight battalions of troops and 15 ships of the line was a formidable challenge. Difficult relations between the New Englanders and the British commanders, nevertheless, did not prevent the assembly of a large force at Boston, including about 1,000 militia, but, on 22–3 August 1711, due to a night-time error in navigation, eight transport ships and nearly 900 men were lost on rocks near Ile aux Oeufs in the St Lawrence estuary. This disaster led to the abandonment of the expedition, even though more than 6,000 troops and most of the fleet had survived. This abandonment ensured that the landward prong of the advance on Canada, from Albany on Montréal, did not set off.

Had Québec been taken, there would have been a determination to retain it in the eventual peace. This is an important counterfactual question in American history. The conquest of Canada without the major effort required in 1755–60 would have ensured that the tensions and costs of those later years would have been avoided. This might have reduced the fiscal pressure that was to inflame Anglo–American relations in 1765–74. Conversely, more of an effort might have been devoted in the 1750s to military operations to the south: to Florida, Louisiana and the West Indies. There might also have been more British settlement in Canada, leading to a more extensive series of settlement colonies, the political consequences of which are unclear.

Canada, however, had not fallen, although the Peace of Utrecht of 1713 left Britain with Nova Scotia, as well as an acceptance of the British position in Newfoundland and Hudson's Bay. These gains increased the British stake in North America and weakened Canada's defences. Given that, in any future war, the British would only have several years campaigning (i.e. the period of the conflict), they could only benefit from not needing to capture Port Royal again.

Yet in Nova Scotia, as a reminder of the difficulties of fixing control, British imperial control, both over Native Americans, particularly the Micmacs, and over French settlers, was to seem precarious, leading eventually in the 1750s to the expulsion of the Acadians of French descent.[33] Conversely, the value to Britain of immigrants was indicated by the presence of more than 300 recent settlers from the Palatinate in Germany in the 1711 expedition against Canada.

Tension with Native Americans over land hunger was particularly acute in the South. The Tuscaroras of northeastern North Carolina responded to the advance of settlers, and to the challenges this posed, by raiding their lands in 1711. Counter-attacks that year and in 1712 failed, with the settlers badly affected by yellow fever in 1712.[34] In 1713, however, with the support of a larger force from South Carolina, of 33 whites and 850 to 900 Native Americans (Cherokees, Yamasees and others), the Tuscaroras' fortress of Neoheroka was successfully stormed and nearly 1,000, a very large number for a Native American society, were killed or enslaved.

This was a defeat that was followed by the advance of British settlement to the Blue Ridge Mountains. The number of Tuscaroras (many of whom had not taken part in the war) fell from 5,000 to 2,500, while the colonies insisted that they handed over runaway slaves. Many Tuscaroras migrated and took refuge with the Iroquois, where they became the Sixth Nation. Those who remained, in a prelude of things to come, were grouped by the colonists in a reservation which, by 1760, contained only about 300 people. Reservations were to prove both cause and aspect of a lack of autonomy linked to cultural degeneration, as well as a serious restriction on the Native American economy.

Further south, provoked by exploitation by Carolina merchants and land-owners, the Yamasees of the Lower Savannah River attacked South Carolina in 1715. The Yamasees, upon whom South Carolina had earlier relied for the defence of its southern frontier, against opposing Native Americans as well as Spain, suffered from enslavement as well as from commercial exploitation, part of a pattern of alliance leading to enslavement. The colony's government was aware of this unreasonable treatment, but did nothing to stop it, a situation that was more generally true of much of North America. As another instance of whites taking advantage of Native Americans, William Penn's son made an agreement with the Delawares in 1737, the 'Walking Purchase', under which the whites would claim land to the west 'as far as a man could walk in a day and a half', and then proceeded to have paths cut and relay runners set up so that a lot more land could be taken.

In 1715, the Yamasees raided to within 12 miles of Charleston, freeing slaves, while other tribes, including the Lower Creeks, Cherokees and Catawbas, provided them with support. The initial South Carolina military response was unsuccessful. North Carolina and Virginia did not send the help requested and the Governor's hope of British regulars proved fruitless. Nevertheless, the Native American alliance was not sustained and Native American disunity greatly helped the colonists. The Cherokees responded to colonial blandishments and came round to help the Carolinians in 1716 and, in 1717; the Creeks deserted the Yamasees. Defeat had a major demographic impact on the Native Americans and from 1715 most of the Yamasees were killed or enslaved by the colonial militia. Strengthening the British position against the Yamasees also helped it with regard to France and Spain.[35] This was a product of the dynamic and potent role of Native American politics within the competing interplay of the European powers.

The Native Americans were hit by their dependence on European munitions. The 'Achilles heel' of the Iroquois in the second half of the seventeenth century, when they were the most powerful military force in the interior of North America, had been their increasing dependence on European firearms and iron weapons, and, in particular, gunpowder. This indicated a major limitation to the argument that the diffusion of European arms to non-Europeans lessened the military advantage enjoyed by Europeans. This was only the case if there was a combination of unlikely circumstances. First, it was necessary to be able to develop the capability to make and repair the arms, and to make any ammunition that might be required. Secondly, it was important to acquire proficiency in their use, either by emulating European tactics, or by integrating the use of European weapons with tactics developed for the particular societies and environments in question. Otherwise, the very adoption of European weaponry would weaken the peoples that were impressed by them. Furthermore, the Native Americans were divided, their politics often factionalized, and they lacked the infrastructure as well as the demography for a sustained, large-scale, organized opposition to the European advance.

Aside from the Yamasees, piracy was another problem for South Carolina. In 1718, 'Blackbeard' (Edward Teach), a Bristol-born thug who had held Charleston to ransom earlier in the year, died after being trapped on the North Carolina coast. The role of piracy was a demonstration of the need to protect the maritime routes that were crucial to the British presence.[36] Unlike the problem facing the Dutch in the East Indies, however, the challenge from piracy was not one mounted by the Native population. Indeed, while the latter was particularly mobile on the rivers and lakes of the interior, there was no significant development of a maritime capability. As a consequence, after the defeat of Blackbeard, piracy was not a major challenge to the colonies, unlike the privateering launched by France and Spain when Britain was at war with either of them.

Although Britain and France were at peace from 1713 to 1744, and indeed were allies from 1716 to 1731, they were also competitors, and particularly so in the colonies. The Ministry of the Marine, the relevant ministry for the French colonies, was more competitive with Britain than the French Foreign Ministry, while in Britain the Board of Trade proved amenable to American concerns about French moves.[37] Replacing their position in Nova Scotia, the French spent large sums on developing a major military and naval base at Louisbourg on Cape Breton Island. This was founded in 1720 in order to support the French presence in the Newfoundland fisheries, and to serve as a halfway port between France and the French West Indies.[38] To Massachusetts, however, it was menacing to have this French base to the north. In 1735, when France and Britain seemed close to hostilities in the War of the Polish Succession, the French considered the possibility of British attacks on Québec and Louisiana.[39]

The expansion of the rival British and French trading networks in the North American interior involved the use of diplomacy, trade and force. Intra-Native American and intra-European rivalries were connected. Cooperation with the Native Americans was a crucial means by which the British and French furthered their interests and influence. The Iroquois allowed the British to build a fort at Oswego in 1727 in response to the Senecas giving the French permission to build one at Niagara in 1719.

The French were particularly active in the interior, being helped by the location of their early bases. Moving north from Louisiana, Bénard de La Harpe reached Oklahoma in 1719 in his search for Native American trade. Further north, interest in the Missouri and the nearby lands led in 1719 to a treaty-making expedition that reached the Pawnees of southern Nebraska, and, five years later, to the establishment of Fort d'Orléans on the north bank of the Missouri near its confluence with the Mississippi. A mission westward from there reached the Padoucas, possibly the Comanches in modern central Kansas, in 1724, and found them willing to trade. The initiative, however, could not be sustained from distant Louisiana, a colony then in difficulties, and in 1728 Fort d'Orléans was abandoned.

West from New France in the 1730s, Pierre Gaultier de la Vérendrye built a series of posts toward the sea then believed to be in western Canada. Fort St Charles (1732) on the Lake of the Woods was followed by Fort Maurepas (1734) at the southern end of Lake Winnipeg, and Fort La Reine (1738) on the Assiniboine River. That year, La Vérendrye set off from the new fort to find the 'great river' reported to run west to the Pacific from near the headwaters of the Missouri. The expedition reached the Missouri near modern Bismarck in North Dakota.[40]

'British' really meant British-Americans, as the home government took only limited interest in the interior of North America. Nevertheless, British newspapers commented on the colonial rivalry with France,[41] and there were diplomatic representations over key episodes and issues.[42] There was also a synergy of public concern in America with press discussion in Britain, as with the British Journal of 11 July (OS) 1724 which reported a representation from the General Assembly of South Carolina.

Direct action drew on and sustained more general concerns. Attacks on Native Americans judged hostile were seen as a way to thwart rival European states, and also registered in the metropoles. In 1724, Lieutenant-Governor William Dummer of Massachusetts sent an expedition into modern Maine to destroy the mission of the French Jesuit Sebastian Râle at Norridgewock, and thus limit French influence among the eastern Abenakis; it had already been burnt during earlier punitive expeditions in 1705 and 1722. Râle was killed in the 1724 raid.

This was a key episode in Dummer's War, a conflict from 1722 to 1727 in which the Abenakis under Grey Lock made repeated raids into Massachusetts and New Hampshire in response to the advancing frontier of settlement. The war revealed a shared inability to triumph as the colonists failed to end Abenaki raids while their opponents suffered from destructive attacks, for example the burning of the Abenaki village of Penobscot in 1725. Each side also suffered from disunity, and New York did not play a role in the fighting.[43]

Conversely, the French were convinced that the British were conspiring with the Fox and Chickasaws against them. With Native American support, the French launched five attacks on the Fox in 1712–34, finally breaking Fox resistance, thanks in particular to a victory on the Illinois Grand Prairie in 1730. Farther south, the French, as an outlier from Louisiana, in 1717, founded Fort Toulouse on the Alabama River system in cooperation with the Creeks, in order to limit British expansion from the Carolinas. In 1736 and 1739, they attacked the Chickasaws, who traded with the British. Failure in the first was followed by success in the second. The Chickasaws agreed to a truce, although they remained aligned with the British. The campaign showed that the French could use the Ohio Valley to move forces from New France to the Mississippi. They followed the route surveyed in 1729 by Chaussegros de Léry, Chief Engineer of New France.[44]

However, the French presence in Louisiana was less threatening than it appeared. After the failure of John Law's bold plans for the Mississippi Company in 1720, there was a loss of interest in Louisiana among both French officials and the public. This led to a less regular dispatch of supplies, with consequent shortages of food and manpower. There were 242 soldiers in the colony in August 1730 and most were of low calibre. Instead of the 600 troops requested to deal with the serious rising by the native Natchez in 1729–31, only 150 men were sent.[45]

Relations with Spain in the New World were more central in British attention due to the importance of the Caribbean. The colonies and trade of the West Indies were seen as more significant both economically and strategically. Lacking naval power, Britain's North American colonists, however, found it easier to strike at Florida. This was to be the case after war broke out in 1739, but already, in 1728 Colonel John Palmer, at the head of 100 Carolinians and 200 Native American allies, had raided the St Augustine area in order to attack the nearby Yamasee villages. Competition with France was also an issue in Florida: in 1718–20, when Britain and France were allied against Spain during the War of the Quadruple Alliance, it was French forces (from Louisiana) that captured, in 1719, Pensacola, the major Spanish base in West Florida. It was returned after the end of the war. The British did not launch a major attack on Florida during this war, although the British and French briefly seized St Catherine's Island.

As an important reminder of the reality underlying European competition, the Spaniards in Pensacola and the French in nearby Mobile had close relations arising from a mutual dependence that reflected a sense of isolation and vulnerability in the face of a hostile environment and uncertain relations with Native Americans. This was accentuated by a lack of news and supplies from home, which encouraged the sharing of both. The British lacked similar interdependence with the French or Spaniards.

The British also expressed concern about economic competition with France in North America. On 20 September (OS) 1718, the *Weekly Medley* warned that the planting of tobacco by the French in their new colony of Louisiana was a threat to the British tobacco trade and thus to the colonies. The French certainly intended this, not least as their consumption of British tobacco exports grew considerably after the Treaty of Utrecht in 1713 and, by 1730, was the largest on the continent.[46] The *Weekly Packet*, in its issue of 26 September (OS) 1719, noted that it would not address the issue of competition lest it be accused of criticizing the French alliance, as it was 'a time when other circumstances oblige us to favour the interest of France'. The value of the colonies was very much considered in competitive terms. In practice, Louisiana found it difficult to develop a profitable export economy, while the protection costs of the colony remained high.

Alongside war and rivalry, the character of the British colonies was changing. Most important was that they were becoming more populous and defined. Thus,

Philadelphia, which had a population of 2,500 in 1685 and 4,000 in 1690, had about 25,000 people by 1760, making it one of the biggest cities in the English-speaking world. A visit to modern Philadelphia underlines this with many buildings of the period still well-preserved, significantly near the river.

Alongside the continued agricultural differentiation, an urban hierarchy emerged clearly among the settlements, and economic links developed between colonies. Moreover, economic links between the colonies and the British Isles strengthened and became more varied. As in Spanish America, a sense of community, separate from, but not opposed to, that of Britain, was increasingly apparent. This sense of community was superimposed on the multitude of identities that colonial life and settlement gave rise to.

The foundation of a colonial press was a clear sign of this. English newspapers were shipped across the Atlantic, but as early as 1704 Boston had the *Boston News Letter*. This was the first regular newspaper in British North America published by authority, although, in 1690, the unlicensed *Public Occurrences Foreign and Domestic* had been published there, only to be swiftly suppressed. The press communicated both pressures for a separate sense of identity and those for Anglicization; both a sense of distinction from Britain and yet also being part of a trans-Atlantic world. The press certainly was part of this world, for newspapers were a major component in the trans-Atlantic information system. Much of this system focused on the details of the voyages that kept links alive. In the colonies, as in Britain, they reported the voyages of individual ships, with predictions of arrival dates and, sometimes, information about cargoes. In addition, many printers crossed the Atlantic to North America.[47] As sailings became quicker and more frequent, so news from London appeared more speedily in the American press.

Newspapers were part of a shared 'mental space': colonial newspapers were frequently dominated by news of the mother country, while imported works were central to bookselling.[48] Cartographic knowledge was also more widely disseminated. Maps of North America came to play a greater role in atlases published in the first half of the century, for example those produced in London by Moll, Senex and Bowen. Laurence Echard's *The Gazeteer's or Newsman's Interpreter ... a Geographical Index ... in Europe*, was followed in 1704 by the first edition of a similar work devoted to Asia, Africa and America. More detailed works also appeared. The different flora and fauna of North America was revealed in publications such as Mark Catesby's *The Natural History of Carolina, Florida, and the Bahama Islands* (1731), which was based on his travels in 1712–25. American plants and trees became fashionable with designers of British landscape gardens, such as Charles Hamilton who developed one at Painshill in Surrey from 1738 until 1773. This included pine plantations.

The press also contributed to the expression of a strong sense of local rights and privileges. Mirroring the situation in Britain, these were seen as the local and necessary encapsulation of British liberties. Partly as a result, disputes over the power and pretensions of governors were widespread and frequent. Although the situation varied greatly by colony, the majority of senior officials were appointed by the British government or from Britain. They were generally products of the British patronage systems and their appointment was often a blow to the interests and aspirations of the colonists. Aside from variations between the colonies, tension between home government and colonists, however, was not continuous, not least because of the protection benefits derived by the colonists from Britain. It also offered a developed, prosperous and protected market for colonial goods. Moreover, trans-Atlantic links were generally close and many colonists were recent immigrants.

Colonists were also part of an economic system that was organized to supply British needs, yet within a context in which colonial leaders sought to ensure that these needs were understood and expressed in terms that were acceptable to them.[49] Salutary neglect by government, and the delegation of oversight, or even policy, to local authorities and agents and chartered bodies, were natural consequences of the dissipation of power over distance and of the range of other government commitments. Yet the strategic, financial, and commercial issues and opportunities involved encouraged government to put effort into overcoming the effects of colonial distance. This was facilitated, and made more apparent, by the importance of colonial towns, which owed much to the significance of overseas trade to the colonial economies, and to the use of slaves in the agricultural workforce. Thus, the key points in the Empire were port-capitals, especially Halifax, Boston, New York, Charleston and Savannah.

Moving from the widely agreed and agreeable nostrums about the mutual benefits of Empire, it was often unclear how best to integrate the colonies into this imperial system in specific terms, but that problem itself testified to the importance of the colonies. In seeking such integration, the need to assess America alongside other issues was a matter for polemic and policy. In 1719, Martin Bladen, an active member of the Board of Trade, was informed by a subordinate about the views of William Lowndes, Senior Secretary to the Treasury and, like Bladen, an MP:

> Mr Lowndes sent to speak with me this morning. I find by what he said to me that he has altered his mind, and is now against taking off the duties on American lumber or timber, upon a supposition that it is not properly naval stores, and that if it should be done it would ruin our trade to the Northern Crowns [Denmark and Sweden]; for if we do not take off their goods, they will not take off ours, and besides if we supply ourselves from our own plantations, there will of consequence the less come from the Northern Crowns, and so the duties on their timber will be considerably lessened to the prejudice of the revenue.[50]

Colonial governors, such as Joseph Dudley of Massachusetts, were more committed to the production of naval stores, and as part of a policy of colonial development.[51]

The colonies were in a suppliant position, obliged to turn to Westminster and Whitehall for changes in the regulatory regime, and, as a result, affected by legal opinions and political pressure in Britain. In 1729, for example, a petition on behalf of Virginia was presented to the House of Commons against legislation which prohibited the import of tobacco in a particular form, and in 1730 a petition on behalf of New York was presented for allowing salt to be imported into it from Europe, rather than via Britain. The Whig monopoly of power in Britain from 1714 left colonial lobbyists with little room for manoeuvre, which encouraged them to fall back onto the resources of their own local constituencies.[52]

The call for state action in economic matters was particularly marked in the early eighteenth century and was characteristic of the economic thought subsequently described as mercantilism.[53] Mercantilist practices in the colonies were an aspect of the system seen in Britain, but attempts could be made to push the process further in the colonies because of the lesser degree of corporate privilege and political power there and also because of the need to devise new systems of regulation.

Mercantilist practices, however, not only clashed with the individualistic pursuit of profit but also focused attention on the bodies issuing and regulating the system, and thus looked toward tensions later in the century. The Navigation Act of 1696 had been intended as a means of strengthening the enforcement of commercial regulations by making it less dependent on local support. Yet the British customs officials lacked the power to fulfil their responsibilities, and unsurprisingly so given the length of coastline. Moreover, legislation as a solution was of limited value in the absence of local consent and support. This lack of support was seen with the actions of colonial assemblies, juries and officials, and combined in an antagonistic duality in which royal was seen as opposed to colonial. Whatever the rhetoric of shared imperial interests, regulation was only sought by the colonists on terms and generally for particular benefit.

Moreover, there were variations in the appeal of mercantilism. Regulation was to seem less desirable in the second half of the century, especially for those colonies whose economic development and aspirations reflected their lack of profitable staple exports,[54] and this attitude toward regulation helped challenge the nature of Anglo–American links.

Already, in the first half of the century, while the colonies offered a useful market for British exports,[55] this was as part of a more difficult relationship. In the colonies, restrictions on their trade with foreign countries and their colonies were resented and evaded. Profits to be gained, or believed to be gained, by trade with the French and Spanish colonies in the West Indies proved particularly attractive. The extent of colonial evasion indeed led to the suggestion from the Board of Trade in 1724 that this trade be connived in, with rice exported direct to the Mediterranean, in order to enable the colonies to pay what they owed Britain in their bilateral trade.[56] Once permitted, this direct export contributed greatly to the prosperity of South Carolina.

In the important fishing industry, New England ports competed with those of the West Country of England in the Newfoundland cod fishery. Given the major significance of exports of dried fish for the economy of Massachusetts, this economic rivalry was important for a more general tension. Moreover, American shipbuilders exploited their access to plentiful timber in order to undersell British competitors.

The financial implications of imperial regulation, for both colonists and government, were significant not least in terms of the serious shortage of liquidity that affected North America throughout the century. This shortage was due to the extent to which the American colonies imported more from Britain than they exported to it. Imports included manufactured goods, for example ironware, such as ploughs and pins, clothing and weapons. Consumers had varied requirements, but the determination of the elite to act like British models of ladies and gentlemen ensured a need for imports such as wine and porcelain.

Imports led to significant levels of debt, as did the need to turn to Britain for investment capital. In the former case, a key issue in debt was that of supporting colonial living standards. These living standards were higher overall than in the West Indies because a smaller proportion of the colonial population was in servitude, but, as the whites were concerned average living standards were probably higher for the white minority in the West Indies. Living standards were linked to credit, and the shortage of liquidity – of both coinage and credit – made the level of taxation an especially serious issue. This also led to acute problems when there were financial problems, as during and after the South Sea Bubble of 1720. The bursting of this speculative bubble caused a serious deflation. In the Chesapeake, the shortage of liquidity was linked to the dominance of the tobacco trade by large British trading houses.[57]

The issue of paper currency by colonial governments in response was particularly unsatisfactory to British merchants who were dubious about its inherent value. This led to tension, with merchants pressing the British government to instruct colonial governors accordingly, but the latter tended to be more aware of the economic, social and political pressures on the ground. In 1733, Massachusetts was forbidden from issuing new bonds.

As far as trade was concerned, the regulatory environment was firm, if not harsh, and was certainly not a case of the salutary neglect sometimes observed in British policy. The 1660 Act banning the export of raw wool and live sheep included the colonies, and was confirmed by the Wool Act of 1699. In 1750, under the Iron Act, the making of steel, the refining of iron, and the manufacture of finished articles from iron, were all prohibited in the colonies. This was of particular importance given the major expansion in iron production from 1715. The Molasses Act of 1733 sought to determine the economic relationship between the West Indies and New England.

These and other regulations and restrictions caused irritation, if not anger, although they were not to have the emotive power and the capacity to focus grievances and a sense of grievance that tea caused in the 1770s. Aside from questions of profit, trade was bound up with practices of consumption through which social worth was expressed and generated. This was a cause of anxiety different to, but linked with, that about wealth.

Yet alongside contradictory definitions of economic interest, as well as simple irritations, there was a common purpose between British and colonial lobbies, and government, as far as re-exports were concerned. The inelastic nature of British demand for tobacco ensured that continental markets were particularly important, and their growth encouraged the spread of tobacco production in North America. British diplomats urged foreign powers to receive re-exports, such as tobacco, and to keep taxes on them low, and also pressed the case in entrepôts such as Hamburg and Livorno. Furthermore, the American colonies benefited from pressure on their West Indies counterparts to heed imperial preference, rather than turning to French sources.[58] Because North American-built and owned ships counted as British under the Navigation Acts, they benefited from their protectionist provisions.

Influenced by eventual independence, it is too easy to underrate the extent to which colonists contributed to the development of the Empire to which they were happy to belong. It is also too easy to underrate the Englishness (and from 1707 Britishness) of early America, and the English context of social development in the Thirteen Colonies, as if the conditions encountered necessarily implied a radical break with the past. In practice, the evolution of Maryland and Virginia society, for example, is incomprehensible without an awareness of English social development. Most settlers were English by birth and upbringing. They established a society based on English laws, government and economic organization, and brought traditional English attitudes towards the social order and religious practices; although the extent of localism in England was such that there was a number of models to draw on. Virginia, for example, drew more on the south-west, where Royalism and Anglicanism were strong, whereas the Puritans of New England drew on a very different heritage in East Anglia, which had been a centre of resistance to the Crown during the Civil War.

Moreover, in the case of the Chesapeake, immigration from England greatly slackened from the 1690s, which was a decade of demographic crisis in the British

Isles, and social contrasts within the white population became more marked. This was linked to a demographic shift in which, thanks to a decline in death rates, the percentage of native-born inhabitants rose. This rise ensured a better balance of men and women, early marriages and thus more children.[59] Correspondingly, a sense of particular community developed; although the sway of the homeland remained strong as a result of the influence of precepts of behaviour alongside imported goods that helped to shape domestic space and time, such as furniture and tea.[60]

Aside from a more distinctive and autonomous social world in the North American colonies, there were also political issues in dispute between Britain and her colonies, as well as between the latter. In the context of a legacy of differing formulations of constitutional practice, personality as well as policy and principle were at stake. For example, in 1708, Sir Nathaniel Johnson, Governor of Carolina, imprisoned Thomas Nairne, the province's first Indian agent, for complaining about his abuse of commercial links with the Native Americans. The expansion of territorial claims and settlement was a particular source of dispute, as it brought issues of authority and interest into play.

Support for imperial defence also proved a vexed matter, not least disputes over who was to meet the considerable cost of fortifications. These disputes opposed not only royal authority to colonial assemblies, for example New Hampshire's unwillingness to pay much toward a fort in Great Island, but also colony with colony. In 1703, Colonel Joseph Dudley, the Governor of Massachusetts, traced his difficulties to the character of the colony's political culture, specifically the extent of representation, claiming that as the colony's Council was:

> of the people's choice ... they are more careful of their election than of the Queen's service and satisfaction, in so much that I have only power to deny anything offered me that is amiss in the Assembly, but no assistance to bring to pass what is necessary for the service, which will be in a great measure altered when Her Majesty will please to assume her just power to name her own Council here as in all the other governments in America.[61]

More generally, governors were under pressure from assemblies, and the latter usurped their powers.[62] Seeing the Westminster Parliament as a model, assemblies interpreted their privileges and competence in terms of Westminster's role, and sought to extend their responsibilities accordingly. Indeed, in some respects, colonial assemblies took forward what was latent in the Revolution Settlement but had not been greatly developed at Westminster, namely the development of executive functions by the legislature. This was seen in particular when assemblies appointed to public offices and took control over public works.[63]

This process was pushed particularly hard in South Carolina where the proprietors lacked local support, not least for their failure to take a role in facing the varied challenges in the 1700s and 1710s. As a result, in 1719, the militia overthrew the Governor and asked George I to replace the proprietors. The role of the Crown as both arbiter and solution looked toward the views expressed by some critics of parliamentary legislation in the early 1770s (see pp. 117–18). In the event, the Board of Trade, happy to see the end of the proprietors in South Carolina, dispatched a royal governor and in 1729 the Crown bought out the proprietors.

Governors, with their prerogative pretensions unsupported by the resources of political management, suffered from their frequent inability to win over important constituencies within American political life. Instead, rather like the King's representatives in Dublin, they were observers in effect of tensions within local politics. In both Ireland and North America, this gave influence to elitist groups able to link up with, and appear to shape, lower status opinion, while employing the deference of the latter to ensure that it did not challenge elite views.[64]

Among the parallels that can be noted, the Westminster Parliament's Declaratory Act of 1720 stated its supremacy over that of Dublin, prefiguring the Act of 1766 with regard to North America. The support of the military was an important issue, but a sense of threat from the Bourbon powers and Ireland's Catholics helped lead to compliance with British wishes: the Irish Parliament had to pay the cost of quartering a large part of the army in Ireland to support the Anglo-Irish establishment. Trade was also a key concern. Legislation in Westminster, the result of protectionist lobbying by English interests, for example the Irish Woollen Export Prohibition Act of 1699, hindered Irish exports.

Particular steps exacerbated the sense of exploitation. In 1722, a Wolverhampton ironmaster, William Wood, purchased a patent to mint copper coins for Ireland, a step that led to bitter complaints with constitutional and political weakness seen as leading to economic problems. Walpole's government was obliged as a result of the agitation to recall the patent, prefiguring the Stamp Act Crisis with North America in 1765–6. The denominational politics of different confessional groups complicated the situation in America, giving politics alignments, issues, and anger,[65] whereas in Ireland there was an Anglican monopoly of power.

The general theme in the political history of the colonies is of growing opposition to aspects of imperial practice and policy, looking toward the crisis of the War of Independence. That narrative is certainly feasible, but it is also possible to chart a parallel between developments in North America and those in the British Isles. Such a parallel draws attention to the range, intensity and impact of public debate, but puts public pressures alongside the complex processes of compromise by which politics also worked to further the business of governance.

A longer timescale moreover clarifies the extent to which there was no clear linear trajectory in political tension. Instead, the divisions and disruptions of the 1640s, 1650s and 1680s were greater than those of the eighteenth century prior to the mid-1770s, and even into the early stages of the crisis then. Although there was political contention, the stability of colonial institutions earlier in the eighteenth century was notable.[66]

Furthermore, both sides of the Atlantic saw the complex and contingent working-through of the Glorious Revolution as the Revolution Settlement was grounded in constitutional, political, dynastic and confessional terms. In Britain, parliamentary monarchy took time to establish, and the dynastic challenge of the Stuarts was only overcome within Britain at Culloden in 1746, while the last attempted French invasion on their behalf was in 1759. In both Ireland and the American colonies, the working through of this Settlement was also uncertain, as it was difficult to revise the arrangements adopted in the aftermath of William III's victory in the Glorious Revolution.

An aspect of subsequent political history can be seen in terms of attempts to revise these arrangements. For America, this is true of the Stamp Act Crisis of 1765–6 and the Declaratory Act of 1766 (see pp. 106–7), while the working through to annual sessions of a Parliament elected at least at regular intervals was only secured in Ireland in 1768.

The idea of distinct trans-Atlantic political chronologies, and the problems these created for imperial governance, can be expanded. For example, ideas from the county studies on mid-seventeenth-century England, with their emphasis on distinct political worlds, can be applied to the varied political cultures of the colonies at that time, and into and throughout the eighteenth century. This emphasis underlines the difficulties of taking common action at a proto-national level when without the focus of an American Parliament with a specific constitutional place. Instead, as far as the colonies were concerned, the Westminster Parliament operated in a fashion that was episodic as well as unpredictable, and the latter risked seeming arbitrary. The Civil War parallel also encompasses mid-seventeenth-century English urban politico-religious radicalism, which can be seen as prefiguring aspects of urban activism in American cities a century later.

These themes of division and disorder, in Britain and its colonies, were not incompatible with a social politics and practice of power that could contain them, bar for the complete overthrow of the monarchical centre and signifier of the system, as occurred in Britain in the 1640s and 1680s. Alongside the role of monarchy as the symbol of political purpose, and the prime source of imperial and colonial authority and patronage, came the role of religious authorities and practices in contributing to this nexus of norms and order, as well as the powerful products of social respect. Well aware of social gradations, colonial society responded, in a world of patronage and clientage, to the wishes of the patricians who acted as public patrons and who dominated government office.

Again, there are powerful similarities with the British Isles, not least in the way in which the potential radicalism of Whig ideas and the example of the Glorious Revolution were adapted to dominant social norms and to a politics of deference. This adaptation did not prevent the disruptions of factionalism and popular activism, but neither, in the early eighteenth century, was in a position to change the political parameters fundamentally, nor indeed sought to do so.

The nature of American politics appeared most significant to governors and British commentators during periods of international tension, as military assistance was considered or sought in an urgent context. Yet this politics was already a constant factor for those interested in imperial issues. For example, a memorandum among the papers of Sir Robert Walpole, the head of the ministry from 1720 to 1742, included one on recently conquered Nova Scotia that drew together ideas of imperial rivalry and colonial governance. In support of the idea of settling Nova Scotia, it was seen as a province that would 'raise a considerable revenue to the Crown, make a frontier against our French neighbours, and drain a great number of inhabitants from New England where they are daily aiming at an independency, and very much interfere with the trade of their mother kingdom'.[67]

This is instructive from the perspective of what were seen as the likely consequences of the conquest of Canada in 1711, although that was the project of a Tory ministry, while Walpole was the head of a Whig one. More broadly, such ideas reflected a tendency on imperial governance to put a stress on the state. Whereas for colonies established by chartered enterprises, this stress had been indirect, there was now a different pattern of governance, one that reflected the development of Crown in Parliament, the Union of the kingdoms, and the establishment in Britain of a strong fiscal system to finance military engagements. As a consequence, from 1713, overseas acquisitions from wars remained under greater metropolitan control than the colonies established by chartered enterprises, and the two patterns of governance created pressures, from both directions, for imperial realignments.

At the same time as these signs of tension, trans-Atlantic links improved. As a consequence, the English Atlantic 'shrank' between 1675 and 1740 with significant improvements, such as the development of postal services, and the invention of the helm wheel, which dramatically increased rudder control on large ships, and thus their manoeuvrability so as to gain advantage of sea and wind conditions. The number of trans-Atlantic voyages doubled in this period and the number of ships that extended or ignored the 'optimum' shipping seasons also increased on several major routes. Inter-colonial shipping trebled.[68]

Ironically, however, 'mariner-resident interaction times' decreased with greater efficiencies in the transport system, as did the degree to which 'average residents experienced colonial societies as maritime societies'.[69] The latter decline, however, owed more to changing settlement patterns than to improved maritime links, for colonial society became less urban and less bound to the coast. From the British perspective, increased links were to help make imperial control appear more viable and visible; but this was to have deleterious political consequences.

2

Imperial Rivalries, 1739–53

North America became more prominent as a subject of British governmental and public attention in the 1740s, although at first, as during the war in the 1700s, it was subordinate to the West Indies in governmental and public concerns. This focus on the West Indies reflected the centrality of confrontation with Spain, with whom the War of Jenkins' Ear had broken out in 1739. This conflict arose from Spanish attempts to preserve its commercial system in the New World and to prevent illegal British trade. It was named after the most prominent of a string of Spanish atrocities, the alleged cutting off by Spanish coastguards of an ear of Robert Jenkins, the captain of an English merchantman.

This conflict continued until 1748, becoming part of the War of the Austrian Succession as fighting also began with France. In the USA, this is known as King George's War. Although Caribbean trade was the key issue in Anglo–Spanish relations, there were also tensions over the North American mainland. These tensions arose from British expansion. The British had spread south from the Carolinas, initially with the construction of Fort King George on the Altamaha River in 1721 in order to forestall possible French influence from Louisiana over the Native Americans. The Spaniards objected that the fort breached the Anglo–Spanish treaty of 1670, South Carolina complained about Spain sheltering escaped slaves, and the crisis eased when the British garrison was withdrawn in 1727.

The situation became more serious with the chartering in 1732 of the colony of Georgia, where indeed British maritime force and interests could more readily be brought to bear. The first settlers arrived in 1733. The key figure was Colonel James Oglethorpe, one of the 21 Georgia Trustees and the only one on site. Savannah was established as the capital, and was followed in 1736 by Augusta.

Georgia appeared to threaten the neighbouring Spanish colony of Florida, which was centred on nearby St Augustine, and Spanish governmental disquiet[1] contributed to the outbreak of the War of Jenkins' Ear. An agreement between the Governor of Florida and Oglethorpe's agent signed in 1736 was unacceptable to the Spanish government, which continued to find the British position in Georgia a menace. In 1738, a British battalion arrived. Like the French naval base of Louisbourg, concern about Florida and Georgia was evidence of increasing investment in the North American contest by European governments.[2]

Tension between Georgia and Florida led to Anglo–Spanish hostilities at the outbreak of the war. After inconclusive skirmishes in 1739, the dynamic Oglethorpe, in May 1740, led an expedition against St Augustine, which Spain had designated a haven for escaped slaves and which was also a major base for privateers. He encountered no serious resistance en route, but his plan for a methodical siege was thwarted by the South Carolina Assembly's insistence on a short campaign. This was an instructive demonstration of the conditional nature of colonial support, not only for the initiatives of the British government but also for those of other colonies. At the same time, the Assembly was representing what was possible within its political parameters.

In an important episode in the political shaping of North America, the Spaniards resisted bravely at St Augustine. They mounted an effective night sortie on 14–15 June, the well-fortified position resisted bombardment, and the British naval blockade failed to prevent the arrival of Spanish supply ships. Once the momentum of advance and success was lost, Oglethorpe's force was struck by desertion, especially on the part of his Native American allies, mostly Creek, and by the troops from South Carolina. Neither Native Americans nor colonists liked long campaigns nor were easy to keep motivated when success seemed a distant prospect. As so often with conflicts in hot and humid environments, the effects of disease exacerbated the situation and on 9 July Oglethorpe retreated.[3] Lieutenant William Horton claimed: 'that the Indians are good to fight against Indians, and to waste the Spanish plantations, but not fit for entering breaches or trenches, or besieging a town regularly'.[4] At any event, the first assault on a rival centre of power in North America since the British expedition against Québec in 1711 had failed.

In July 1742, the Spaniards counter-attacked, invading Georgia with 1,900 men and capturing St Simon's Island. Oglethorpe, however, used the wooded terrain effectively to ambush their force at the Battle of Bloody Marsh. The Spaniards, also discouraged by reports of British naval reinforcements, retreated. In September 1742, in turn, there was an unsuccessful British naval attack on St Augustine.

Thereafter, the situation became a matter of raids, such as that mounted on the St Augustine area in March 1743. That year, Oglethorpe returned to Britain, never to revisit Georgia. The effective end to operations reflected the limited local military resources on both sides and the unwillingness of distant imperial sources of military power to provide sufficient additional resources. This was due to the greater appeal and importance of operations in the Caribbean. Compared to the military resources sent there in 1739–41, particularly, in 1741, in the unsuccessful British siege of Cartagena, on the coast of modern Colombia, the British ignored Florida.

Florida anyway was of slight economic significance, much of it being covered by swamps,[5] while, in the interior, Native Americans were a powerful element, such as the Yamasee who destroyed the trading post of Mount Venture on the Altamaha River in 1742. Operations on the mainland also served no domestic political imperative within Britain, which again greatly contrasted with the situation in the Caribbean. Admiral Vernon's success at Porto Bello in 1739 attracted widespread and favourable comment, but there was no comparable interest in Britain in the position on the North American mainland. The situation was to be very different in 1754–6.

The British campaigns in the Caribbean were largely dependent on troops from Britain. The South did not produce an effort comparable to that repeatedly mounted against French bases by New England. In part, this reflected the lack of local naval and maritime resources compared to New England, while Louisiana and the French and Spanish West Indies were more distant than Nova Scotia, Cape Breton and Canada. There was also a racial dimension with the extent to which Southern manpower was black, and the unwillingness to arm blacks. They were used as labour to build fortifications, but not as soldiers. In contrast, drawing on escaped slaves, the Spaniards created a free militia based at Fort Mose near St Augustine.

A bold prospectus for relations between the British colonies as part of a geopolitical whole had been suggested in 1741, when Colonel John Stewart wrote from Jamaica:

> If ever Britain strikes any considerable stroke in this part of the world, the blow must come from the North American colonies not by bringing raw men from … [Britain], but by sending officers of experience and good corps to incorporate with and discipline the men to be raised there, these troops as the passage from thence is much shorter might be transported directly to any part of the Spanish West Indies and arrive there with the health and vigour necessary for action, whereas troops sent from home as our own experience has taught us, are by the length of the passage one half disabled with the scurvy and the other half laid up with diseases contracted by confinement and the feeding of salt provisions.[6]

Indeed, the Cartagena expedition carried 3,700 American recruits as well as 5,800 British troops. The Americans, under William Gooch, Virginia's Governor, included vagrants drafted in Virginia and Pennsylvanians fleeing indentured service, but most were volunteers. Due to disease, however, only about 10 per cent of the Americans returned home. It is possible that a consciousness of difference between Britons and colonists was accentuated by contrasting treatment during the expedition, and some Americans certainly felt comparatively worse treated.

To the north, in the 1740s, there was a revival of the British attempt to encompass North America imaginatively and practically by discovering a navigable North-West Passage to the Pacific. James Knight had failed to do so or to discover gold in 1719, dying with his entire expedition, but the attempt was revived in the 1740s. Individuals and institutions both played a role. In 1741, the Admiralty sent the *Discovery* and the *Furnace* to Hudson Bay under Christopher Middleton. The following year, he sailed further north along the west coast of that inhospitable region than any previous European explorer, but could not find the entrance to a North-West Passage. The naming of Repulse Bay testified to Middleton's frustration.

The problems of exploration were not the sole issue. Organization, profit and politics were intertwined, as the controlling role of the Hudson's Bay Company caused anger and concern in Britain. There was criticism of the company's apparent ineffectiveness in upholding national interests in the face of French competition, and of its alleged lack of commitment to expansion into the interior of Canada. These led, in 1749, to a parliamentary enquiry and, in 1752, to an unsuccessful attempt by London merchants to obtain trading privileges in Labrador.

In 1746–7, William Moor, who was sent by the North-West Committee organized by Arthur Dobbs, a critic of the Hudson's Bay Company, also failed to find a Passage. One consequence of these attempts was a scattering of the names of British ministers along the coast of Hudson Bay, with Chesterfield Inlet and Wager Bay.[7] It was only in 1778 that James Cook sailed from the Pacific to a new farthest north – 70° 44' N at Icy Cape, Alaska, and proved that pack ice blocked any possible North-West Passage.

Meanwhile, in their expansion into the interior, the French were seeking a route to the Pacific alongside dominance of the fur trade. Fort Boubon (1739) took the French presence to the north-west shore of Lake Winnipeg. Fort Dauphin (1741) established their presence on the western shore of Lake Winnipegosis, and Fort la Corne (1753) was built near the Fords of the Saskatchewan, a crucial node of Native American trade routes first reached by French explorers in 1739–40. These explorations enhanced the French position in the fur trade, but did not bring the hoped-for route to the Pacific. In 1742–3, La Vérendrye sent two of his sons on a further search for the Pacific. They crossed much of the Dakotas before turning back short of the River Platte because their Native American companions feared attack.

The fur trade proved more effective than exploration in transmitting European wishes. Although mediated in terms of local interests and concepts, the response in terms of the provision of furs paralleled that of slave traders in the African interior. Moreover, just as European demand for furs led to increased pressure on the ecology, particularly on the beaver population, so also with the greater demand for slaves in Africa. European trade goods were important to each process, but they were obtained on terms that the non-Western population influenced, and therefore the latter were important in determining how these goods were used.[8] Trade, moreover, should be seen alongside gift-giving, and thus as an aspect of diplomacy in which power was expressed in accordance with particular conventions.

Tensions over Anglo–Spanish hostilities had nearly led France into conflict with Britain in 1740–1, but this had been avoided. Instead, it was not till 1743 that hostilities between Britain and France began. They started in Europe (and war was declared the following year), leading to conflict in North America, rather than, as in 1754–6, conflict in North America leading to war at home. Indeed, in 1743–8, fighting was largely restricted to the Atlantic littoral. This owed much to the nature of the military aid sent from Britain or the metropole (naval rather than army), to pressure for neutrality from the Iroquois, and for the maintenance of peaceful trade with Canada from the Albany Dutch and from major landholders in the region such as the Livingstones. These factors kept the peace south-east of the Great Lakes, while distances between the Carolinas and French positions along the Mississippi were too great for any significant operations there. The French-backed Abenaki of what was to become Vermont, New Hampshire and Maine raided British settlements in New England, drove the settlers from what was to be Vermont, and ambushed militia patrols, but the French lacked regular troops to support large-scale offensive operations in this region. They were heavily committed in Europe, against Austria, the Dutch and the kingdom of Sardinia, as well as Britain. Nevertheless, Massachusetts devoted much effort in 1744–5 to building forts to cover its northern frontier.

In 1745 and 1746, the French and Native American forces launched inland offensives against New York and Massachusetts, capturing Saratoga and Fort Massachusetts respectively. This ended the de facto neutrality on the New York frontier and, looking toward the situation in 1749–54 and 1756–7, reflected the degree to which the French were able to take the initiative in the interior. Their base at Fort St Frédéric (Crown Point), at the southern end of Lake Champlain, threatened the Hudson valley. In 1746, the British planned a joint attack with the Iroquois on Canada, beginning with the capture of Fort St Frédéric, but the British forces did not arrive and most of the Iroquois remained neutral. War began between France and the Mohawks (one of the Iroquois tribes), and the latter, encouraged by William Johnson, New York's active agent with the Iroquois, raided far to the north, but an Anglo–Mohawk raiding party was ambushed at the Cascades of the St Lawrence in June 1747.

For the European powers, sea power could both lessen distance and permit the concentrated application of force, each offering an improvement on inland offensives. The French acted first on the Atlantic littoral. Taking the initiative on the outbreak of war in 1744, warships from Louisbourg, the major French base on Ile Royale (Cape Breton Island), attacked the British position in Nova Scotia. Louisbourg and its warships were, in turn, challenged by New England troops under General William Pepperrell, supported by the small Leeward Islands squadron of the Royal Navy under Commodore Peter Warren, William Johnson's uncle, and the husband of the New York heiress Susannah DeLancey.

Warren's support testified to a capacity to ensure an integrated nature of British military effort in the New World. Indeed, warships were rotated between the Caribbean in the winter and North American waters. In turn, this capacity created an expectation that such integration would be the case, although such cooperation posed serious problems of military command and control, as well as issues of political acceptability and accountability in the direction and support of effort.

Louisbourg was the best-fortified position in New France, its defences newly created on the Vauban plan for major French fortresses. Louisbourg was designed, however, to resist attack from the sea, was more vulnerable by land, and the morale of the garrison was low. In April 1745, Warren blockaded the harbour, and the New England militia was able to land safely in Gabarus Bay. The attackers bombarded the land defences, while Warren's blockade reduced the food available to the defenders. With the walls breached and Warren also able to force his way into the harbour, the Governor capitulated in June. The Massachusetts forces had acted like European regulars; the siege of Louisbourg was not an exercise in wilderness warfare. Its fall was a considerable achievement, not least because it was a stronger position than Port Royal.

Warren sought to consolidate the new conquest by pressing for the establishment of a civil government and for naming Louisbourg as a free port. To encourage settlement further, Warren proposed that religious toleration be offered to Protestant Dissenters.[9] Each of these steps was indicative of the nature of British imperialism: alongside its many flaws, it was more committed to commerce and liberty than other contemporary empires.

The capture of Louisbourg suggested new possibilities for British and colonial commentators, and was contrasted with the government's unpopular concern to fight the French in the Low Countries (Belgium and the Dutch Republic). The *Universal Spectator*, a London newspaper, of 27 July (OS) 1745 stated:

> It is presumed our success at Cape Breton, which the French have so much interest in defending, will encourage us to some farther attempts upon their settlements in America: by which we might more effectively distress them, and serve ourselves, than by showing them our backsides in Flanders.

Pepperrell next suggested an invasion of Canada proper. The British government agreed in April 1746 and planned to send six regiments of troops to sail up the St Lawrence, with two more coming from American units stationed at Louisbourg. Other colonial troops would advance north from Albany. The colonies raised about 7,000 men, the largest contingent from Massachusetts, but there were a series of delays. Instead, the port of Lorient in France was attacked, while it was the French who sent a major fleet to North America in 1746, although this attempt to regain Louisbourg fell victim to bad weather, disease and inadequate supplies. The French faced very serious organizational and operational problems in mounting trans-Atlantic expeditions and had less experience in such operations than the British; this gap was to become more important in the next war.

The planned British St Lawrence expedition was postponed until 1747 and then cancelled. However, the capture of Louisbourg had deprived the French of a base and, instead, enabled the British, again dominant at sea, to blockade the St Lawrence. This cut supplies to Canada and destroyed the basis of the French fur trade, because alliances with the Native Americans were sustained by presents and trade goods. Instead, British fur traders were now able to undersell the French dramatically, and this encouraged both the Miami and the Hurons to break with the French, while the Choctaws signed a treaty with Governor James Glen of South Carolina in 1747. The Miami sacked Fort Miami in 1747 and Fort Vincennes in 1751. The two battles off Cape Finisterre, serious French naval defeats in European waters in 1747, accentuated the situation by confirming British mastery at sea.

In Britain, the capture of Louisbourg led to a marked increase in public discussion of North America,[10] and, crucially, of this rather than the West Indies. Popular interest in the New World rose. For example, in 1747, *Felix Farley's Bristol Journal* announced that it had engaged Boston and Philadelphia correspondents.[11] It was indicative that such a step was seen as worthy of notice. It testified not only to the close commercial relations across the Atlantic, but also to the understanding that this had consequences in terms of public interest.

The *Westminster Journal* of 6 February (OS) 1748, a copy of which was acquired by the French government, argued that, thanks to its island character, Britain was safe from French attack, but that the North American colonies were not, and that Canada must therefore be seized:

> Whatever the creed of some persons may be, mine, that of the British Americans, and of all Englishmen who judge with knowledge and impartiality, is that to people and secure New Scotland [Nova Scotia], to reduce Canada, and open a communication betwixt our settlements in Hudson's Bay and those on the [Atlantic] Ocean, should be one of the principal objects in view in a war against France. Let us turn out these bad neighbours while we have power and lawful authority ... It is of much more concern to us than who has the possession of Italy, I had almost said of the Netherlands.[12]

The government, however, was unimpressed. Instead, it agreed, by the Peace of Aix-la-Chapelle (1748), to return Louisbourg in order to persuade France, in turn, to return its own captures: both in the Low Countries, and Madras in India to the British East India Company. This decision was much to the fury of New

Englanders, who had played a key role in Louisbourg's capture and who were the colonists most concerned about Canada.[13] If this fury reflected a New England failure to appreciate the exigencies of an imperial system that faced major difficulties in its struggle with the Bourbons, that did not demonstrate a gap between Britain and her colonies, because this fury was widely shared in Britain. Nevertheless, as with shared critical trans-Atlantic responses to British imperial legislation in the 1760s and early 1770s, the consequences played a greater and different role in North America, and an angry alienation developed. Parliament, which had appropriated funds for the purpose in 1747, sought to lessen the anger by awarding Massachusetts £180,000 for its costs in the war.

Although an American identity was forming, and the term American began to be used,[14] the expression 'British North America' captures the extent to which Britain and her colonies were seen as part of the same world. The languages of Britishness and Empire provided the conception of a larger community, with the full range of English-speaking territories in the western hemisphere being members of a single body, the Empire. This was a potent ideology that accorded with other developments within British public culture that encompassed Britain and the colonies. These focused on the linkage of Protestantism, trade, maritime range and liberty, their role in British identity, and their positive synergy.

The vision and, increasingly, reality of a maritime commercial empire identified the success of a trading nation with the liberty of its government, and distinguished this process (in a positive fashion) from a simple emphasis on territorial conquest, which was attributed to France and Spain. British writers saw this supposed character of their Empire as ensuring that the corruptions and debilities discerned in classical and modern republics, and associated with a lack of liberty and with conquest, need not destroy British liberties. This focus on liberty integrated the British world, creating a potent trans-Atlantic ideology, and yet also had the potential of creating tensions within it, as the threat to British liberties could be presented as coming from British government.[15]

Liberty, however, was not simply a secular construction, ideology and language. There was also a powerful religious dimension, with liberty almost defined by anti-Catholicism. Moreover, this had clear political consequences, as in a ready linkage between anti-Catholicism and opposition to Catholic states. The anniversary sermons of the Georgia Trustees made this clear. The purpose of Empire was also a religious theme, one, furthermore, that encompassed commerce and the state:

> The essentially spiritual condition of tenure for their empire as a requirement for its continued colonial wealth that these eighteenth-century Anglicans constructed necessitated the English also accepting responsibility for the eternal destinies of their colonists.[16]

Such arguments are a reminder of the flexibility and applicability of religious themes, and indeed of the need for both flexibility and applicability given the tendency to see and express moral and ideological issues in religious terms and language. There was, however, a paradox: that the British loathed Catholicism in part because of its overseas allegiance to the Papacy but, in their own colonies, replicated an overseas sovereignty themselves.

Presenting British expansionism as a response to Bourbon aggression, and therefore as necessary, was also important. It contributed to what the *Westminster Journal* of 1 April (OS) 1749 termed 'the principle of take and hold in America'. Trade and territory could thus be linked in what was seen as a dynamic concept of Empire, one that emphasized relationships that provided important and sustaining links. Moreover, the fall of Louisbourg had shown that it could be captured, and thus suggested the expansionist potential for British North America.

Linking trade and territory, however, led also to the argument that to be weak in any particular aspect might destroy the entire system. Thus, in 1749, Admiral Edward Vernon, the victor at Porto Bello in 1739 and an opposition MP, wrote to a colleague:

> I look on the fate of this country to be drawing to a speedy period whenever France should attain to a superior maritime power to Britain, which by the present of Cape Breton, we have given them an extensive foundation for … I may say without the spirit of prophecy that whenever they think themselves so, the first blow they will strike, will be to strip us, of every one of our sugar colonies, which I know to be easily attainable by them, whenever they have a superior force by sea; and that the natural consequence of that will be, that you will by the same blow, lose all your American colonies as to their dependence on Britain. And then what must become of a nation … with eighty millions of debt, and deprived of those branches of commerce that principally produced the revenues, to pay the interest of those debts, is a melancholy consideration.[17]

Thus, naval power, the West Indies, America, and British finances were all linked. In the early 1770s, the crucial addition was to be Britain's economic and fiscal interests in India in the form of American imports of East India Company tea.

Earlier attempts to translate the idea of Empire into policy had mixed success. This was seen, for example, with the long-discussed idea that naval supplies from the North American colonies could replace imports from Sweden, especially tar. Colonial output was built up in the 1730s, in part as a result of the granting of subsidies to New England production from 1729, and, in 1732, the Board of Trade pressed for import substitution from America.[18] Despite concern in Sweden about North American imports, however, there was no such chance of comparable substitution for Swedish iron. Moreover, British merchants handling Swedish iron imports were opposed to moves to substitute North American production.

The transport costs of colonial tar were far higher than for its Swedish competitor and, as a result, the Royal Navy, which preferred Swedish tar, opposed the subsidies. This ensured that there was a major dispute over policy within Britain, with the Board of Trade subject to contrary pressures. Bristol merchants, for example, supported colonial production, as they were best placed to import the tar, whereas London merchants could readily dominate trade with the Baltic. Further complications included concern about the quality of colonial tar, with the government unable to ensure that it was satisfactory.

Moreover, Spanish and French privateering during the wars of 1739–48 made the import of colonial tar less profitable as freight rates and insurance rose.[19] This was an instance of the way in which war could hit imperial links. Indeed, the export of tobacco and rice from the Chesapeake and South Carolina was affected, while, in 1747–8, Bourbon privateers off the Delaware Capes brought Philadelphia's trade to a halt.[20]

Yet the relationship between war and trade was more complex than one of simple hindrance. For example, during this period of warfare, there was a degree of import substitution. Indeed, it became more profitable to export indigo (for dye) from South Carolina, as it was a lighter good for the same value, and therefore required less shipping, while the production of indigo there developed as a substitute for British imports from the French West Indies and from Jamaica. Indigo therefore became an important complement to the rising rice exports from South Carolina; although tobacco exports from the Chesapeake remained the most important agricultural staple.

These exports were not only significant for trans-Atlantic trade but also brought Britain an important role in the comparative advantage that the West was gaining in the world economy. Indeed, the New World offered a host of advantages, including relatively low protection costs in the face of native peoples unable to threaten their core settlements, as well as important economic benefits, not least soils, many of these rich, that had not yet been denuded by intensive cultivation, and that, instead, served as a good basis for improved agricultural practices. The benefit was largely from the Southern colonies as these produced plantation goods. These had a high value in Western (although not non-Western) markets. As these goods could not be readily produced within Europe, this trade was very profitable and helped to underscore the growth of financial and mercantile capital and organization.[21]

Alongside developments in particular trades, individual interests and networks successfully spanned the Atlantic. William Baker (1705–70) was a prime example of the London merchant-politicians who bonded government, trade and Empire. The eldest son of a London draper, he was very active in trading with North America, not least with New York, and was also a major entrepreneur, buying land in Georgia and South Carolina. Prominent in the East India and Hudson's Bay

Companies, an MP, a London alderman, and a government contractor supplying troops in Nova Scotia from 1746, Baker was also consulted by ministers on colonial matters, not least on the repeal of the Stamp Act in 1766.

In the 1750s, there was also a growing ministerial conviction of the economic value of America, and indeed this was an aspect of the different constituencies, on both sides of the Atlantic, who had an interest in deriving benefit from the growth in colonial trade. As this trade expanded, so the opportunities became greater. In 1756, Robert, 4th Earl of Holdernesse, Secretary of State for the Northern Department, claimed that 'the extensive navigation of England ... takes its source from those very American colonies which France is now endeavouring forcibly and unjustly to invade.'[22] At the same time, there was an awareness of tension. *Some Reflections on the Trade Between Great Britain and Sweden*, an anonymously written pamphlet of that year, urging the import of iron from America rather than Sweden, discussed the objection that:

> it would occasion a vast increase of people and wealth, and consequently of power in those countries that in time might become rivals to their mother country, prejudice her interests, and become at last independent of her. But however plausible this objection may appear, there can be no just foundation for it, since ... it will be always in our power to subject them by our fleets, and still more by refusing them supplies of many of the necessaries of life.[23]

Naval power and economic controls were thus seen as a way to bring any rebellious colonists to heel.

There were a number of points in dispute between Britain and France in North America. The Congress of Aix-la-Chapelle of 1748 had failed to settle differences between Britain and France over North American boundaries, and the issue was referred to commissioners, who, however, could not resolve the matter. These differences led to anxiety on both sides and fostered fears. The return of Louisbourg threw attention on Nova Scotia, where the British were concerned about the stability of their position. The peace treaty had confirmed its cession to Britain, but had not specified its boundaries, and this provided a basis for dissension, especially, but not only, in 1750–1. In 1749, the government founded the port-fortress of Halifax in order to strengthen the British position. A naval dockyard was to follow there.

In 1750, Joseph Yorke, the envoy in Paris, expressed concern, but was also less alarmist than William Shirley, Governor of Massachusetts, an influential advocate of a forward policy in North America, who argued, in Yorke's words, that the fate of 'North America and indeed of our marine depends on the success of Nova Scotia.'[24] However, the front-page essay in the opposition London newspaper *Old England*, on 15 December 1750, referred to 'the all-grasping views of the House of Bourbon' and 'the practices now on foot to wrest from us the best part of Nova Scotia'. In December 1750, in turn, Brûlart, Marquis de Puysieulx, the French Foreign Minister, claimed that Britain appeared to be preparing an invasion of Canada.[25]

More consistently, the French feared that the pressure of British westward expansion would undermine the security of their colonies. In 1750, François-Marie Durand, the perceptive French Chargé d'Affaires in London, urged his government to pay attention to the large number of emigrants going to British North America.[26]

Growing French assertiveness was to help lead to crisis, but the French saw this as a necessary response to British policy, as well as a way to recover from the last stage of the recent war. Interest in the containment of the British colonies led the French, in 1749, to send a small force into the Ohio Valley which offered a shorter route from Canada to the French settlements in the Illinois Country, and then on to Louisiana. However, the Ohio Valley was also attractive to Virginians seeking land, as well as to imperial strategists thinking of how best to provide protection for the colonies and to disrupt French plans. Indeed, in 1747–8, the Virginia House of Assembly and the British government had given the Ohio Company, a newly chartered group of Virginia landowners and London merchants, title to a third of a million acres. This was a vast stake that represented a bold land speculation and its capacity to engender confrontation.

In 1747–9, the French recovered their position among the Choctaws, while, in 1752–4, they drove out British traders from the Ohio Valley, intimidated Britain's Native American allies, and constructed forts between Lake Erie and the junction of the Allegheny and Monongahela Rivers. In 1753, Fort de la Presque Isle and Fort Le Boeuf were built in Erie and Waterford, Pennsylvania respectively, Fort Duquesne following at the forks in the Ohio in 1754. The last was where the Ohio Company had also planned to erect a fort. In 1752, the Miami were forced back into an alliance with France, although French attacks on the Chickasaws in 1752 and 1753 failed. In a far less threatening fashion, the Spaniards encouraged settlement in Florida in order to strengthen its ability to resist British attack.

The renewal of French activity threatened to exclude the British not only from the Ohio Valley, but also from the entire interior of the continent: by 1753, a line of French posts lay across canoe routes to Hudson Bay. This was both economic and political warfare: for Britain and France, the fur trade interacted with Native American alliances.[27] Both sides were convinced that the other was stirring up Native American hostility and acting in a hostile fashion.

At the same time, the narrative and analysis of Anglo–Native American relations should not be expressed only in terms of a wider sphere in which France played a key role, let alone subordinated to this interpretation. Instead, hostile relations between Native Americans played a role as in the Creek–Cherokee conflict of the 1750s, a conflict that led the Cherokees to press for the construction of a fort. This resulted in James Glen, the Governor of South Carolina, building Fort Prince George in Cherokee country in 1753. Fort Loudoun, to protect the Overhill Cherokee Towns (in modern east Tennessee), followed in 1756.

Owing to the assertive French stance,[28] it proved harder for the two powers to disengage. Although the British government had no wish for war, it could not accept French claims in the Ohio Valley. In 1753, Robert Dinwiddie, the Lieutenant Governor of Virginia, was ordered to use force to defend British claims. George Washington, a Virginia militia officer, (small) landowner and land-speculator, was sent by him to demand that the French evacuate the area. Thus, the basis was laid for the Seven Years' War, which is known in the USA as the French and Indian War. Dinwiddie himself was a supporter of westward expansion, the Ohio Company and George Washington. In July 1754, the veteran diplomat Horatio Walpole, wrote to Dinwiddie of his

> concern at the unjust attempts of the French upon the boundaries of our colonies; if they go on the project they seem to have in view they will encompass all our northern colonies in the back by a chain of communication between the rivers Canada, and Mississippi, and become masters of all the Indians, and the trade on that continent, which requires our utmost attention and exertion of strength to prevent it, but as it is a common cause to all our northern colonies … they might, I am fully persuaded, considering their connection and the number of their inhabitants, soon disperse the French and their Indians, and disappoint their dangerous schemes, which at the beginning may be done, if cordially undertaken, without any great expense, and they might think fit to retire at once; before the councils of France shall have openly owned it, and made it a matter of state; but if they are suffered to make a strong settlement there and get together forces enough to support it, it may occasion troubles between the two nations of such expense and extent as may make it difficult to put an end to.[29]

Meanwhile, the pressure of immigration and the process of settlement continued in the British colonies, with the schemes of land speculators helping stimulate population flows. Alongside English immigrants, there were large numbers of Scots–Irish and Germans. The Scots–Irish were Ulster Presbyterians of Scots descent who suffered both political and religious disabilities under the 1704 Test Act and were affected by downturns in the local economy.

These high rates of immigration underlined the heterogeneous character of American society and ensured that direct links with Old World influences remained very powerful. These were not separate to the domestic formation of American culture, but, instead, part of it. These high rates ensured that much of the white population was starting anew with scant capital assets. From within the colonies, there were, however, expressions of opposition to the high rates of immigration, most significantly Benjamin Franklin's 'Observations concerning the Increase of Mankind, Peopling of Countries, etc.' (1755).[30] It is probable, that alongside such expressions, there was a more general disquiet, although the need for settlers for both labour and defence would have been a given.

As before, settlement spread geographically, both westward and also into the gaps between the earlier coastal enclaves, processes that helped ensure that British America was becoming less urban. In already-farmed regions, there was also an intensification of settlement, with the clearing and burning of woodland again providing an opportunity to benefit from fertile soil. This process also led to driving away Native Americans, for example into the Iroquois lands in northern Pennsylvania, as a key aspect of clearing the land. To the west, the New River Valley in the south of the Valley of Virginia, west of the Blue Ridge Mountains, was settled from the 1740s. In the more settled lands east of the mountains, new towns included Charlottesville (1744) and Charlotte (1750). However, round the Chesapeake there was as yet no major port, no focus of the trans-Atlantic trade,[31] that could serve as a sphere for urban mass-politicization.

After 1730, as readily cultivatable land grew scarcer in Maryland, Pennsylvania and Virginia, settlers travelled down the Great Philadelphia Wagon Road, through the Shenandoah Valley and the James River and Roanoke Gaps, to enter the Piedmont of North and South Carolina. This was a migration stream that was different in its composition from that which supplied people to the Tidewater, or coastal plain, of both colonies, and a stream that altered the demographic geography of the Carolinas. Although German settlers played a role in developing this route in the 1740s, it was exploited most by the Scots–Irish. Marrying young, their numbers increased greatly in the colonies.

The Piedmont borderland proved an area that was to be particularly free of control even by American standards. In the absence of effective civil and ecclesiastical authorities, the emphasis was on the role of family and extended kinship system, alongside ethical injunctions by evangelical preachers. This was a society that rejected outside authority.

The new migration drove up the population: that of North Carolina from 30,000 whites and 6,000 African Americans in 1730, to 65,000 and 19,000 respecitvely in 1755 and 124,000 and 41,000 in 1767.[32] These figures reflect the extent to which North Carolina was not a plantation society like South Carolina, where the rice plantations required large labour forces and two-thirds of the population in 1740 were slaves. Slaves were particularly numerous in low-country parishes in South Carolina, which were the centre of rice production. Instead, underlining the variety of colonial economies, pine-based timber products were among the most important exports of North Carolina; as they were not from South Carolina. Based on the valley of the Cape Fear River in the south of the state, the rice plantations in North Carolina were less important than those in South Carolina. Georgia, in contrast, remained less populous, and its combined population of blacks and whites (but not Native Americans) was estimated as 33,000 by 1773.[33]

Alongside economic variety there was social variety in the colonies, and thus tension. Much of the settler population was poor and lacking in power. Many settlers were indentured servants, most of whom went to America as labourers. In return for their passage, indentured servants bound themselves to service for a number of years, and, in some respects, they were traded like slaves.[34] By the mid-eighteenth century, indentured servitude was largely limited to Pennsylvania, but, more generally, some settlers were badly off wage labourers or impoverished farmers. Although they had opportunities to challenge their conditions by abandoning their employment or by labour protest, and cannot really be considered as white slaves, their circumstances were often difficult.[35]

Indeed, it is necessary to note the role of social tensions within settler communities, alongside the race relations that attract so much modern attention. Yeomen clashed with gentry over a range of issues, including political representation and economic interests. Moreover, far from being unrelated, racial issues were often driven by social tensions within the settler community. Opposition to the import of slaves and a desire to drive Native Americans from the land both, in part, reflected the particular interests of poor whites.[36]

Such whites were also an important element in the towns. Their position there reflected political and social disabilities as well as economic hardship. This was an aspect of a more general process of differentiation among the settler population. Thus, in Philadelphia, apprentices were banned from taverns by law alongside slaves and Native Americans, while, as another instance of discriminatory practice as well as choice, women generally were absent.[37] Despite white poverty, the average standard of living among whites was higher than in the British Isles. This was a matter not only of current circumstances, such as diet and accommodation, but also of prospects. Opportunities, crucially, were better for whites in the colonies. Indeed, the possibility of migrating there was one of the sole opportunities that was valuable to their British counterparts. A ready measure of the contrast in living standards was provided by height, which was a function of diet. Colonial militia were on average about two inches taller than British regulars.

Discussion of advancing frontiers of settlement can underplay the extent to which British North America also involved cooperation with the Native Americans, and can thus lead to a simplification of frontier society and 'the frontier'. Indeed, frontier society is an aspect of British North America that receives insufficient attention because better records survive for those of the colonial population who lived in port cities. Moreover, they, and their trade with Britain, engaged most fully the attention of the British government. Thus, the Anglo–French crisis of the mid-1750s, which arose from the rivalry over the remote Ohio Valley, was an aberration for the British government. Looked at differently, the extent to which the British government in this crisis was largely responding to developments, in part, reflected its earlier lack of attention to the frontier issues. Yet what became a new determination to take these issues into its hands, and to enforce its views in the borderlands of Empire, clashed with colonists' assumptions, not least a zeal for land speculation.[38]

Another reason for the underrating of the frontier is that its economy and society were inherently unstable and prone to be absorbed by the controls, practices and ethos of more colonized areas, especially as immigration gathered pace. Nevertheless, however, unstable, frontier societies were not some mere fag-end of Empire. Instead, the phrase encapsulates complex relationships, both between colonists and Native Americans, and between colonists and their governments.

Furthermore, these frontier societies have been presented as providing what has been termed a 'middle ground' of shared cultural space between colonists (especially if traders rather than settlers) and Native Americans. In this space, individuals and groups have been seen as playing an active role in organizing relations, instead of being simply victims of a distant imperial power. This is part of an understanding of Empire in terms of processes rather than structures. These were processes in which not only those immediately engaged in colonization played a crucial role but also those affected by imperialism.[39] Moreover, there was a Native American pursuit of advantage that can be seen as a variant on imperialism.

Many individuals prominent in the 'middle ground' were the product of European–Native American marriages, which helped them to act as translators and to play a major role in trade. In addition, as more mixed-race children were born, so the prospects of marrying mixed-race women increased. The process of participation in the 'middle ground' and, more generally, in the imperial system, however, was both unstable and unequal. European mores were strongly asserted, and Native American views were slighted. As a consequence, mixed-race relationships faced opposition to what was seen as concubinage.

The 'middle ground' with the Native Americans was key to the reality, if not concept, of the frontier, but the slave economy was more central to the trans-Atlantic links of the British Empire. This economy also involved violence, not only in the purchase of slaves in Africa and their crossing to North America, during which they were incarcerated, crowded together and held in poor, especially insanitary, conditions, but also in the plantations. Punishment there was generally harsh.

Few options were available to the slaves. Some chose flight and some suicide. Circumstances did not favour slave risings, as the whites restricted the availability of firearms and tried to prevent slaves plotting.[40] Indeed, slaves were unable to coordinate action, except in very small areas. In 1739, in the Stono Rebellion in

South Carolina, close to Charleston, 100 slaves rebelled and killed 20 colonists, before being defeated by the militia and their Native American allies. The determination of some of the slaves to escape to Spanish Florida helped spark the rebellion.

The Stono Rebellion led the South Carolina Assembly to increase the duty on new slave imports, in order to limit their number. It was also cited by the Trustees of Georgia in defence of their ban on slavery in the colony, but they capitulated to pro-slavery pressure in 1750, arguing that, since Spain had been unsuccessful in 1742 when it invaded Georgia, it was safe to import slaves.[41] This compromise followed concessions by the Trustees on other restrictions in the colony, such as land tenure and alcohol consumption (1742), although their regulations anyway had been largely ignored in the key trading settlement of Augusta. The 1742 compromise was an aspect of the collapse of the Trustees' position, and they surrendered their charter in 1752, although fears that Georgia would be absorbed into South Carolina were assuaged. These fears had led to several petitions to Parliament by the Trustees and their agent Edward Gray in the late 1740s and early 1750s.

Hindered by poor sandy soils and the cost of white labour, the Trustees' objective of a colony of small farmers had not been realized. Yet, it reflected the range of ideas that influenced American colonization. This objective prefigured the later goal of Thomas Jefferson for the USA as a whole, and, in this, also reflected the sense that such a community was more virtuous, self-reliant and resilient, and thus better able to prevail against opponents. The economy of Georgia, however, only came close to being a success after the Trustee era. Rice cultivation then spread south from South Carolina. However, real wealth in Georgia had to wait for King Cotton.[42]

The politics of Georgia is a reminder of the extent to which imperial politics were local at the same time as local politics were imperial. If the British Empire in practice entailed the dissipation of power over distance, then this dissipation did not prevent the search for validation through the use of imperial authority. This was a process that involved both imperial and local action.

More profoundly, growing colonial wealth, however socially skewed, helped encourage the assertion of social groups, especially elites. This assertion was not necessarily directed against Empire or Crown, but required both to adapt to its aspirations. Neither was to be able to do so in the 1760s–70s, but, conversely, royal government had become stronger in mid-century as governors succeeded in working with assemblies with singularly few crises.[43] Yet, looking ahead, difficulties were posed by colonial assertion, and there were the related political tensions of an Anglicization in which colonists, whatever their origin, were resolved to ensure and preserve their position as English people, with all that meant in terms of political, social and religious liberties. Indeed, the right of colonial assemblies to make their own laws encouraged a sense that the colonists were well-placed to define what was legally appropriate. It was but a short step to argue that they were best placed to do so.

The state of British North America on the eve of the Seven Years' War contains clues to the later dissolution of political links, but they were more than counterweighted by the many and strong signs of vital trans-Atlantic links. These were to be of great importance in the war for Empire.

3

The Defeat of France, 1754–60

Small groups of men on the frontiers of empires provoked and precipitated the great mid-century war between Britain and France. In 1754, their actions, building on the tensions of recent years, led to the use of force in what was to prove an irreversible fashion. On 17 April, a 500-strong French force obliged the small colonial garrison of 40 men in Fort Prince George (near modern Pittsburgh) to surrender. In turn, George Washington, who, as a land speculator, was keenly committed to westward expansion,[1] advanced as colonel at the head of a small force of 40 Virginia militia supported by 12 Native Americans, into the contested area. He surprised and defeated a smaller French detachment on 28 May, killing ten and capturing the other 20.

The French, in response, advanced south in greater numbers and, on 3 July, Washington was obliged to surrender at Fort Necessity. He was outnumbered, 700 (including 200 Native Americans) to 400, but, more seriously, was outfought, his force taking shelter in weak entrenchments where they were exposed to French musket fire. Having taken much heavier casualties (200 to over 100), Washington accepted the reasonably generous French capitulation terms which included the evacuation of the Ohio region for a year and a day.[2]

In response to events in the Ohio Valley, a sense of threat was readily felt across the colonies, leading to calls for unity. On 9 May 1754, the *Pennsylvania Gazette*, a very successful newspaper edited by Benjamin Franklin, published a woodcut emblem (what would later be called a cartoon) in which a segmented snake appeared, the segments bearing initials for colonies or regions, above the motto 'Join or Die'. Franklin also wrote an accompanying text which drew attention to French aggression and claimed that French confidence 'seems well-grounded on the present disunited state of the British colonies, and the extreme difficulty of bringing so many different governments and assemblies to agree in any speedy and effectual measures for our common defence and security'.

Indeed, at a colonial conference held at Albany from 19 June to 11 July, in response to a request by the Board of Trade, Franklin, drawing on ideas he had formulated in 1751, urged union, amounting to a colonial federation with a Grand Council, in order best to repel the common threat. This, however, clashed with the colonial desire for autonomy. As a result, Pennsylvania rejected the plan in August. The other colonies failed to counteract this, but the conference set the pattern for congresses representing all or most of the colonies. Anxious that a colonial union would weaken the imperial link, the British ministry was concerned that Franklin's scheme gave too much power to the projected Grand Council.[3]

Franklin was not alone. Dinwiddie, the Lieutenant Governor of Virginia, sought to increase colonial union, not least by creating two confederacies for the colonies, although he also wanted to increase imperial direction, including with the institution of a poll tax levied on the colonists by Parliament for defence needs. Such ideas reflected the extent to which proposals for imperial reform or indeed transformation did not have to wait until after the Seven Years' War.

The defeat at Fort Necessity also resonated across the Atlantic, registering with the British public. Indeed, Thomas, Duke of Newcastle, the head of the ministry, first heard the news when he read the *London Evening Post*.[4]

The crisis rapidly spread. That summer, Native Americans from Canada, as well as pro-French Abenakis, raided settlements in Massachusetts, near New Hampshire and in New York, advancing to within 15 miles of Albany. At that point, the vulnerable British had fewer than 900 regular troops in North America. Commenting on their weakness, Charles Townshend, a Lord of the Admiralty, proposed that local troops be raised to confront the situation: 'If a regiment should be sent from hence, the transportation will be extremely expensive, and the men both new to the service and strangers to the climate. But if a regiment should be raised there, the expense will be much less, and the men not only accustomed to the climate, but in a degree to the service.'

Rather than resting on the defensive, and offering inadequate protection, the memorandum proposed an advance to cut the forward French positions and their Native American supporters off from Montréal. It was claimed that only offensive operations would deter the French from future attacks.[5]

As an instance of the danger of segmenting history, and, in this case, separating the Seven Years' War and the apotheosis of Empire, from the crisis leading to the War of American Independence, Townshend was to be prominent as the Chancellor of the Exchequer responsible for the duties of 1767 that greatly exacerbated Anglo–American relations (see pp. 107–8). His memorandum also reflected what was to be a continued theme in these relations, the best way to raise, control and finance military forces in North America.

In 1754, the ministers did not appreciate that maintaining British interests would lead to a protracted war. At that stage, the conquest of Canada was not the plan. Indeed, there was no agreed goal other than protecting rights and possessions.[6] This was within a context in which French policy was viewed as very threatening. For example, it could be seen in terms of a desire to seize the trade of North America as a stage in dominating world commerce,[7] which would necessarily hit the prosperity, and thus wealth, of Britain.

The French Foreign Minister, Antoine-Louis Rouillé, certain that the French were only maintaining their rights and repelling the British use of force with force, argued that border problems could be dealt with by the commissioners already empowered to do so. Rouillé stressed French moderation, adding ominously, but accurately, that the chance of successful negotiations was ended by the British refusal to suspend military steps and that, once clashes had begun, their consequences would be difficult to contain.[8]

Drawing attention to the specific geographical details all-too-often lacking in European ministerial discussion of North America, Rouillé also pointed out that the Appalachians were a considerable obstacle to any French threat to the British colonies.[9] This was true, but only to a point, as French expansion threatened to energize Native American opposition to the British colonists, as well as to block efforts by the latter to expand. As a powerful limitation to any chance of compromise, these efforts were inseparable from the colonies, which indeed took on much of their character from their dynamism.

Despite French assurances, the British government decided, in late September 1754, to send two regiments to America in order to conduct offensive operations there. Domestic political pressures, particularly the role of George II's son, William, Duke of Cumberland, the Captain-General of the army, as well as George, 2nd Earl of Halifax, President of the Board of Trade, and Henry Fox, the Secretary-at-War, politicians critical of Newcastle, obliged the government to adopt a firm attitude in 1755 and to support a series of attacks.[10] Having decided not to attempt the major French bases of Louisbourg and in the St Lawrence, the British, instead, dissipated their strength with three separate attacks, although this separation also reflected the varied concerns and priorities of the northern colonies. Indeed, these colonies produced appreciable numbers of the troops involved.

The most successful campaign was that in which naval power could be used, an attack on the French forts that threatened Nova Scotia: Fort Beauséjour fell on 16 June 1755, to a force of 250 regulars and 2,000 New England militia under Lieutenant-Colonel Robert Monckton, and, two days later, Fort Gaspereau surrendered.[11] The British marked their presence by renaming the forts Cumberland and Monckton, but, more harshly, by deporting the Acadians. These French settlers in Nova Scotia, ruled by Britain since 1713, were suspected of disloyalty. In 1755, more than half the 13,000 Acadians were deported, others following in 1758. Their treatment was less harsh than that of the Native Americans, but it served as a clear indication that the victims of British power were not only non-Europeans. Reflecting security concerns, the deportation was ordered by British officials in Nova Scotia, not London, and was an indication of the extent to which policy was set at the imperial periphery.[12] Many of the Acadians ended up as Cajuns in Louisiana and helped strengthen the French cultural legacy there.

Another force, largely of regulars under the inexperienced Major-General Edward Braddock, however, was defeated on 9 July 1755 near Fort Duquesne by the outnumbered French and their Native American allies, who made excellent use of tree cover. Braddock's army, fresh from Britain, lacked experience of North American operations, and Braddock had deprived himself of the possibility of effective Native American backing by refusing support from Shingas, the Delaware chief. As a reminder of the many groups with a stake in the future Ohio Valley, Shingas had sought a promise that the Ohio region should remain in Native American hands. From a Native American viewpoint, one crucial issue was whether the British or French posed the greater threat to their position in the Ohio river systems and hinterland. As a result of Braddock's attitude, he had very few Native American auxiliaries, and none of the expected Cherokees and Catawbas. Braddock also lacked light infantry, which the British Army had as yet failed adequately to develop. The Virginia militia in his force had very little experience of frontier warfare.

Braddock left Fort Cumberland on 30 May 1755, cutting a road through the trees in order to move his cannon and supplies. By 9 July, he was within ten miles of his target. Fort Duquesne would have been vulnerable to cannon – indeed, in 1758, the French were to abandon and destroy it before such an attack could be mounted – but, in 1755, they took the tactical advantage from the British operational and strategic offensives by advancing to attack. The British response to the resulting ambush was inadequate, unsurprisingly so, as they were not prepared for such an engagement. Instead of advancing into the forest and attacking the ambushing forces, they held their ground, thus offering excellent targets. Lieutenant-Colonel Thomas Gage, who was to be in command of the British forces in Boston in 1775, like Townshend a reminder of continuity between generations, reported:

> a visible terror and confusion appeared amongst the men ... The same infatuation attended the whole; none would form a line of battle, and the whole army was very soon mixed together, twelve or fourteen deep, firing away at nothing but trees, and killing many of our own men and officers. The cannon were soon deserted by those that covered them. The artillery did their duty perfectly well, but, from the nature of the country, could do little execution ... the enemy always giving way, whenever they advanced even on the most faint attack ... I can't ascribe their behaviour to any other cause than the talk of the country people, ever since our arrival in America – the woodsmen and Indian traders, who were continually telling the soldiers, that if they attempted to fight Indians in a regular manner, they would certainly be defeated ... the only excuse I can get from them is that they were quite dispirited from the great fatigue they had undergone and not receiving a sufficient quantity of food; and further that they did not expect the enemy would come down so suddenly.

Although this was an attempt to exculpate his own conduct by blaming the men, it captured the confusion of the encounter. Braddock was mortally wounded and his force fled after two and a half hours. Of the 1,459 British troops, 977 were killed or wounded; whereas the French lost only 40 men from their force of about 250 regulars and militia and 640 Native Americans.

Braddock's defeat led to Native American attacks which that November forced Pennsylvania to allocate £60,000 for the construction of a series of forts. This was part of a more general process of fortification in the mid-1750s as colonies sought protection against Native Americans allied with the French. For example, North Carolina built Fort Dobbs in 1756 in order to provide protection against the Shawnees. Organization was also seen as a key response, with the appointment, in 1755, of two Indian Superintendents by the British government, in order to recruit and direct Native American support.

Braddock's defeat also posed the challenge of how best to operate in North America. Major-General, Lord George Sackville (later, as Lord George Germain, responsible for British strategy during the War of American Independence) had expressed the confidence of a regular soldier that the conflict would be a conventional matter of sieges, while James Delancey, Lieutenant-Governor of New York, responded to the defeat by emphasizing the need for central direction and the value of artillery: 'the expediency of having, at all times, in this city, as being nearly the centre of the British colonies, a number of cannon and arms, and a large quantity of ammunition ready, on all occasions, to be disposed of for such services, as the general His Majesty shall think fit to appoint for North America, shall judge proper'. This represented a call for militarized unity. In contrast, Horatio Sharp, the Governor of Maryland, took note of frontier conditions and suggested that 'in case of another campaign against Fort Duquesne … there ought to be two, or at least one, thousand of our woodsmen or hunters, who are marksmen and used to rifles, to precede the army and engage the Indians in their own way'.[13]

Not only regulars were defeated. A militia force under William Johnson, Superintendent for the northern Indian Department, advancing from Albany towards Fort St Frédéric, was ambushed near Lake George on 8 September 1755, the French commander, Baron Dieskau trying to repeat Braddock's defeat. Much of the militia force, however, was able to flee back to Johnson's camp. The French then attacked the camp, but were unsuccessful and took heavy casualties from cannon and musket fire: they no longer enjoyed surprise and were now fighting on ground of Johnson's choosing. Fortified positions gave a marked edge to defenders, but only if the battle came to them. Johnson's advance was abandoned, but the British saw the battle as a victory, not least because the wounded Dieskau was captured.

War between Britain and France was formally declared in 1756, the British declaring war on 17 May. Significantly, the declaration was not a product of the fighting in North America in 1754–6, nor of the largely unsuccessful naval attack on French reinforcements for Canada sailing across the Atlantic on 10 June 1755. Instead, it was the result of the successful French invasion of the British-ruled Mediterranean island of Minorca the following year. Increased French interest in Canada, nevertheless, had led to a growth in the size of the Louisbourg garrison to 2,500 regulars, with a supporting naval squadron. Six battalions, totalling 3,000 men, had been sent to Canada in 1755, although 330 troops were captured when two ships were seized by Admiral Boscawen on 10 June. Louisbourg and Québec were well fortified, and work on the former was actively pressed forward in 1755–7.[14] The French were outnumbered, however, both in regulars and in local militia, the latter a reflection of greater British settlement in North America.

Nevertheless, their new commander, Louis Joseph, Marquis de Montcalm, a Major-General with no experience in North American warfare, decided that it was best to take the initiative and thus counter the British numerical advantage by achieving a local superiority in strength. After Fort Bull was taken in March 1756, in August 1756, he captured Forts Ontario, George and Oswego, taking 1,620 prisoners for the loss of only 30 men. The British were thereby driven from Lake Ontario. The French also established Fort Carillon (Ticonderoga) as an advanced base at the southern end of Lake Champlain. These French successes increased concern in British America, accentuating a sense of vulnerability, and there was press criticism of Braddock. The French appeared much more threatening than in the previous war. They had regained the initiative, and had killed or captured an appreciable portion of the British forces. This reflected the extent to which these units were located in frontier areas, rather than in the centres of population.

That year, the British did not mount an effective response. In London, the government was weak and demoralized, and also concerned about the defence of Britain from possible invasion. Moreover, the new commander in North America, John, 4th Earl of Loudoun, a protégé of the Duke of Cumberland, was unwilling to search for a compromise on the reimbursement and control of colonial troops and, as a result, there was scant cooperation between Loudoun and the colonies. This was crippling as the British were dependent on such cooperation, particularly if they were to raise forces for operations in the interior. Loudoun, moreover, did not put an emphasis on training for conflict in North America.

In 1757, in contrast, a large fleet was sent to Halifax, Nova Scotia. This was designed for an expedition against, first, nearby Louisbourg and then Québec. In February, William Pitt the Elder, the most dynamic of the ministers, wrote to Loudoun, that he should be able to

form, early in the spring, an army of near 17,000 men. His Majesty [George II] doubts not, but with such a force, supplied with artillery, and supported with a strong squadron, your Lordship will find yourself in a condition to push, with the utmost vigour, an offensive war, and to effectuate some great and essential impression on the enemy. The King is of opinion, that the taking of Louisbourg and Quebec can alone prove decisive.

The colonies were ordered to provide military assistance.[15]

As so often, it proved easier to plan victory than to secure it. Poor weather helped to ensure that the British force did not assemble at Halifax until July. By then, the French had succeeded in assembling a superior fleet at Louisbourg, a consequence of the British failure to blockade the main French Atlantic naval base of Brest. The Council of War summoned by Loudoun decided not to risk disaster by landing on Cape Breton Island, so late in the year and in the face of a French fleet. This failure contributed to a sense of crisis in North America, with charges of mismanagement in what was called the 'Cabbage Planting Expedition', colouring attitudes.

Instead of the capture of Louisbourg, it was Montcalm who advanced, besieging Fort William Henry at the head of Lake George with a far larger force. The fort was bombarded with 30 cannon that Montcalm had had hauled overland, and it fell rapidly, with the surrender of 2,400 troops and militia. The viability of the French–Native American alliance was abundantly demonstrated. Anxieties about this alliance were underlined by the subsequent killing of about 30 prisoners by the Native Americans, although this step greatly offended Montcalm, while the Native Americans carried off a much greater number of prisoners.[16]

As a reminder, however, of the problems of organizing effective operations, Montcalm did not only face the difficulty of managing Native American allies. He was also critical of the Canadian troops under his command. The basis of his criticism was similar to tensions between British regulars and colonial militia,[17] although the tensions within the French command were more serious.

As a result of three years of operations, British forces had secured Acadia/Nova Scotia, but made no impact on Louisbourg, while, in the interior, the Ohio River valley remained in French hands and, farther north, Montcalm had driven the British from Lake Ontario and back towards the Hudson. He had successfully taken and retained the initiative. British failure led to criticism in Britain and to attacks on poor leadership. The *Herald* claimed in its issue of 20 October 1757:

> With a vast land and sea force in North America, nothing has been done. And with the odds of twenty inhabitants to one against the French on that continent, our forts are taken, the out-settlements of our colonies continually ravaged, and the whole body of every one of them kept in perpetual terror and alarm!

An unimpressed Pitt was determined to do better. Linked with his recent enemy Newcastle, Pitt now headed a strong ministry which remained in power from late 1757 to 1761.[18] He had Loudoun, whom he blamed for failure, removed, promised to provide funds from Britain and restricted the authority of Loudoun's successor over the colonial authorities. In 1758, Pitt took a leading role in planning a massive three-pronged offensive on New France that took the initiative from the French. Separate expeditions were to attack Louisbourg, Carillon, and Fort Duquesne. The largest force was sent under General James Abercromby against Carillon,[19] but it was the smaller Louisbourg force, under Generals Jeffrey Amherst and James Wolfe, and Admiral Boscawen, that was successful. It contained first-rate regular units (and relatively few colonial troops) and the intention was for it to proceed that same summer to capture Québec.

Troops were landed on Cape Breton Island on 8 June 1758. This is a bland remark that gives no sense of the nature of the task. The journal of Richard Humphrys of the 28th Regiment provides more indication:

> About three in the morning the men of war began to play against their batteries and breastworks, and the troops being in their boats two hours before day … about six the signal was made to land, when the whole set off with the greatest eagerness and a terrible fire began on both sides, that nothing was seen or heard for one hour but the thundering of cannon and flashes of lightning, where the never daunted spirits of British soldiers landed and forced their way through the batteries and breastworks. As soon as the enemy found that we had landed, and that they could not make any farther resistance, they gave way and began to retreat in great disorder leaving us to take possession of all their works. The attackers on the right behaved gallantly and forced their way through the rocks, but unfortunately as one of the boats was making for the shore a wave took her and she overset, being loaded with grenadiers.

All bar one died.[20]

As in 1745, the troops then concentrated on the landward defences of Louisbourg. British cannon breached the walls and Louisbourg surrendered on 26 July. The British force of 13,000 suffered 560 killed or wounded, but 3,000 French troops were taken prisoner. In addition, the French naval squadron of five warships was lost – three to bombardment by the British artillery, and two when British warships penetrated the harbour on the night of 25–6 July – and thus there was no challenge to British naval operations in the St Lawrence.

In contrast, the main British advance, against Carillon, was a costly failure. A frontal assault on the French position, an 'unlucky ill-conducted attack',[21] on 8 July 1758, led to heavy casualties. The British then abandoned the operation having lost 1,900 killed or wounded out of a force of 6,400 regulars and 9,000 American colonial troops. Most of the casualties were from the regulars. Montcalm's 3,500 strong force suffered only 400 casualties.

The third offensive, however, was successful. An army of 7,000 (1,600 regulars, the rest Pennsylvania and Virginia militia), under Brigadier-General John Forbes, advanced on Fort Duquesne, building a road as they moved forward, and the

300 poorly supplied defenders blew up the fort on 24 November. The advance indicated the value of experience and the ability to learn from mistakes. Forbes was determined to learn from Braddock. He took a shorter route and cautiously advanced from one fortified position to another.

French prospects, moreover, were harmed when, in October, at the Easton Conference, Pennsylvania authorities and the British government promised the Native Americans that they would not occupy land west of the Alleghenies. The consequent shift of Native American support obliged the French to give up the Ohio region. Forbes' success, in turn, strengthened Native American advocates of conciliating Britain. Viewed from Europe, this was still a two-sided conflict, whereas on the ground, especially to the west of the mountains, the shifting support and fears of Native American groups could be decisive. The captured and rebuilt Fort Duquesne was named Fort Pitt.[22] At the same time, relations between the Cherokees and South Carolina were deteriorating, although conflict did not break out until 1759.

In August 1758, another British force, composed largely of colonial troops under Lieutenant-Colonel John Bradstreet (the largest group from New York), sailed across Lake Ontario from Oswego and destroyed crucial French supplies and the French lake squadron at Fort Frontenac. Bradstreet commanded 2,820 colonials, 150 regulars and 40 Native Americans, while the weak fort had a garrison of only 110. Under cannon fire, the fort surrendered on 27 August. It was demolished before Bradstreet withdrew. Alongside Forbes' advance, this under-lined the value of provincial troops, and it was indicative of the geopolitics of empire, as well as of military politics of the war and their impact on deployments, that these troops took the more westerly tasks, those that were furthest from the sea. Bradstreet's success hit French support among the Native Americans.

Further east, also in August 1758, a British amphibious force from Louisbourg captured Ile Saint-Jean, which was renamed Prince Edward Island. On the pattern of Acadia/Nova Scotia, its population was largely deported to France. British raiding parties from Louisbourg also successfully raided the French fishing stations on the Gaspé Peninsula that September.

Despite these successes, British strategy and its execution were weak in 1758, although there were serious constraints affecting coherent command and communications, and also logistical problems with massing strength on one axis. The British offensives had failed to provide mutual support and Montcalm had been able to concentrate his efforts against Abercromby. The length of time taken to capture Louisbourg had postponed options for an attack up the St Lawrence, but, looking to the future, the loss of the port increased the danger of a British amphibious attack up the river, while the fall of Forts Frontenac and Duquesne exacerbated the vulnerability of the French on and near Lakes Erie and Ontario and hit French supply links, rendering the French positions to the west of the

Appalachians indefensible. These problems undermined Montcalm's defensive success at Carillon.

Yet had the war ended in the winter of 1758–9, the British would have had relatively little to show for their campaigning. This was a point that Richard Rush, Comptroller of the Treasury, was to make during the War of 1812, when arguing that the USA should persist in its unsuccessful attacks on Canada,[23] attacks that indicated anew the difficulty of such a task. Indeed, the British campaigns in 1758–60 were to be the sole conquest of Canada to result from the many attempts launched or projected in 1689–1815.

The political dimension also played a key role in the military situation. The British government would certainly have had a major political problem had the war ended in early 1759, because there would have been considerable pressure to secure the gains made hitherto. The *Monitor*, in its issue of 19 November 1757, condemned the restoration of Cape Breton in 1748, while that of 7 October 1758 stressed the necessity of retaining Cape Breton at the eventual peace whatever the requirements of Britain's ally Prussia. As far as this influential London newspaper was concerned, there was to be no compromising exchange of gains, as in 1748, and no return to an unsatisfactory past. This served as a reminder of the political significance of North American campaigns, a significance that was to hang over and play a background role in post-war debates concerning how best to defend North America.

In 1758, the British had made the Hudson–Lake Champlain axis their first priority. In 1759, it was to be the St Lawrence, and it was there that British naval power could be used most effectively.[24] American provincial troops garrisoned Louisbourg, freeing regulars for the advance on Québec. Benefiting from reliable pilots and nearby harbour facilities at Halifax, both of which had been lacking in 1690 and 1711, the navy convoyed a force of 8,600 men under James Wolfe to near Québec. Although young, Wolfe (1727–59) was very experienced and had a well-deserved reputation for energy and determination.

Wolfe arrived near Québec on 26 June 1759, but his operations along the Beauport shore were initially unsuccessful. On 31 July, an attack on French positions was repelled by Montcalm's larger army, with the British suffering 440 casualties to the French 60. As winter approached, it seemed increasingly likely that the British would fail to capture the city, which had formidable natural and man-made defences.

Wolfe risked a bold move. James Cook, later famous as the explorer of the Pacific, had thoroughly surveyed the St Lawrence, charting its rocks, and British warships had passed beyond Québec from 18 July onwards and made upriver raids on 8 August. The army was to follow. On 1–3 September, British troops left the Montmorency camp and moved along the southern bank of the river opposite Québec. On 10 September, Wolfe, having reconnoitred the river, decided to land at Anse au Foulon to the west of the city. After delays due to the weather, the British landed in the early hours of 13 September. Some 200 light infantry scaled the cliffs and successfully attacked a French camp of 100 men. The remainder of the British force, fewer than 4,500 men, then landed and advanced to the Plains of Abraham to the south-west of the city.

Montcalm, with a total of 13,000 men in the area, was in a strong position, with fresh troops approaching Wolfe's rear, but, instead of waiting on the defensive and uniting his forces, Montcalm chose to attack with the men immediately available. Richard Humphrys of the 28th Foot noted:

> The French lined the bushes in their front with one thousand five hundred Indians and Canadians where they also placed their best marksmen, who kept up a very galling, though irregular fire upon the whole British line, who bore it with the greatest patience and good order, reserving their fire for the main body of the French, now advancing, this fire was however checked by the posts in General Wolfe's front .... The general exhorted his troops to reserve their fire, and at forty yards distance they gave it, which took place in its full extent, and made terrible havoc amongst the French. It was supported with as much vivacity as it was begun and the enemy everywhere yielded to it.[25]

British volley fire put paid to the French column advance, after which a bayonet charge drove the disordered French from the field. British troops indeed were adept at both volley fire and bayonet charges. Both generals were killed in the battle. An anonymous British participant recorded:

> About nine o'clock the French army had drawn up under the walls of the town, and advanced towards us briskly and in good order. We stood to receive them; they began their fire at a distance, we reserved ours, and as they came nearer fired on them by divisions, this did execution and seemed to check them a little. However they still advanced pretty quick, we increased our fire without altering our position, and, when they were within less than an hundred yards, gave them a full fire, fixed our bayonets, and, under cover of the smoke, the whole line charged.[26]

French morale was shattered. Although Québec had not been captured and more French troops arrived immediately after the battle, the French officers decided at a council of war not to risk battle again, but to retreat upriver. The decision to retreat was reversed a few days later, but, even as a French relief force approached Québec, it surrendered on 18 September. The British were also successful in 1759 on the Hudson–Lake Champlain axis, Amherst capturing Carillon (which the French had blown up) on 27 July, and building a fort at Crown Fort. Wolfe's attack on the St Lawrence ensured that the French facing Amherst were short of men and supplies, which made Amherst's failure to advance farther a disappointment.

The death of Wolfe and the capture of Québec are generally seen as marking the end of New France. This is mistaken. The caveat, had the war ended then, is especially appropriate in 1759, given that that was the year of the planned French invasion of Britain. Indeed, had French forces landed, the British troops in North America would have been sorely missed. Pitt was taking a risk in sending so many troops to North America, for the defence of Britain was more than a sub-text in the struggle for North America. Instead, it was a key element, both in strategic planning and in the politics entailed in judging between commitments.

Moreover, to underline the extent to which the fall of Québec did not end the struggle, the French forces left in Canada, although cut off from supplies and reinforcements from France, were no passive victims. Six months after the fall of Québec, the substantial French army still in Canada under Lévis, advanced to recapture the city. Brigadier James Murray had been left in command of a garrison of 4,000 troops, but his position was weakened by the closure of the St Lawrence by ice, which deprived him of both naval support and supplies. The latter contributed to the scurvy that weakened the garrison; other diseases also caused serious inroads.

When Lévis's much larger army advanced to threaten British outposts, Murray repeated Montcalm's mistake, engaging on the Plains of Abraham when it would have been wiser to remain on the defensive in the city. In the Battle of Sainte-Foy (28 April 1760), the French carried the day with a bayonet charge that benefited from disorder on the advancing British flank, and the British, 'obliged to yield to superior numbers' in Humphrys' phrase,[27] retreated with heavier casualties into Québec: 1,088 dead and wounded out of 3,866 troops, compared to 833 French casualties. The British also had to abandon most of their cannon. The battle is one of the numerous engagements forgotten in the teleological account of Britain's imperial rise, not least in this period.

Québec was then besieged, but the French batteries did not begin firing until 11 May 1760. They had little time to do damage: a British fleet arrived with reinforcements on 16 May. The French ships in the St Lawrence supporting the siege fled and ran aground. As a result of the fleet's arrival, Lévis raised the siege and fell back to Montréal. The fleet had 'sealed the fate of Canada'. Humphrys had noted 'that had a French fleet appeared first in the river the place must certainly have fell'.[28]

In the summer of 1760, the three-pronged British advance finally triumphed, bringing the power of the wider British Empire to bear in the interior of North America, in a key episode in the geopolitics of power. Troops advanced from Québec, Crown Point and, in largest numbers, Lake Ontario, under Murray, Colonel William Haviland and General Jeffrey Amherst respectively. The outnumbered French abandoned most of their positions, although there was fighting around Fort Lévis in August. The surrender of the position at Chambly on 1 September opened the way for Haviland. By 6 September, Amherst's force lay above Montréal on the St Lawrence, Murray's below it, and Haviland was approaching overland.

On 8 September, the Marquis de Vaudreuil, the Governor-General of New France, and the 3,520 French troops in Montréal surrendered to Amherst's force of 17,000. Trois Rivières capitulated three days later. New France had fallen.

The 1760 campaign was an impressive triumph of resources and planning, and indicated the accumulated skill of the British Army in North America. Amherst's logistical organization of the 1760 campaign, which involved the coordination of large forces, was especially impressive.[29] Humphrys noted: 'History can hardly produce a more striking instance of excellent military conduct in three separate expeditions against one place, by different routes, without any communication with each other, and through such a dangerous and difficult country, meeting almost at the same time, at the destined rendezvous'.[30]

Had the war ended in 1758, then it would have been nowhere near as successful for the British. Naval predominance and success in European waters, however, meant an ability to grasp the initiative outside Europe. That was the crucial interconnectedness of British power. It was not so much, as was sometimes said, that the French had lost Canada in Germany (or North America in Europe) – that the concentration of French effort there from 1757, against, first, Hanover, then Prussia, and then the British forces in Germany, deprived Montcalm of men – as that the British conquered Canada off Brest. The blockade of this, the leading French naval base, a blockade that led ultimately to naval victory in Quiberon Bay in 1759, made it difficult for France to retain the initiative in North America, to send substantial reinforcements to their colonies, or to maintain important trade links with them. As an indication, French insurance premiums for ships to Québec rose from about 5 per cent in 1755 to 50 per cent or more in 1758 and were seldom obtainable in 1759, a year in which many of the merchantmen sent to Canada were captured. The French were unable to provide their Native American allies with the gunpowder and trade goods they expected and needed and this led to a falling off of their allies.

Thus, the French imperial system collapsed before the British captured the colonies. The control and organization of maritime links was vital for demographic, economic, organizational and military factors. Without a large hinterland, French colonies were vulnerable, while, thanks to British naval strength, the French ability to attack key British positions, such as Québec in 1760, was limited.

The French also deployed fewer resources in North America than the British. In 1758, the British had 24,000 regulars and 22,500 provincial troops in North America, the French 6,600 *troupes de terre*, 2,900 *compagnies franches de la marine*, and about 15,000 militia. Even these numbers pressed hard on food supplies which were themselves hit by a series of poor harvests. The demand caused serious inflation in Canada and led to an enormous increase in expenditure in the province that, in turn, helped to lead to financial crisis. Moreover, the warships launched by the French in Canada were few and not particularly effective.

The size of the respective forces was not the sole determinant of success: the Canadian militia in French service was very good and had more experience in wilderness warfare than their New England opponents. Moreover, the large British armies faced logistical problems, while, in the operations near Québec in 1759–60, it was not numbers alone that were crucial. More generally, the relatively small forces involved in transoceanic operations, and the close similarity of their weapons and methods of fighting, put a great premium on leadership, as well as an ability to understand and exploit terrain, morale, and unit cohesion and firepower. The British were usually adept at all of these, but so also were the French, and sometimes more so. Montcalm made effective use of French troops and Native American allies, and understood how best to operate in the interior of North America. Furthermore, British naval strength did not prevent the arrival of six French battalions to Canada in 1755, two in 1756, two in 1757, and another two in 1758.

Nevertheless, the exceptionally large resources devoted to the struggle in Canada by the British in 1758–60 stacked the odds against New France. The British spent far more on the struggle there.[31] This expenditure was in part required in order to fund the major logistical support that the army required. In order to minimize risk, the British focused on securing lines of communications and on creating a flexible support system to support their advance.[32] This expenditure brought a lot of money into the Thirteen Colonies, as they were crucial in the provision and transportation of supplies. This was particularly so because of the effort devoted to overland attacks on Canada. Furthermore, government purchases were in cash, and thus brought liquidity into the colonial economy. They were of added significance because they were concentrated in the northern colonies, which were the ones that were both most short of money and most dependent on credit. This, however, was to ensure that the cut in expenditure once Canada had been conquered had a particularly sharp impact.

The financial commitment encouraged British public interest in North America, but so also did the lengthy nature of the struggle with alternating despair and euphoria. An officer in North America was informed by a London correspondent in 1758 that 'the great and favourite object is your continent of North America.'[33] This was the case due to the war, but it is also relevant to note the extent to which other factors in Anglo–American relations remained in play, although, of course, they were, in turn, affected by the fact and course of the conflict.

Trade, for example continued to be a key factor, but the role of French privateering and the prospects of profit from American privateering focused attention on both beneficial and irritating aspects of relations. British warships helped offer protection from French privateers, but American privateering was affected by the requirements of officialdom. The latter also came into play with the wartime extension of the British Empire in the West Indies as most of the French islands were captured. This affected the position of American smugglers and, if it opened up opportunities for other American trade, it did so within the unwelcome constraints of British officialdom.

A less chronologically specific element was provided by the religious cross-currents of mid-century, particularly in New England. The extent to which anti-episcopalian sentiment played a role in encouraging opposition to British rule in the run-up to the War of Independence is a staple of the literature. What is less noted is that, alongside these tensions, there was both a degree of loyalism among those opposed to bishops and also growing support for the Church of England. In New England, the latter was in the unusual position of not being the established Church and, instead, of being opposed to the Congregationalist establishment. It was only in 1691 that Anglicans were granted official toleration in New England.

Moreover, the Church of England did well there in the 1740s and 1750s, in part in reaction against the Calvinistic revivalism of the Great Awakening of those years, with its stress on conversion and spirituality focused on a revival of an avowedly primitive form of Puritan Calvinism. The Church of England employed the techniques seen in Nonconformity elsewhere, for example an extensive use of the culture of print, and of reaching out through preaching to groups outside the mainstream, not least through the 'field preaching' so disapproved of at home. This suggests both that the Church of England might have done well had there not been an American Revolution and, indeed, that trans-Atlantic links could have become closer as a result.[34] More generally, the Society for the Propagation of the Gospel in Foreign Parts, the missionary focus of the Church of England, established in 1701, founded close to 150 congregations between 1740 and 1770, and was active among both African and Native Americans.

The widespread use of the culture of print and the extent of itinerant preaching reflected the need to devise means of communication and persuasion for a rapidly growing society. This was true both for religious issues and movements, and for their political counterparts. Thus the revivalism of the Great Awakening, and its equivalent for the Church of England, helped create links within and between colonies. Community revivalism was located by these wider links.

The Great Awakening itself also was an intercolonial movement at the same time that it strengthened trans-Atlantic ties. The latter were crucial to the course of the Great Awakening in North America. Aside from the important German links, prominent British figures were also involved. Howell Harris had links in North America,[35] while John and Charles Wesley left England for Georgia in October 1735, with Benjamin Ingham and Charles Delamotte. All four were American clergy recruited by Oglethorpe for the colony. The journey took three months. Once arrived, Charles Wesley, who served as Secretary of Indian Affairs, attempted a mission to Fort Frederica on St Simon's Island, but his admonitions to a strict religious life were rejected and he returned to England in August 1736.

John Wesley fared no better. He spent most of his time in Savannah, but also toured around the colony. By 1736, he declared that his mission was to convert the Native Americans, but, before he could do so, he became embroiled in a controversial relationship with Sophy Hopkey, whom he eventually decided not to marry. In the autumn of 1737, Wesley gave up and returned to England. The significance of the Wesleys' failure was that even the most enthusiastically motivated clerics needed to work with the colonists, not to be counsels of perfection. They had to adjust their expectations to colonial life, rather than treating colonists as recalcitrant Oxford undergraduates.

The career of the charismatic George Whitefield (1714–70), an evangelist who became the leader of Calvinistic Methodism, indicated not only the strength and development of trans-Atlantic ties, but also that a degree of success that had eluded the Wesleys could be obtained. Educated at Oxford, he became a deacon of the Church of England, and, inspired by the hopes focused on the new colony, went on mission to Georgia in 1738, founding churches and an orphanage school. In trouble in England for heterodox opinions and preaching without licence, Whitefield, a charismatic speaker, went on a lengthy preaching tour in America in 1739–41. This indicated the extent to which America could constitute a unit, for, calling for repentance and offering rebirth through so doing, he visited the colonies from Boston to Savannah, preaching largely in Presbyterian meeting houses and in the open, and being listened to by many Americans, including Benjamin Franklin. In Savannah, Whitefield began work on the orphanage, the financing of which had been a major goal of his preaching. The Great Awakening was therefore important not only in New England but also further south. Freemasonry was also a major link between Britain and Georgia, with a Masonic temple constructed in Savannah soon after settlement began. Whitefield was a strong proponent of bringing slavery into Georgia: he wanted cheap labour to build his orphanage, Bethesda, but claimed that the presence of slaves would give him the opportunity to convert them.

At the same time, Whitefield was involved in ecclesiastical disputes that spanned the Atlantic and were also specific to America. Although nominally, from 1739, the Anglican incumbent at Savannah, Whitefield's preaching at large and his links with Dissenters caused controversy and, in 1740, he was questioned before the Commissary in Charleston. As was so often the case with the complex web of clerical authority, a situation accentuated by Empire, the hearing led to disputes over jurisdiction. Later in 1740, Whitefield preached in Boston against the liberalism in Harvard and, instead, underlined Calvinist doctrine. Returning to Britain, Whitefield went on fresh preaching missions before he visited America again in 1744–8, 1751–2, 1754–5, 1763–5 and 1769–70, dying on his last preaching tour, which took him from Savannah to Massachusetts.[36] Ironically, there were parallels between the revivalist preaching of Whitefield and others, and the call for purity and faith by Native Americans such as the charismatic Neolin.

The diversity of Christian practice was linked to ethnic variety among the settler population. This, in turn, led to a pragmatic religious toleration, at least for Protestants, that was a continuing characteristic of British America.[37] This was also true of the British Isles, but this toleration was taken further in America, particularly in the Middle Colonies. Government made messy compromises, officials implementing policy found the situation complex, and the people sought accommodations as they had to find ways of living with heterodox neighbours. Furthermore, such compromises became more widespread, and, by the 1760s, dissenters to established churches were generally treated more leniently.

Yet compromise as a moral choice was rejected by those who sought revival. The result was to divide congregations, as the urgent drive for salvation led to the abandonment of what might be acceptable to friends and neighbours. This had subversive possibilities, as the opting out, in favour of a trans-Atlantic city on the hill, which had been the possibility for Puritans settling in New England in the seventeenth century, was now presented across the colonies. Furthermore, the emphasis on free will and individual responsibility that Whitefield and others advanced offered a political prospect in which deference was rejected in favour of meritorious liberty.

The ability of many of the colonists to organize themselves for religious ends reflected not simply the sense of a society in creation and flux, but also the flexibility provided by the weaknesses of existing institutions. For the Church of England, this included the absence of an episcopal structure and the large size of the parishes.

Attention to the nature of religious activity serves to underline the extent to which variations between colonies were not a matter of differences in the degree to which a common theme had been adopted, but, instead, reflected distinctive dynamics that were frequently at cross purposes. This then raises the question whether it is pertinent to speak of a common American experience and, if so, how it should be characterized. There is a particular tension between an emphasis on New England and one on the Chesapeake. The extent to which they established models that influenced developments elsewhere is a matter of controversy. It is certainly clear that there were significant elements in each that were different from the other. The stress on land in the Chesapeake was more influential elsewhere than that on towns in New England because it resonated with themes of social and cultural aspiration, order and hierarchy.

Yet however much the Chesapeake provided a model for patterns of development that lessened differences between colonies, and thus made possible the articulation of an American cultural order,[38] it would be misleading to see colonial populations as shoehorned into any particular model. It is also pertinent to note the extent to which New England did not have a static social pattern. Thus, wealthy Boston merchants became interested in presenting themselves, like their Virginian counterparts, as gentlemen farmers.[39] This matched British patterns. The cultural order was captured by American portraitists, although, in a significant difference of tone, their work was more vigorous and naturalistic than most British counterparts.[40]

It remained to be seen what the consequences of the fall of New France would be for the British colonies farther south, although the issue, initially, was not a pressing one for British ministers who focused, instead, on the global struggle with France and, from 1762, Spain also. Towns in Massachusetts and New Hampshire were named after Amherst, who had been welcomed in New York as a hero after the capture of Louisbourg, while the fall of Québec had been much celebrated in British North America, not least in New England, and Wolfe was seen as a martyr to a common cause.[41]

Yet there were tensions already between the colonies and the British government. In part, these arose from the legacy of wartime differences over funding, military service, and command.[42] Indeed, there is no clear divide between the close of the war and the beginning of imperial unrest because the latter was already significant.[43] Thus, in Virginia, the theme of no taxation without representation had been much expressed in response to the order by Dinwiddie, the Lieutenant-Governor, in 1752 that a payment be levied on land patents bearing his seal and signature. When the Attorney General, Peyton Randolph, was sent by the House of Burgesses to Britain to complain, he was dismissed by Dinwiddie. Finally, in 1756, on the instructions of the Board of Trade, the fee was abandoned and Randolph reinstated.

More lastingly, there was the question of how much credit the colonists deserved and, even, who bore the principal responsibility for victory: regulars or provincials, Britain or its colonies. This was a debt of honour, and therefore a credit, that was seen in the colonies as more significant than the financial burdens that Britain had incurred. In Britain, in contrast, due to war expenditure, the national debt had risen to an unprecedented height, putting great pressure not only on government borrowing, but also on governmental and political confidence in the future. Indeed, in 1771, David Hume queried the value of the acquisitions gained with this borrowing, and challenged the idea 'that the practice of contracting debts has produced the greatness of England. Without that practice indeed we should not have had four such long wars with France as we have undertaken since the Revolution [of 1688–9]: But what acquisitions have we made by these wars, except Canada, which some people think scarce worth acquiring.'[44]

This financial burden encouraged the idea that the colonies were in debt to Britain. These contrasting ideas of credit and debt were important from the outset of imperial expansion. They were internalized further in the colonies because of the tension between, on the one hand, the sense of opportunity provided by plentiful land and related expansion, and, on the other, the pressing reality of individual debt that was integral to the trans-Atlantic commercial economy.

Contrasting ideas of credit and debt also overlapped with the question of how, and how far, Empire was to be redefined after Britain had won its struggle for France, and what this was to mean in North America. Indeed, the effort involved in the conquest of Canada was important in a reconceptualization of the British Empire towards a more territorial idea of power. Canada would be British by conquest, not trade, and Québec would obviously have to be held by force. This was unsettling for those in Britain and the Thirteen Colonies whose conception of the Empire was as a force of and for commerce and liberty. Indeed, there was anxiety that a new more authoritarian Empire would threaten the liberty of settlers.

4

Gathering Crisis, 1760–74

Services and sermons of thanksgiving in Britain and British North America alike greeted victory over France, as well as the accession of George III in 1760 and his marriage the following year. Failure and civil war did not seem a prospect. While the breakdown of the trans-Atlantic relationship is the major theme of this chapter, such a coverage has to confront major problems. First, knowing the outcome always affects the discussion, and, secondly, there were several themes at play in this period aside from growing tensions in relations between the British government and its colonists.

The changing position of the Native Americans was a significant element in the situation. Important in its own right, this issue also interacted with that of relations between government and colonists. A common theme to both was that of reacting to the epiphany of British imperial success in the Seven Years' War. This conflict concluded with the Peace of Paris of 1763 under which Britain was ceded Canada by France. Moreover, Florida was acquired from Spain which, in compensation, gained Louisiana from France. Spain had come into the war on France's side in 1762, leading Georgia to build Fort George in order to protect the entrance to the Savannah River. The British had not conquered, or sought to conquer, Florida, but after heavy casualties, which were largely due to disease, they had successfully besieged Havana, a more strategically important gain. Its return was secured by Spain, but only by ceding East and West Florida.

The British Empire had never been so extensive as in 1763, but, alongside comparisons with imperial Rome, this left uncertainty about the stability and sustainability of what seemed a new system. There was concern about challenges from within and threats from without. Indeed, the prospect of a Bourbon war of *revanche* to reverse French and Spanish losses had been held out before the Seven Years' War ended. 'Ibericus', writing in the *London Chronicle* of 7 January 1762, pressed for the conquest of Florida and Louisiana in order to complete the Empire in North America: 'it will fix our colony's security beyond the reach of rival states in future times to endanger'. In the *London Evening Post* of 25 May 1762, 'Anglicus' made the same point about Louisiana. The assumption was that the British Empire could only be challenged by attack from neighbouring colonies, as in 1754. The challenge that soon emerged, rebellion supported by foreign naval power, was not anticipated.

Empire gained lent a celebratory goal to the account of Britain's role. Nevertheless, this left many questions about the terms under which those who could be held to constitute Britain took part in Empire. It is conventional to focus on the colonists who were the cause of rebellion in 1775, but it is also appropriate to remember the others involved in British North America. In demographic terms, both Native and African Americans were significant.

Difficult relations with Native Americans, or rather with several prominent tribes, spanned the Peace of Paris, serving to underline the problems created by conflicting assumptions about the role of Native Americans in the British world. The dynamic was set by the colonists' hunger for land and also by a distrust of Native Americans which, for example, wrecked the attempt by the Moravians to undertake missionary work among the Delaware of Pennsylvania.[1] The Seven Years' War encouraged the militarization of relations, in part because there were links with the conflict with France, but, in part, due to the availability of troops, which was very different to the pre-war situation. In 1759, Amherst had sent 200 American Rangers under Major Robert Rogers to surprise and destroy St François, the main village of the Abenakis, France's traditional ally, near New England. This was a task they successfully accomplished, although a collapse of supply arrangements on their retreat forced the men to eat the corpses of colleagues. The raid on their hitherto invulnerable base greatly wrecked Abenaki confidence.[2]

In 1759, war broke out with the Cherokees. This was a very different struggle to that against the French regulars in Canada, but, in terms of the immediate threat to some colonies, it was a more urgent struggle. They were a generally pro-British tribe whose hunting lands in modern east Tennessee and west North Carolina were under pressure from the advancing frontier of European activity, control and settlement. Mistreatment by Virginian frontiersmen, who in 1758 killed Cherokees returning from helping against the French, led to an upsurge in violence, which was seriously exacerbated in 1759 with the imprisonment of a delegation of Cherokee headmen by Governor William Lyttleton of South Carolina. In turn, Cherokee action against Fort Prince George resulted in the killing of hostages by the troops and led the Governor, who was ready for war, to plead with Amherst for military assistance. In contrast, the French at Fort Toulouse on the Alabama River were unable to respond to Cherokee requests for aid.

A force of 1,300 regulars, including 400 Scottish Highlanders under Colonel Archibald Montgomery, that was sent by Amherst in the spring of 1760 to suppress the Cherokees faced serious logistical problems and also met guerrilla resistance organized by Oconostota, being ambushed and then retreating. As a result, Montgomery brought devastation without ending the conflict. He had also been instructed to return for the campaign against the French in Canada, and the Cherokee rifles were more effective than the British muskets.

In turn, the Cherokees, who had laid siege to Fort Loudoun on the Lower Tennessee River, captured the starving garrison on 8 August as it retreated. The garrison had surrendered the fort a day earlier, on the promise of a safe pass to Fort Prince George, but many of the Cherokees wanted revenge for the earlier murder of some of their kinsmen held as hostages, and some of the captives were killed.

British commentators linked the conflict to the war with France, John Leland fearing 'if the war should continue that the French will molest our Southern colonies, as South Carolina is already attacked by Indians instigated by them'.[3] Such claims reflected the general tendency to underrate Native American autonomy and their ability to take their own decisions. This tendency exacerbated the difficulties facing the Native Americans as it led to calls to extirpate the threat they allegedly posed as the representative of hostile forces. The Americans were to employ this argument with reference to an alleged British–Native American matrix, developing the earlier argument of a French–Native American matrix.

After a truce, the British invaded Cherokee country again in 1761, with a mixed force of regular troops, Carolina Rangers, and allied Native Americans under Lieutenant-Colonel James Grant. The eastern Chickasaws backed the British. A scorched-earth policy, in which settlements and crops were burnt,[4] was countered by Cherokee resistance based on highland hideouts, and Grant felt it unwise to advance to the Overhill towns.

However, food shortages, disease and destruction led the Cherokees that September to agree to terms and return Fort Loudoun, although the demand that four Cherokees be executed was dropped.[5] Governor William Bull of South Carolina reported in 1761 that Anglo-American prisoners released by the Cherokees claimed that

> their young men from their past observations express no very respectable opinion of our manner of fighting them, as, by our close order, we present a large object to their fire, and our platoons do little execution as the Indians are thinly scattered and concealed behind bushes or trees; though they acknowledged our troops thereby show they are not afraid, and that our numbers would be formidable in open ground, where they will never give us an opportunity of engaging them.[6]

Further south, Creek concern about settlement in the Georgia backcountry led to attacks on settlers in 1761, causing hostilities that were settled for a while by the Augusta Conference in 1763 where the Governors of Virginia, North Carolina, South Carolina and Georgia met with the Native American representatives.

The Peace of Paris of 1763, however, was followed by renewed tension with Native Americans. The terms had not taken note of Native American views and territorial interests. This was normal in negotiations between European powers, and the implications became more serious with the advance of the frontier of settlement. Tension rose as the British failed to provide the Native Americans with customary presents, which were seen by the Native Americans as compensation for the right to trade and travel. Moreover, British American merchants acted in an arbitrary fashion, and settlers moved into Native American lands, breaking agreements. For example, in 1759, the Delaware had been promised that the British would depart from their lands in the Ohio Valley, which, however, was not the intention of the Ohio Company.

The British were very fortunate that the crisis followed the Seven Years' War. They would have found war with the French very difficult had they had to face a major Native American rising, while French support would have made such a rising far more serious. Similarly, sequential, rather than simultaneous, conflicts were an important element in British success in India, with the British trying to fight opponents such as the Marathas separately to others such as Mysore.

Mounting tension led to Pontiac's War (1763–4), a conflict between British forces and a number of tribes, especially the Ottawas under Pontiac, but also the Saulteaux, Sauks, Miamis, Mississaugas, Wyandots, Delawares and Shawnees, most of whom were former allies. As with earlier Native American resistance, this was not a united response. The 'northern nations' were generally quiescent, while there was no unified effort among the Native Americans who fought. Pontiac's influence was, in fact, limited. Attempts at securing Native American unity centred less around him than around nativist religious revival leaders, such as Neolin, the Delaware prophet. This revival began a movement for unified resistance to Anglo-American expansion which continued until its destruction in the War of 1812. The revival also drew on ideas that were similar to the Great Awakening, and, indeed, the nativist revival was a blend of traditional beliefs with Christian concepts. Looking toward the radical ideas that were to be seen in the American Revolution, these nativists, like George Whitefield, stressed spiritual equality.

A series of attacks was launched by the Native Americans in May 1763. Many settlers fled back over the Appalachians, although about 2,000 traders and settlers were killed or captured in the uprising. The army was left to hold the forts to the south of the Great Lakes. Most of the forts were small and not designed for large garrisons, and most of the garrisons were undermanned and unable to hold their positions. The 16 defenders of Fort Sandusky were killed by the Wyandots on 16 May and the fort was burned. Fort Miami fell to the Miamis on 27 May: one of the defenders was killed, the other 11 captured. The Miamis pressed on to capture Fort Ouiatenon on 31 May. All 21 defenders were taken prisoner.

More forts fell the following month, largely as a result of ruses. The Sauks and Saulteaux captured Fort Michilimackinac on 2 June after gaining entry to follow a lacrosse ball: 18 of the defenders were killed, the other ten taken prisoner. The defenders of Fort Venango were killed on 13 June when the Delaware-Seneca captured it. Other forts were abandoned: Edward Augusta (15 June), Le Boeuf (18 June), and Lyttleton (20 June): the forts thus failed as a system of control and forward defence.

The Native Americans were helped by the small size of the British Army in North America and the vast area it had to cover. A series of Native American victories in battle also prevented the British from relieving besieged forts, hit their communications and lessened their confidence in their ability to move troops safely. Unaware that fighting had begun, 96 troops from Fort Niagara, sailing in 18 small boats along Lake Erie towards Detroit, were ambushed at Point Pelée on 28 May 1763, and 63 were killed or captured. On 5–6 August, 350 regulars and 110 American militia, advancing to relieve Fort Pitt, were ambushed at Bushy Run; 118 were killed or wounded, but their opponents suffered only 60 casualties.

However, Fort Pitt was still relieved. At Bushy Run, the British force was far more effective in forest warfare than Braddock's had been. Instead of milling around as confused targets, Lieutenant-Colonel Henry Bouquet's men retained operational effectiveness, mounting a bayonet attack, and a feinted retreat; the latter was effective in causing Native American casualties on the second day of the battle because the Native Americans abandoned their distant fighting tactics and came within reach of the British bayonets. Nevertheless, Bouquet's force had been hard hit and was unable to mount further operations that year. In addition, on 14 September, in the 'Devil's Hole Massacre', 139 British regulars were ambushed near Fort Niagara and 127 were killed.

Despite these Native American successes, the major forts, with their sizeable garrisons and artillery, resisted siege. The Native Americans lacked cannon, and their ethos and method of warfare were not well suited to the lengthy, methodical, arduous and unheroic nature of siegecraft, although they also displayed an adaptability that included waging siege warfare.[7] Detroit held out from 9 May 1763 until the unsuccessful siege was lifted on 31 October, Fort Pitt from 26 June until the siege ended on 7 August. Despite hit and run attacks in June, Forts Ligonier and Bedford did not fall, while the forts on Lake Ontario – Niagara and Oswego – remained in British hands.

Their opponents were affected by shortages of supplies. Owing to the British conquest of Canada, Native Americans opposed to the British had lost their French supporters, and the Native Americans had no access to firearms other than those they captured. The Anglo–French rivalry had given a measure of opportunity, providing, for example, arms and ammunition to the Abenakis, but the conquest of Canada had ended this rivalry as far as the North American interior was concerned. By 1764 the Native Americans were probably short of gunpowder: the British received reports to this effect. This had also been a serious problem for the Cherokees in 1761. Moreover, it proved difficult for the

Native American tribes to sustain cooperation, which was not surprising, given the vast area at stake, and, in addition, many important tribes did not take part in the rising.

The Native Americans found it difficult to sustain long conflicts, an instance of the advantage that professional permanent forces had over societies in which conflict involved the bulk of the adult male population. The British also distributed at least two blankets infected with smallpox – an early example of biological warfare – and whether this was crucial or not, the Delawares were ravaged by a smallpox epidemic.[8] Although the Delawares and Shawnees continued to attack the frontier until August 1764, the 1763 Royal Proclamation offered a way forward. It established a line beyond which colonial settlement was prohibited, a measure, however, that was resented in the American colonies and that proved difficult to enforce. Moreover, in 1764, a British threat to Native American towns in the Muskingum Valley encouraged the Native Americans to negotiate. As, more generally, a threat to opponents' bases was more effective than encounter warfare.

The conflict was settled in a series of treaties, for example one in August with the Senecas and another in November with the Delawares and Shawnees. The Royal Proclamation – and the resumption of presents to the Native Americans – indicated that, although the British authorities assured themselves that their terms were imposed,[9] the settlement was a compromise. The Native Americans returned all prisoners, but ceded no land.[10]

In the war, Amherst had lacked flexibility in his treatment of the Native Americans and failed to appreciate the potential of the colonial American militia. Yet the ability to retain hold of key fortresses at the beginning of the rising and also to prevent the Native Americans from rolling up the supply route to Fort Pitt ensured that, once the initial energy of the rising had been spent, the British were well placed to mount a response. Raids on Forts Ligonier and Bedford were not sufficient to dislodge their garrisons and, further east, Fort London, Carlisle and Lancaster remained under British control, and could serve as bases for counter-moves. Attacks on settlements in rural Pennsylvania and neighbouring colonies did not translate into an assault on the region of cultivation and settlement that was serious and systematic enough to force the British to adopt a reactive strategy in which they had to concentrate their troops on holding defensive positions to the east and south of the areas of Native American settlement.

Indeed, the very weakness of the Native American position in areas that had been colonized was a vital resource for the British. The major rise in the colonial population through immigration ensured that the Native Americans were heavily outnumbered, repeating the advantage seen, for example, in King Philip's War of 1675–6.[11] The capacity of regulars and colonials in 1763–4 to respond to Native American successes and to mount fresh efforts was indicative of the manpower resources they enjoyed. Within areas where settlers were numerous, the Native Americans had to adapt if they were to survive.[12] The combination of demographic and economic factors led Adam Smith to suggest that, although the Native Americans 'may plague them [European settlers] and hurt some of the back settlements, they could never injure the body of the people'.[13] Yet, the backcountry was also of significance. A recent study has emphasized that greater Native American unity could have ensured that the Allegheny Mountains were a more effective barrier against white expansion, and has also stressed colonial reluctance to help Britain defend the frontier.[14]

In the American War of Independence, the situation was to be very different: the British did not enjoy a safe base-area for recruitment, supply, communications and manoeuvre similar to that they had benefited from during Pontiac's War. Indeed, that conflict highlights, by contrast, the nature of the military challenge in the War of Independence. The latter was at the centre of Britain's North American empire, not at its margins.

Pontiac's War underlined the need for the government to take care of relations with Native Americans, but these relations were put under pressure from colonists. The latter had little sympathy for the idea of the Crown's responsibility to, and agreements with, the Native Americans. Thus, in 1764, in Pennsylvania, the Scots–Irish 'Paxton Boys' claimed that they were exposed to border raids and attacked Christian Native Americans. Tension therefore brought out issues of authority. The 1763 Royal Proclamation was of particular importance, because the colonists' practice of uniting in expansion at the expense of the Native Americans was directly opposed to this policy. The government thus both checked the interests of colonists and also challenged their sense of unity through this struggle. Land and race, the issues at stake, involved property in the sense of wealth but also the property of values. If the former entailed the dispossession of others, the latter also implied it. Wills, 2nd Viscount Hillsborough, President of the Board of Trade in 1763–5, 1766 and 1768–72, and Secretary of State for the Colonies from 1768 to 1772, a keen opponent of colonial expansion, resigned in 1772 when the government shifted in favour of settlement in the Ohio Valley.

Other issues of authority were also bound up in the treatment of the Native Americans. For example, in 1771, a consortium of traders to whom the Cherokees owed money got them to cede, in return for ending the debt, a large amount of land along tributaries of the Savannah River in Georgia. Governor James Wright, however, argued that such a cession could only be legally conducted with the government. This occurred in 1773: the land was ceded to Georgia, which reimbursed the traders, intending to compensate itself by selling the land to settlers.[15]

White activity could lead to a violent response, as in 1768 when Emistisiguo, a key and pro-British figure in the Upper Creek towns, attacked illegal traders. Far more seriously, in 1774, 1,500 Virginia militia advanced against the Shawnees, who had attacked settlers in their territory and had ambushed a volunteer force that went to their assistance. The Shawnees were defeated at the Battle of Point Pleasant.

At the same time, the Native American issue was much less prominent in the early 1770s than it had been a decade earlier. In place of the extended network of forts, defended portages and roads created by British troops then, there were, by the 1770s, few posts. In part, this reflected growing anxiety, instead, about the loyalty of the colonists.[16] The cost of the Shawnee conflict, however, reawakened concerns about the costs of defence.

The expansion of European control involved not only dominion over Native Americans but also the use of Africans and whites. Thus, in the lower Mississippi in the 1760s, Spain and Britain, the new rulers in Louisiana and West Florida respectively, took measures to increase the number of colonial inhabitants, both white settlers and black slaves, and an export economy developed based on indigo, tobacco and timber.[17] The British were now able to base trade in Mobile and Pensacola. The small size of the white population made the attitude of the local Native American tribes particularly important, but they neither joined nor imitated Pontiac's War. The Governor, George Johnstone, took care to seek Native American support.

As another aspect of consolidating power over Florida, George Gauld, from 1764 to 1781, charted the Gulf of Mexico in response to instructions from the Admiralty, while William De Brahm, the Surveyor General of East Florida, mapped the Atlantic coast from 1765.[18] Alongside official reports the public discussion of the wider world focused on utility: channels to navigate, harbours to use as ports, lands to cultivate, and so on. Thus, the *St James's Chronicle* of 24 July 1766 printed a letter, dated Mobile 21 February, that was from Thomas Miller, who was trying to develop a plantation, to John Ellis, King's Agent for West Florida. Having stressed the quantity of wood available, he continued:

> Those swamps appear to me to be good lands, capable of producing either rice, hemp, flax, indigo, or cotton; indeed indigo and cotton I have seen succeed in them very well. The whole face of the country is covered with grass of so good a kind that cattle fat to good beef on it … the woods abound with deer, turkeys, quails, rabbits, etc. … I never saw a place so full of fine fish as this Bay of Mobile.

By 1767, Miller had developed a rice plantation. The British were therefore taking over the possibilities previously open to France and Spain. French traders who continued to develop the river routes from the Great Lakes were now working for British entrepreneurs.

A different type of margin to the 'Middle Ground' with Native Americans was provided by slave society, but this society was a matter for local control and coercion rather than providing serious challenges to British authority. The system of oversight was firm. In Pensacola in West Florida, which was under British rule from 1763, no slave was allowed out without his owner's written permission, and meetings of more than six slaves were forbidden after 9 pm.[19]

Flight was a more common form of resistance, and, in aggregate, an often serious challenge to detailed patterns of control and authority.[20] The *Briton*, a London newspaper, in its issue of 11 December 1762, argued that gaining St Augustine from Spain would prevent 'the desertion of our Negro slaves' from Georgia. Further north, slaves fled to the Dismal Swamp on the Virginia North Carolina border. Concern about slave flight ensured that patrols were a regular means of supervision. Hunting runaways, indeed, was an activity in which many whites engaged, and it helped underline the role of violence in American society.

Rising prices for slaves from mid-century indicate that demand from the growing colonial economy was outstripping supply. This is a reminder of the extent to which control over labour was as important an element in power politics as that over land, particularly in local power politics. This was less the case in New England, where the family economy provided labour, but was true elsewhere where single males predominated and operated by controlling bound labour. In labour-poor areas, indeed, the key goal of control was over labour.

Moreover, aside from overall demand, differing needs for slaves were a key aspect of the variety of this economy and of the sophisticated demand–response interactions of the trade. For example, the Ibo shipped from the Bight of Biafra were favoured by Virginia planters, but were seen as insufficiently strong by Carolina and Georgia planters, who preferred Bambara and Malimke from Senegambia, or Angolans. The rice cultivation of South Carolina and Georgia was more arduous than the tobacco cultivation of the Chesapeake. By the mid-1770s, the rise in the latter's slave population through natural increase was such that few slaves were being imported there.

This created an easier environment for Christian proselytism, and missionary activity among slaves, as well as to free blacks, increased and became more successful. Servitude did not preclude Christian practice. This was also politically significant, as within a general context of coercion and force it was to ease the presence of African Americans as a significant section of the American population.

For whites, a rhetoric of a threat to liberty that prefigured servitude was to be an incitement to action against British rule, but, given the coercive environment, the disorientation of enslavement and the variety of slave environments, it is scarcely surprising that African Americans were not in a position to witness an independent nativist religious revival outside white control comparable to that of the Native Americans. The absence of such an independent revival was an important aspect of race relations, of religious developments, and of frontiers of control within the colonies.

The relationship between slavery and economic development was complex. There were disagreements about the desirability of slave labour. In South Carolina, Georgia, and East Florida, opinion among planters was divided. The better established commercial agriculture was, the more its participants wanted to reform or diversify it, particularly to prevent greater dependence on slavery. Conversely, newer settlers welcomed such dependence.[21]

At the level of the Atlantic economy, it would not have benefited the slaves to know that they were part of a dynamic economic system, in which consumerism, capital accumulation, and investment in industrialization were all linked. For example, profits accumulated in Glasgow from tobacco trading helped fund the development of the chemical industry in west-central Scotland, and also increased the liquidity of Scottish banks. This was an aspect of the extent to which the British Atlantic stood out from the other European Atlantics in terms of the combined degree and intensity of the processes of exchange and linkage.[22] As a reminder of the widespread impact of slavery, it was important not only to Chesapeake tobacco exports but also to the oceanic trade of New England, which subsequently did its best to ignore its role.

Problems in frontier or backcountry areas were not restricted to relations with Native Americans, although there was a common concern about what was seen as lawlessness. In some cases this was true, for example of the violence and banditry in the South Carolina backcountry. In addition, the role of royal officials and linked interests, based on ports and colonial centres, in directing backcountry areas led to complaints, many of which focused on taxation. In North Carolina in 1766–71, the royal government was attacked by the backcountry farmers of the Piedmont who sought to 'regulate' local officials, but the Regulators' attack on regressive taxation and a lack of consultation was unsuccessful, and they were defeated in battle at Alamance.

This rebellion can be seen as a throwback to a tradition of sectional assertion, a reaction on the frontiers of Empire that is inconsequential to the story of the development of the USA, but that is unduly to minimize the significance of the leading violent episode in the decade prior to the Revolution. In some respects, the complaints in North Carolina were specific to the processes of government, especially the combination of officialdom, the courts and mercantile credit. Yet there were also more wideranging issues and concerns arising from these complaints, including anxiety about the nature of power and an encoding of the militancy of the Great Awakening in political action. Debt and power were moral as well as economic issues.[23]

More generally, there was a strongly pronounced localism that arose from the prime attachment to local neighbourhoods and the economic context of small-scale agriculture.[24] This localism could be seen not only in frontier areas, but also in others that were under-represented and only partly integrated into the dominant power system, for example the eastern shore of the Chesapeake. Such areas can be understood not only in terms of localism but also with reference to the concept of the internal frontier employed by Jos Gommans in his work on Mughal India.[25]

Marginal economic zones, especially on or close to the frontier of settlement, could reject aspects of the governmental authority of the centres of power, not least their control over networks of trade, credit and debt. The most common form of opposition was the refusal to pay debt. Violent resistance, as in North Carolina, however, was a continuing tradition that led, after British authority was rejected, to Shays' Rebellion in Massachusetts in 1786–7 and the Whiskey Rebellion in Pennsylvania in 1794. For the imperial government, such risings were less troublesome than defiance in the port cities, not least because the latter resonated, through the culture of print, more clearly with domestic concerns and criticisms. Thus, despite the value of North Carolina as a source of timber, Massachusetts was of greater concern to the British government.

At the same time, there were links between the two, with the North Carolina Regulators drawing on the example of the protestors against the Stamp Act. Moreover, although the Tidewater elite disliked the backcountry, not least disparaging its recent Scots–Irish settlers, they also sought to win its support. This attempt was seen in a popularization of politics that was also important to the development of American electoral conduct. This popularization lent itself to the rhetoric of liberty.

Thus, while an approach to the American Revolution that centres on crises on the periphery would be mistaken, these crises, whether focusing on Native Americans, territorial expansion, or backcountry dissidence, were related to the dynamics of politics, or at least the anxieties of liberty, of the coastlands. Similarly, albeit at a different scale of significance and prominence, at the same time as noting the strength of localism within colonies such as Massachusetts,[26] it is necessary to appreciate their wider importance.

This entails a concentration on the defiance of royal authority in the centres of American society and government, a process dramatized with the Boston Tea Party on 16 December 1773. The issues here relate to another narrative of the working out of the consequences of the Seven Years' War, although other factors also played a major part. Some were co-terminous with the consequences of the recent war, but others were of longer genesis. Before turning to the issues, it is pertinent to give a sense of the general context.

The origins of the American Revolution looked back to seventeenth-century British traditions of resistance to unreasonable royal demands, and, in some respects, it was a second version of the civil conflict of 1638–52, and, like that, a war of religion. In this new war of religion, non-Anglicans played the key role in resistance, while the principal source of support within the colonies for royal authority came from Anglicans, although this was not true of the Southern elites. George III's support for authority and order was seen in large part, by both him and others, as influenced by religious considerations.

It was not only the role of religion that was reminiscent of 1638–52. The latter had begun as a rejection of the authority of the royal government in Scotland, and a sense of alienation from authority as a result of the interventionism of royal government played a major role in America in the 1770s. Angered by their consequences, many colonists resisted Parliament's efforts to project its sovereign authority across the Atlantic. These efforts, however, were seen as natural in Britain in order to secure the coherence of the Empire.

The debate over the terms of the Empire that grew out of the Seven Years' War became, in North America, an effort to limit the exercise of state power by defining and asserting the natural and constitutional rights of individuals and groups within the body politic, albeit individuals and groups that, due to the position of African and Native Americans, did not include much of the population. These disagreements over the colonial bond cut to the core of the nature of the Empire, which was that of a reciprocal benefit controlled by the state, as expressed through the sovereignty of Parliament. This understanding of Empire was challenged by autonomous tendencies in the colonies, that, in turn, led to uneasiness in the metropole. Joseph Yorke, a well-connected diplomat and MP, remarked in 1763: 'I cannot bear the thought of the North Americans selling powder to the savages to murder the King's troops whilst they look on,'[27] an approach to Pontiac's War that saw the Americans as an aspect of the problem.

Tension also arose from other developments within the colonies, including the disruptive consequences of rapid population growth, as well as the Calvinistic revivalism of the Great Awakening (see pp. 83–5). One result of the former was that the relative share of the colonial population in the British Empire increased, but without any comparable increase in the fiscal support provided by the colonists or any change in their political position. The Great Awakening ensured that rumours about the possible establishment of an Anglican episcopacy in North America (in contrast to the previous position in which George II had denied resident suffragan bishops for America) were greeted with strong hostility by the large number of non-Anglicans, while many lay Anglicans were determined to ensure their continued power over the clergy. Thus, anti-clericalism played a role in the opposition to Britain.[28] In practice, the British government's political agenda came foremost, and ecclesiastical organization was not seen as a key issue by the ministry. This was what was crucial, not worry about the critical response from Dissenters in New England and Britain.

In America, Protestant concerns made the granting of rights to French-speaking Catholics under the Québec Act of 1774 a matter of particular sensitivity, as it compromised notions of Protestant nationhood and threatened American opportunities to expand west of the Appalachians. There was an echo of anxiety about the authoritarian views on Church government held by Archbishop Laud (see p. 4) and about the apparently Catholicizing nature of Charles I's court. The idea of Protestant nationhood was strong in the Thirteen Colonies where there were only about 30,000 Catholics. Most lived in Maryland or Pennsylvania and, elsewhere, colonists met few Catholics of any social prominence.

Concern about Québec brought together old, but not dormant, anti-Catholicism, anxieties about the lands to the north and west, still active worries about Native Americans, and a sense that a potentially tyrannical British state was looking for a base and basis of support for action against the Thirteen Colonies. As such, this concern reprised English anxieties about the situation in Ireland at the time both of the outbreak of the English Civil War and in the aftermath of the Glorious Revolution. In October 1774, the First Continental Congress presented the Act as a way for 'a wicked ministry' to recruit Québecois support against 'the free Protestant colonies'.[29] In short, the shots might not yet have been fired, but the army was already recruited.

More generally, in the Thirteen Colonies, in the early 1770s, there were challenges to established patterns and practices of authority and social influence. These necessarily involved the prestige and authority of the Crown. This was certainly true of the ultimately violent opposition in Massachusetts to Thomas Hutchinson, the Governor, in the early 1770s.[30] These challenges stemmed in part from the nature of society. The Great Awakening released and energized democratizing forces, while Puritanism in New England was, to some extent, becoming secularized.

These tensions were not clearly separated in American minds. For example, what has been written of the Massachusetts' lawyer Josiah Quincy, is more generally true: 'Quincy conflated what modern historians have made distinct. For him there was no sharp distinction between the divine and what was inherent in nature, nor were charter rights discrete from more elusive constitutional rights; what is more, a violation of one could threaten all of the others'.[31]

The challenge to establish patterns and practices of authority matched that in Britain, but acquired greater saliency because in the colonies it was also possible to encapsulate the issue by extrapolating authority to its British base and thus making it seem foreign. This foreignness owed something to a sense of betrayal by the British government and elite, a betrayal that took up themes of cultural treason already central in British discourse.[32] These themes readily overlapped with, and supported, arguments of political corruption and religious authoritarianism.

A significant source of tension was provided by the problems that attended the economic growth of the period, problems that made British fiscal pressures particularly difficult. For example, alongside growing tobacco exports, there was pressure on tobacco prices, especially in 1760–3, even though exports to France and Spain continued under license.[33] Moreover, the rise of the direct tobacco trade controlled by Scottish syndicates and, conversely, the diminishing share of the market controlled by consignment merchants, was linked to a tightening of credit and to a persistence of debt that ensured that tobacco played as big a part in the Revolution as tea. That tobacco was not an issue in New England underlined the continued regional nature of problems, but there was a common theme in anger with British interests.[34]

Prior to the Revolution, British America was already understood by Europeans as very different to their societies. Ignoring the hardship undergone by African and Native Americans, they saw it as a new land of liberty and of freedom from many of the burdens of the Old World, albeit one that was culturally backward. Modern research has supported contemporary views that, compared to Europe, there were significantly higher proportions of property holders, higher rates of family formation (owing something to an earlier average age of marriage), broader opportunities for achieving economic independence and personal 'empowerment', less poverty, fewer and less rigid social distinctions, and less powerful and obtrusive political and religious establishments. This situation was not incompatible with much poverty and considerable social differences in America: it is the comparative picture that is instructive. Height is a key indicator of widespread prosperity, at least in terms of a lack of malnutrition.[35] From this perspective, white Americans born there were a particularly successful group.[36]

The contemporary sense of America as a land of opportunity greatly encouraged migration, which increased after the Seven Years' War, such that approximately 10 per cent of the population there in 1775 had arrived since 1760. The pattern of emigration changed also with a marked rise in emigration from Scotland and Ireland. In contrast, as annual net emigration from England was reasonably constant, its impact diminished as the population rose. By the 1760s, the numbers emigrating from England were considerably less than those from Scotland and, even more, Ireland. Heavy rent rises contributed to the emigration of about 20,000 Scots to North America between 1769 and 1774. The Reverend William Thom claimed, in his *Candid Inquiry into the Causes of the Late and Intended Migrations from Scotland* (1771), that 'in whatever country the whole property is engrossed by a few, there the people must be wretched'. Whatever the cause of emigration, more recent immigrants to the colonies were to prove particularly loyal during the War of Independence.

Immigration brought opportunities, with the settlers able to move forward across the Alleghenies as well as to settle areas to their east. Yet within the colonies there was a sense that opportunities were slackening close to the Atlantic, with the lands there already allocated. Work could be found there, but not the status that went with land ownership. This encouraged demand for landward expansion, not least on behalf of younger sons, so that it was not solely a product of the requirements of new immigrants. This forward movement increased pressure on the Native Americans, and demonstrated the inconsistencies and weakness of British policy toward them. In some respects, this replicated the inconsistencies and problems of British fiscal-mercantile policy toward the colonies.

The notion of America as a land to which freedom was natural underwent a powerful revival among European commentators during the era of the Revolution, when American exceptionalism took on political weight in North America and Europe.[37] Nevertheless, the Revolution did not occur because of a general desire to fight for liberty. The situation was more complex. One element was the definition of power – 'whether ultimate power should rest in Britain or among the ruling classes in the colonies', with the latter pursuing not only liberty from British autocracy, but also 'determined to break free from the British empire in order to establish their own empire'.[38] A hesitant (if not unwilling) yet hostile response on the part of many to the confused tergiversations of British policy was also crucial.

This hesitation puts a question mark against any idea of an inevitable clash. Indeed, it is necessary to underline the continued similarities between the societies of Britain and British North America, and also the colonists' sense of themselves as British. This was not a revolution in what became the pattern of nineteenth-century assertions of liberal nationalism.

Justified fear of French ambitions for *revanche* underlay the government's contentious desire to build up the defensive strength of the colonies. The future of Empire and the fate of trade were still understood in a competitive environment. International rivalry and, even more, a perception of such rivalry, was the basic condition of thought abut Empire, and led to urgent concern about how best to strengthen it. Yet from the 1760s the emphasis on foreign threats became less pronounced and was increasingly set alongside serious divisions over how best to organize Empire. The ways in which policy, and regulation as an aspect of it, were to be framed, formulated and enforced, were matters of contention to a far greater degree than before, or during, the mid-century wars. As a result, the importance of foreign policy in framing discussion about trade and Empire, or in expressing views about them, declined in importance.

Policy changes, which arose as apparent remedies for the fiscal burden of imperial defence, were sought by the British government in the context of heavy national indebtedness, but, to the colonists, these policy changes apparently pointed the way to new forms of imperial governance. This led in the colonies to a pervasiveness and depth of alienation that was seriously underrated in Britain, at least by the government, or that was misleadingly seen as restricted to a few troublemakers.

After the Seven Years' War, there was significant governmental support for attempts to reform the workings of Empire and, at least partly, to seek an imperial solution for the accumulated debts of war. This represented a revival of pre-war ideas, but these had been shelved by Pitt and Newcastle. Their revival reflected the severity of the fiscal situation and also a 'dominant view of American incapacity and turpitude'.[39] In 1762, John, 4th Duke of Bedford had linked agreement on the peace terms with France, which he had negotiated, to the opportunity, and need, to focus on American affairs:

> I most heartily wish that this event may so far strengthen the hands of administration, as to enable the King to carry most effectually into execution such plans of government, as the great increase of territory in America, and the present circumstances of the rest of his dominions may require for the good of his people harassed by a long, bloody and expensive war.[40]

George III was more concerned initially with the security of the new acquisitions (Canada from France and Florida from Spain), arguing, in February 1763, that 10,000 troops should be stationed in North America to protect it in the event of a new war with France. George made no reference to the use of troops to overawe the older colonies, but he came to support his ministers' views that the colonists should pay for their security. This was a measure seen as necessary in order to respond to the concerns of British Tory politicians about the allocation of such a force, not least due to the cost. Yet George and his key adviser, John, 3rd Earl of Bute, who headed the ministry from 1762 to 1763, failed to appreciate the likely risks of this legislation in North America, and also ignored the views of experienced British ministers. Bute's predecessor, Newcastle, felt that the planned force was too large and therefore overly expensive, while Henry Legge, until 1761 Chancellor of the Exchequer, was concerned about the extension of ministerial powers.[41]

Bute was succeeded as First Lord of the Treasury in 1763 by the bullying George Grenville, and the latter's policies caused the first major crisis in Anglo–American relations. With a background in government finance, Grenville was more worried about 'the exhausted state of the public revenues' than the 'clamour of opposition of any individuals whatsoever',[42] but this led to the Stamp Act, fiscal legislation that greatly increased 'clamour'.

Commerce, indeed, was central to the colonies, with external trade accounting for nearly 20 per cent of the total income of the North American colonies on the eve of the Revolution. However, no such thing as a single colonial economy developed until the end of the era, after coastal trade had helped integrate the colonies; instead, there were sets of colonial economies, each linked more closely with London than with each other.[43] The significance of the colonies as a market and a potential source of revenue rose with their population, which rapidly increased after the Seven Years' War.

Aside from separate economies, a particularly blunt demonstration of colonial disunity was provided by serious disputes over frontiers between individual colonies. Rivers were very important in the establishment of frontiers, but they could not be used everywhere, and there were also the challenges posed in allocating lands to the west, whether occupied or expected. At the same time, agreements could be reached. As so often with historical scholarship, it is possible to place the emphasis on division or on settlement. To take the case of Pennsylvania, despite tentative agreements between it and Maryland in 1732 and 1739, neither resulted in a permanent solution. In 1763, David Rittenhouse made the first survey of the Delaware Curve, but it would not be defined satisfactorily until 1892, although the remainder of the Pennsylvania–Maryland boundary was settled by Charles Mason and Jeremiah Dixon in 1764–7. Violent disputes between Connecticut and Pennsylvania, beginning in 1769, were only settled by Congress's acceptance of the Pennsylvania claim in 1782.[44]

A less pointed aspect of differentiation rather than division was provided by regional dialects. These became more pronounced, with the link between kinship networks and senses of place entrenching differences in dialect and vocabulary. This was also the case with trans-Atlantic differences and ones within the British Isles.[45]

Yet there were also significant moves towards colonial integration. Both a top-down and a more diffuse account can be offered. For the former, the improvement in postal services pushed hard by Benjamin Franklin, Deputy Postmaster-General for the Colonies, was important in enhancing links between the colonies. More generally, in Philadelphia, there was a link between interest in the enlightened improvement of America's society and economy, and activism directed against measures of the British government.[46] Moreover, inter-regional and intercolonial trade was longstanding and significant. It encompassed both local products and imports from outside North America, and also reflected the trade arising from the differences of function between towns and country, ports and hinterlands, merchants and farmers, and so on. The resulting links created a sense of shared interest within and between colonies. This, however, could also serve to transmit problems, such as bad debt, round the economic system.[47]

Trans-Atlantic economic and political links registered pressures which were exacerbated by legislation that, if not inappropriate, was designed for different purposes than keeping the colonies happy. This was the case most prominently with the sequence of fiscal legislation that began with the Stamp Act of 1765. Already in 1764, however, the Currency Act had indicated the problems created by imperial legislation for an economic system whose interdependence both rested on and accentuated sensitive financial weaknesses. By banning the additional issue of paper notes, the Act cut the money supply in the Thirteen Colonies, which hit the debt-management crucial to so many individual and family fortunes and strategies. This also threatened land values, which further challenged not only these strategies but also the sense of security of local elites. If debt had to be covered by specie, then social position and personal consumption would both be challenged, and the role of Americans in the imperial system would become unsteady.

As a reminder of colonial diversity, different aspects of legislation and judicial activism were of greater concern in particular colonies. Thus, in Massachusetts, the enforcement by the colony's Superior Court of parliamentary legislation of the late seventeenth century designed to help implement the Navigation Acts was a key issue, as standing general search warrants were seen as a disruption to commerce and a threat to liberty. This focused anxieties about the unfair nature of the imperial trading system and its particular implications for Massachusetts. The lawyer James Otis played a key role in this dispute in 1760–1, and indicated how the rhetorical strategies of individuals could help radicalize the situation. His critique of the pretensions of government led to an implicit questioning of parliamentary sovereignty which was the basis of the writs he challenged and Otis went on to advance an ideological alternative in his *The Rights of the Colonies Asserted* (1764).

The Sugar Act of 1764, and the naval enforcement put in place to support it, also hit New England by taxing the import, and hindering the smuggling, of molasses from the French West Indies for the production of rum. This led to serious financial problems including a tightening of credit and a number of prominent bankruptcies.

The Stamp Act of 1765 imposed a series of fiscal duties on the colonies, nearly the same stamp duties already established in England. The crisis over the Act was greater than that within England over the highly unpopular cider tax, because it raised the question of parliamentary authority in America. The Act, which was supported by George III,[48] easily passed both Houses of Parliament, but the response in most of the colonies was hostile. In America, Nova Scotia and the Leeward Island (but not in the major West Indian colonies), the levying of taxation for revenue purposes by a Parliament that included no colonial representatives was regarded as a dangerous innovation, and was seen to threaten colonial rights in the shape of consent by their assemblies. This was accompanied by anger about any departure from the traditionally lax enforcement of existing commercial regulations and about restrictions on smuggling with non-British territories. In a letter that made clear a gulf in views, Edward Sedgwick, an Under Secretary, wrote in February 1765, when the House of Commons agreed the Act, about the refractoriness of the colonies ... there are several resolutions of American assemblies, in which they almost deny or strongly remonstrate against the right of the Parliament to tax them, which are directed by order in Council to be laid before the Parliament. But first it is thought proper to establish that right by a new exertion of it, and in the strongest instance, an internal tax, that of the Stamp Duty. It is remarkable that the colonies can find no champion to oppose that measure, and that there are petitions in town from some of them to the two Houses which they can not get any member to present.[49]

'All America is in confusion' was the news back in Britain about the Stamp Act.[50] Indeed, mob action led the intimidated stamp distributors to resign, wrecking the measure, while the establishment of the Stamp Act Congress reflected a more coherent opposition. This probably would not have swayed the Grenville ministry, but George's anger with Grenville's domineering treatment of him led, in July 1765, to the formation of a new ministry under Charles, 2nd Marquess of Rockingham, and it did not feel committed to the legislation. Concerned about the violent response in America, and influenced by pressure from British merchants anxious abut the crisis and worried about an American boycott of British goods,[51] the new ministry favoured the abandonment of the tax but, at the same time, insisted, by means of a Declaratory Act, on the principle of parliamentary sovereignty. A worried Edward Sedgwick wrote on Christmas Eve 1765:

> I am, like you, full of anxiety with regard to the consequences of the American dispute. The evil is in all respects of such a magnitude, that I cannot presume to guess what are the measures proper to be pursued for remedying it. The only thing I am clear in, and that I have been from the beginning is that the right of the British legislature to tax the colonies is clear and incontestable, and that it, must not, cannot be given up without annihilating the British constitution in British America.[52]

The Stamp Act indeed was repealed in March 1766, but the Declaratory Act stated that Parliament 'had, hath, and of right ought to have full power and authority to make laws and statutes of sufficient form and validity to bind the colonies and people of America in all cases whatsoever'.[53]

This was unwelcome in America where, alongside a reduction in tension after repeal, there was a conviction that the ministry would repeat its effort. Moreover, the Sugar Act remained in force and, as altered by the Revenue Act of 1766, which covered all molasses imported into the colonies, became a useful source of revenue. As a tax on trade, this seemed more bearable than a duty on internal acts, such as the Stamp Act.

In turn, the Chatham ministry (under William Pitt the Elder, now Earl of Chatham), which replaced that of Rockingham in 1766, imposed customs duties in the colonies on a variety of goods, paper, paint, lead, glass and, most valuably, tea. This was imported by the East India Company and was to provide half the

revenue that was to be raised. The Revenue Act of 1766, drawn up by Charles
Townshend, the Chancellor of the Exchequer, which imposed these duties, was
designed to pay the costs of civil government in the northern colonies, and thus
end the dependence of officials and judges on the colonial assemblies: in the
southern colonies, fixed salaries were already paid to the governors. A Board of
Customs Commissioners based in Boston was to enforce the duties. The legislation easily passed Parliament and received the royal assent on 2 July 1767. The
previous month, Sedgwick observed:

> The appointment of American commissioners of customs, (if, as you observe, they
> escape hanging) will be found, I am persuaded, a very wise and beneficial measure. But,
> above all, I applaud Mr Charles Townshend for having provided for the expense of the
> whole civil administration in the colonies, and made the several officers concerned in it
> independent of the people. This step ought to have been taken for the want of it has been
> sufficiently felt, many years ago. Without it, it was absurd ever to think of preventing
> smuggling or collecting any revenue whether old or new. But now we may hope to see
> the laws observed and many evils corrected which have hitherto been incorrigible.[54]

Thus, there was no equivalent to the situation in Ireland in the 1720s. There,
the crisis over Wood's patent (see p. 47) had been followed by greater British
care for Irish sensitivities.[55] In contrast, Chatham and his ministry failed to give
coherence to Britain's American policy, let alone to devise a new policy that would
help to repair recent differences and give a new direction, or even to advance a
vision of Empire that would win American support. Chatham turned down the
idea of a Secretary of State for American affairs, a suggestion that would have
offered coherence in the implementation of policy, as well as a source of ideas and
an agency for links with the colonies. Instead, he showed relatively little interest
in America or in American views. In 1767, when the New York Assembly had
refused to enforce the Mutiny Act in full, the Cabinet, with Chatham's backing,
decided to insist on obedience and to suspend the Assembly, although as the latter
yielded, the crisis was averted.[56]

The Townshend Duties led to a serious deterioration in relations between the
British government and its American critics, reversing the reduction in tension
that had followed the repeal of the Stamp Act. Unlike the West Indies, where
the legislation was accepted, the Americans eventually responded with a non-
importation agreement. This was political in intention and economic in force,
but boycotts also expressed a powerful cultural rejection of what was seen as
American dependence on British luxury. As such, they mirrored earlier English
anxiety about the debilitating consequences of the elite's interest in continental
European culture.

On 11 February 1768, the Massachusetts Assembly agreed that the Townshend
Duties infringed the rights of 'American subjects'. Most of the other colonies

proved reluctant to follow Massachusetts' lead, but its circular letter to other assemblies eventually won a favourable reception, which led governors to dissolve the assemblies. However hesitant in practice, the theme of America as a distinctive space and interest was much voiced. These political tensions in the colonies undercut the role of trans-Atlantic lobbies, making compromise and the search for agreement harder, and leading to confrontation in place of nuance.[57]

The capacity for a firm British response to the earlier Stamp Act crisis had been gravely limited by the paucity of troops in the east coast cities. In contrast, now, in response to disturbances in Boston in 1768, the British ministry, in turn, decided to send troops and warships to Boston in order to force Massachusetts to back down. This was an initiative, however, that was to increase tension and to have serious consequences. The troops were stationed there, but not as a police force. They had no clear duties, and no authority to act independent of civil authority. The troops' presence led, on 5 March 1770, to the 'Boston Massacre' in which five Bostonians were killed by troops firing in self-defence. This was seen by many Americans as proof of the militarization and corruption of British authority in the colonies, although it accorded with conventional British conduct in crisis situations, as in Edinburgh in 1736 and London in 1768.

The Townshend Duties were blamed in North America on a Parliament corrupted by the ministry. Instead of an individual ministry, it now appeared that Parliament itself was the problem. This encouraged a notion of the contrast between the branches of government (malign ministry in Parliament versus benign Crown) a contrast linked to a sense of the division of sovereignty between Parliament and Crown. Due to a focus on opposition to Parliament, before 1774 there was limited criticism of George III, and the King was not blamed for the failings of the ministry. Support for the radical Wilkesite cause, which had bitterly criticized George in England, existed in America,[58] but John Wilkes' blasphemy, and the violence associated with his supporters in England, did not recommend the cause to many Americans.

News about Wilkes in the comparatively well-developed American press, however, was extensive, and certainly fostered the sense that the British political system was unsuccessful, if not pernicious. General Thomas Gage, the Commander-in-Chief in North America, observed to the Secretary at War in 1772: 'Your papers are stuffed with infamous paragraphs which the American printers, especially those of Boston, seldom fail to copy with American additions'. Two years later, he added from Boston: 'The seditious here have raised flame in every colony which your speeches, writings, and protests in England have greatly encouraged'.[59] Indeed, the failure of the British government to tackle the issue of rebellious American views in the years before the Revolution was probably due to their failure to control the domestic press in Britain. These were years in which the freedom of the press was being asserted in legal and political challenges.[60]

Pressure on Britain's reputation in North America was due not so much to the impact in America of the domestic British critique, by Wilkes and others, of the supposedly autocratic policies of George III and his ministers, as to the actual measures being followed in America in order to sustain the furthering of the integrated imperial policy. Specifically, the British government had found its authority at issue because of the measures it took to strengthen the Empire by influencing relations between its parts.

These measures focused on trade, more particularly tea, the consumption of which was a prime aspect of the consumer revolution that arose from a desire for goods and, in particular, imported goods.[61] Far from proving a cash cow, the viability of the mid-century conquests in India, especially Bengal, and indeed of the entire position of the East India Company, was challenged by the combination of dividend demands by the company's shareholders, the costs of defence, the difficulties of revenue collection there, and weakness in the market for tea, a major source of company finances. This hit governmental fiscal expectations, particularly when the company sought both the rescheduling of customs payments and a loan.[62]

Tea was imported from China, but the British East India Company did not have a monopoly of the China trade. Moreover, peace in 1763 meant that the wartime limitations affecting competition from other states with the world's leading naval power were no longer pertinent. In Europe, British tea re-exports were affected by protectionist measures by other tea-trading states, as well as by their competition in major *entrepôt* markets such as Hamburg.

Tea imports into North America apparently offered a way to tackle company finances, as well as to provide, through import duties, a means of paying the salaries of colonial officials, thus ending their dependence on the colonial assemblies. This was a measure seen as particularly threatening by many colonists. The tea duty had been retained in 1769 (on a Cabinet vote of five to four) when the other duties introduced by Townshend in 1767 were repealed, a conciliatory measure George approved. Indeed, talk of repeal began as early as September 1767 when Frederick, Lord North succeeded Townshend (who had died) as Chancellor of the Exchequer.

The tea duty, however, symbolized Parliament's right to tax, and public finances benefited from this duty. This was a key point, not least because the American boycott of British imports, introduced in 1768, failed in 1770, although the boycott of tea continued.[63] The taxation of tea was scarcely new, having been included in the very first Excise Act, of 1660, but the political context was now highly charged.

As a reminder of the competitive international context, smuggled Dutch tea challenged company sales. In response, in 1773, the government passed a Tea Act that abolished British duties on the tea re-exported to America and allowed the company to sell its tea directly to consignees to the American colonies. This was a measure designed to cut the cost of tea there, and thus boost sales, helping the company. Tea was thus both reality and symbol of the process by which 'India became an integral part of the empire in tandem with attempts to integrate America more firmly into it'.[64]

The Americans, however, would still have to pay duty on the imported tea, the duty introduced by Townshend. This was condemned by activists, who were unwilling to accept Parliament's right to impose direct taxes on the colonies and who were concerned about the political implications of a greater governmental revenue in America. They also rejected the monopolistic structuring of the trade around company and consignees. The legalization made tea cheaper for consumers, but imposed a monopoly, which cut out those American importers who did not smuggle their goods into port. It was the merchant class, which was well represented in the assemblies and the Sons of Liberty, that felt victimized by the Act.

Opposition to the Act led to the resignation of intimidated consignees and to the departure of tea ships without having landed their cargo. It culminated in the Boston Tea Party on 16 December 1773, when the Sons of Liberty, led by Samuel Adams, seized 342 chests of tea from three ships in Boston harbour and threw them into the water.

Boston like other cities, such as Philadelphia, was affected by the pressure on the poor caused by economic shifts, not least the depression following the Seven Years' War. Social differentiation remained an aspect of economic and population growth, and the net effect was not only widespread hardship, but also an underlining of the risks of downward mobility.[65] Combined with the relative lack of wealth in the form of the human capital of slaves, this meant that white per capita wealth was lower than in the South. Moreover, the harsher agricultural conditions of New England helped ensure that white per capita wealth was lower there than in the Middle Colonies. The division of land among sons – partible inheritance – contributed to the economic problems of New England families. Given the importance of property to contemporary understanding of freedom and identity, these pressures were of more than simply economic importance.

In the Tea Party, colonial protesters had fashioned a powerful symbol of resistance, one that dramatized the breakdown of imperial authority for at least some of the colonists. This breakdown was the first stage of a more general collapse in European control in the New World, and a fresh non-importation movement directed against Britain followed in December 1774. Like the 1768–70 boycott, this hit British merchants, who tended to prefer commercial continuity to the defence of imperial authority.

Thus, the process of reaching, and endlessly redefining, a consensus that underlay and often constituted government in this period, had broken down.

The extent to which American writers invoked Charles I's efforts to tax without parliamentary consent in the 1630s, a clear touchstone of tyranny in contemporary minds, was indicative of a wider breakdown.[66] The frame of reference also reflected the widespread access of white males to education. Moreover, their literacy rate, especially in New England, was higher than that of their British counterparts.

Yet, at the same time, the process did not break down for most British colonists. Many in America were loyal. This could be defined to include not solely ready compliance but also, in contrast, an expectation that support for actions critical of government would lead to a change in British policy, and thus permit the maintenance of loyal obedience.

The British government, however, failed to understand the situation, not least the dynamics of American society and its developing aspirations; not that these were uniform and without important cross-currents. There was also a failure to appreciate the degree to which the individual colonies were joining together in response to successive crises, making joint action on their part increasingly an option. Indeed, in response to British efforts to bring Rhode Islanders to justice for destroying the *Gaspée*, a customs boat, in 1772, all the colonies bar Pennsylvania established committees of correspondence to coordinate responses to British actions.

This British failure of appreciation was exacerbated in 1774 by the view that concessions would be seen as weakness and lead only to fresh demands. On 22 March 1774, when the Duc d'Aiguillon, the French Foreign Minister, mentioned America for the first time to the British envoy, David, Viscount Stormont, the latter replied that the troubles were 'of such a nature as spirit, firmness and temper would certainly cure', adding, for the benefit of the British Secretary of State reading the dispatch, the reflection that in 'such emergencies the middle way is no way at all… procrastination and irresolution have produced numberless evils, but never cured one'.[67]

The legislation of 1774, the Coercive or Intolerable Acts, terms used to describe what were unpopular laws, was designed to provide exemplary punishment and a remedy for disorder. It stemmed from a belief that disorder arose from the actions of a small number, rather than from widespread disaffection; in short that conspiracy and agitation were at issue, not revolution. This was a key aspect of a general inability to appreciate the depth of alienation. Thus, in 1768, Sir James Porter, a former diplomat, claimed that 'whatever measures government may adopt with the Americans they will succeed without any great difficulty. It is at Boston, but two or three degenerate wretches who occasion the bustle and when it comes to the push I dare say they will fear the rod.'[68]

The Boston Port Act, passed in March 1774, closing the port and moving the customs house for overseas trade until the East India Company was reimbursed for the tea, was designed to protect trade and customs officials from harassment, but it was also a severe punishment. The Massachusetts Government Act, passed in May, was intended to strengthen the executive, particularly by reducing the elective character of the legislature; while the Administration of Justice and Quartering Acts were intended to make it easier to enforce order.

These measures struck colonists across the Thirteen Colonies as an infringement of charter rights that threatened the liberties of all colonies,[69] and were criticized by the opposition in Britain as excessive. The cartoon 'The able Doctor, or America Swallowing the Bitter Draught', published in the *London Magazine* in May 1774, showed America spewing back into Lord North's face the tea he is pouring down her throat while she is held down. Nevertheless, the legislation was passed by Parliament with overwhelming majorities. The Boston Port Act was unopposed in Parliament, and the opposition motion to repeal the tea duty was defeated in the House of Commons by 182 votes to 49. The distinction, in American eyes, between what was legal and what was constitutional[70] was now glaring.

Also in 1774, the grant of civil recognition to Québec's Catholics by the Québec Act passed that July, while intended to strengthen imperial stability there, accentuated New England concerns about governmental intentions.[71] The establishment of the French civil law without a jury, the recognition of the Catholic establishment in Québec, the granting of the right to collect tithes, and the absence of any element of popular government acting through an elected assembly were all unwelcome in New England, as was the extension of the province's boundaries to include the country between the Great Lakes and the Ohio and Mississippi rivers, which challenged those already concerned about governmental policy beyond the Appalachians. These western lands became part of Canada, but without formally invalidating existing claims by land speculators. The drafters of the legislation tried to reassure investors like those in the Ohio Company and colonies like Virginia that nothing was being taken away from them. The territory was declared part of Québec:

> Provided always, that nothing herein contained relative to the boundary of the province of Québec shall in anywise affect the boundaries of any other colony. Provided always, and be it enacted, that nothing in this act contained shall extend, or be construed to extend, to make void, or to vary or alter any right, title, or possession, derived under any grant, conveyance, or otherwise howsoever, of or to any lands within the said province, or the provinces thereto adjoining; but that the same shall remain and be in force, and have effect, as if this act had never been made.

This extension of Québec was designed to shore up the stability of the interior by lessening tensions between Native Americans and whites. Recent experience had demonstrated that relations between Québec's whites and the Native Americans were better than those with whites from the Thirteen Colonies, while the military governor and council provided for by the Québec Act could also be expected to ease tensions with the Native Americans.[72]

This, however, helped ensure that the tension over the interior between colonists and the British government, which had been a factor for a decade, was now impacted into narratives of British threat. As a related point, this was a threat to American interest in exploiting the interior to create a branch of the British Empire that was very much under the control of their interests, in short an American Empire.[73] Thus the interior demonstrated that the British Empire was also a spoils system, the operation of which divided metropolitan and provincial elites. Control over the interior was an important issue in the background to the War of Independence.[74]

Such an account suggests an escalating list of grievances. That was indeed the case, but these grievances also highlighted tensions between specific colonial tendencies and controversies. In particular, the social politics and religious views of New England were seen as unwelcome to many in the Chesapeake and vice versa. This was exacerbated by personality differences between prominent would-be leaders. Some of these tensions were captured in the satire *The First Book of the American Chronicle of the Times, 1774–1775* written by John Leacock, a Philadelphia silversmith turned gentleman farmer. He was critical of New England politicians on the grounds that they were millenarians, and thus, like the British government, a threat.[75] At the same time, millenarian ideas were potent because they could also cohere with political pressures for change.[76]

The variety in colonial views reflected differences between colonies that interacted with distinctive migration flows that continued right into the period of conflict. Single, young men dominated in emigration from London and southern England, while from the north and Scotland the focus was on families, and the heads of these families were older than the southern males. There were also differences in destination, with the southerners going to Maryland, Pennsylvania and Virginia, and those from the north to New York, North Carolina and Nova Scotia.[77]

The wider context was troubling to British commentators. American autonomy, let alone independence, was seen, both by supporters and critics of government policy, as a threat to the integrity of the Empire. American criticism of Parliament's regulation of imperial trade was regarded as politically unacceptable and a threat to Empire. The political, strategic and economic interdependency of the constituent parts of Empire was taken for granted, and it was widely felt that economic and political strength were related, that the monopoly of American trade supported British power – most crucially in any conflict with the Bourbons (France and Spain) – and that, without political links, it would be impossible to maintain economic relationships.

Alongside the Whig legacy, the imperial dimension influenced Chatham, who remained a powerful voice, albeit one in opposition. He was, and is, also of symbolic importance, given his role in helping ensure the conquest of Canada. Chatham's desire for conciliation, and his criticism of specific acts of governmental policy in the worsening American crisis, combined with genuine admiration for those colonists who, in defending their liberties, seemed to be asserting the cause of liberty and affirming the Whig tradition, although he was opposed to the American use of violence. Benjamin Franklin, an assiduous wooer of the prominent, who visited Chatham at his house in Hayes in August 1774, recorded:

> That truly great man received me with abundance of civility, inquired particularly into the situation of affairs in America, spoke feelingly of the severity of the late laws against Massachusetts ... and expressed great regard and esteem for the people of that country, who he hopes would continue firm and united in defending by all peaceable and legal means their constitutional rights. I assured him, that I made no doubt they would do so.

Franklin appealed to Chatham's sense of imperial mission, arguing that, but for wrong policies:

> we might have gone on extending our western empire, adding province to province as far as the South Sea [Pacific] ... He replied ... that my idea of extending our empire in that manner was a sound one, worthy of a great, benevolent and comprehensive mind. He wished with me for a good understanding among the different parts of the opposition here, as a means of restoring the ancient harmony of the two countries, which he most earnestly desired; ... he expressed much satisfaction ... in the assurances I had given him that America did not aim at independence.

This notion of American territorial expansion linked longstanding interest to new possibilities created by British exploration in the Pacific, especially by Captain Cook.

When he saw Franklin at Hayes on 26 December 1774, Chatham praised the Continental Congress, which had been formed to coordinate resistance to the coercive legislation passed in 1774, meeting in Philadelphia that September. He said:

> They had acted with so much temper, moderation and wisdom, that he thought it the most honorable assembly of statesmen since those of the ancient Greeks and Romans in the most virtuous times. That there were not in their whole proceedings above one or two things he could have wished otherwise; perhaps but one, and that was their assertion that the keeping up a standing army in the colonies in time of peace, without consent of their legislatures was against the law ... He expressed a great regard and warm affection for that country, with hearty wishes for their prosperity, and that government here might soon come to see its mistakes and rectify them.[78]

Chatham did not appreciate that the Americans were increasingly interested in independence, but the account was indicative both of the continued importance of control over the military and of the habit, shared in Britain and America, of seeing politics as an expression of Classical virtue. Similarly, the Rockingham Whigs, also in opposition, looked back, seeking to use the crisis to justify their past policies and their sense of an appropriate order, rather than responding to changing aspirations in America. This, for example, was the case with Edmund Burke, who devoted much attention to defending the role of the Rockinghamites in passing the Declaratory Act of 1766.[79]

On 20 January 1775, Chatham pressed in the House of Lords for conciliation, particularly for the withdrawal of the troops sent to intimidate Boston, and correctly warned that France might exploit the situation. Failing, however, to build a bridge to the ministerial position, he declared the Americans to have a right not to be taxed without consent and attributed this not only to 'the constitution', but also to 'God and nature', a radical position. His motion was defeated by 68 votes to 18.[80]

The situation was deteriorating, with increasing hostility in the colonies to British authority. The establishment of the Continental Congress indicated that the powerful localism of the colonies did not preclude unity. This localism played a different role in particular colonies, which reflected the character of their politics. Indeed, alongside the theme of growing criticism of aspects of the imperial link, came the continued prominence of imperial diversity. It was easier to advance colony-wide politics, let alone those for all the Thirteen Colonies, in certain colonies than others. This was not so much overcome by the calling of the Continental Congress as overlaid by it, as the dissension in 1776 over declaring independence was to indicate.

Moreover, supplementing the localism, and again illustrating the ability of colonial politicians to devise political practice and thus constitutional precept, was the role of colonial legislatures in addressing public issues. As a consequence, the legislatures developed an ability to supplement and eventually vie with practices of imperial direction. The crisis of the 1760s and 1770s provided opportunities for the assemblies to develop their public roles in the direction of representative vigour, a vigour linked to the acceptance of their place as the adjudicators of best practice. This tested patterns of deference, both within the colonies and toward Britain. The assemblies indeed came to play a greater role in a dynamic political system that challenged imperial government rather than providing it with new opportunities.[81]

This was seen as a particular problem in Massachusetts. More troops were sent there, while General Thomas Gage was appointed Governor of the colony, in order to use force to restore royal authority. This was a significant militarization of policy and Gage's career itself reflected the shift in British priorities. The second son of an Irish peer, he had fought the Jacobites at Culloden in 1746, and had commanded the advance guard in Braddock's unsuccessful advance on Fort Duquesne in 1755. He also held a command position in the failed advance on Ticonderoga in 1758, but had better success against the French in 1759–60, and was then appointed Governor of Montréal, before becoming acting Commander-in-Chief in North America in 1763. Holding this post until 1772, he had responsibility for the military deployment in Boston in 1768.

Returning there in 1774, he found a far more difficult situation. The Massachusetts Government Act was rejected by a population who acted to preserve their existing system and to thwart the new one. Gage was unwilling to accept this, which led to the election of a Provincial Congress, based in Concord, with an executive Committee of Public Safety. This Congress, not Gage, won the resulting struggle for control, with taxes flowing to the former and the militia accepting its control.

A collapse of authority seemed to threaten Britain's position as a great power. New England was seen as the centre of opposition and the focus therefore for government action; and the extent of opposition elsewhere was minimized. This was an analysis that was to have a fatal effect for these colonial governors in 1775 as it left them with insufficient support to resist violent attacks on their position.

The conviction of the need for firmness was strengthened by George III's belief that the repeal of the Stamp Act in 1766 had caused many of the problems in North America, and should not be repeated. He saw toleration as weakness. Royal determination interacted with that of Parliament. Thus Parliament supported firmness and the maintenance of its authority and the rule of law. Had George taken a different view, then the existing practice of imperial parliamentary monarchy would have been put under great pressure, but there was no chance of the King following the advice of Thomas Jefferson (in his critical 1774 pamphlet *A Summary View of the Rights of British America*) and vetoing parliamentary legislation that affected American rights and interests. Jefferson called on George to accept a theory of kingship that was actually in accordance with many of the King's assumptions, but to an end he could not accept:

> That these are our grievances which we have thus laid before his majesty, with that freedom of language and sentiment which becomes a free people claiming their rights, as derived from the laws of nature, and not as the gift of their chief magistrate. Let those flatter who fear; it is not an American art … kings are the servants, not the proprietors of the people. Open your breast, sire, to liberal and expanded thought. Let not the name of George the third be a blot in the page of history.[82]

Jefferson offered a view of the Empire as a series of parts, each with rights under the care of the Crown. This was what he meant when he urged George to 'deal out to all equal and impartial right'. Liberties were to be preserved within the British Empire, and opportunity was thus to be pursued within and through it, not least expansion into the American hinterland.

Yet such a system, let alone the republican monarchy proposed by John Adams in March 1775,[83] was scarcely politically practical in the 1770s whatever was to be the later case with the Dominions, such as Canada, Australia and New Zealand, and, subsequently, with the British Commonwealth. Crucially, the Westminster Parliament, and, indeed, many British ministers, would not have accepted an increase in royal power that would have stemmed from the King 'holding the balance' of the Empire, as he arbitrated between its parts. To them, royal authority was a matter of the Crown-in-Parliament, and this could not be separated without loss to both, as a more powerful Crown risked becoming a tyranny, and thus losing support and becoming weaker.[84]

Yet such ideas about imperial government did not exist in a vacuum. More generally, instead, mutual suspicion, a product of a loss of the sense of political, cultural and economic community between Britain and the American colonies, was a key problem.[85] This was seen with the First Continental Congress, which convened in Philadelphia in September 1774 with representatives from the colonies bar Georgia. It established the Continental Association, an organization that was designed to ensure not only the economic boycotts, of imports, consumption and exports, but also a policy for renewal that would separate virtuous Americans from corrupt Britons.

There was also, however, a great reluctance to fight, a reluctance shared in Britain, where it led to a large-scale petitioning movement against war.[86] Opposition in Britain was particularly strongly expressed by Dissenters. The Unitarian Theophilus Lindsey, who had links with many critics of the Establishment in Church and State, praised Chatham's motion on 20 January 1775, noted the ministerial determination to use force, and saw providence and progress at work in a future of American liberty:

> Providence seems to permit our present ministry to hasten our ruin and the independence of America. And it may be; if so, certainly will be for the best: and we may all of us have reason to rejoice, that there will be a place in the globe where Englishmen may be free.[87]

Such a remark serves as a reminder not only of the variety of views in Britain, but also of the different aspirations focused on America within the British world.

The Jeffersonian prospectus was also inappropriate, in that it wrongly implied that the same policies would not have been adopted had George been conscious of his duties to all his subjects. Instead, the King's view of the necessary interdependence of the Empire was not one that was opposed to the government's fiscal policies; policies, however, which were unwelcome to many Americans.

Furthermore, George's stress on the need for order and, in particular, on the importance of defending it when challenged, would have ensured problems in responding as the colonists wanted, whatever the role of Parliament, and even if it was only a question of supporting existing authorities within the colonies.

Eventually, the British government was to adopt the path of imperial conciliation. It did so unsuccessfully in America in 1778, when the Carlisle Commission was sent to try to negotiate a settlement, but successfully in Ireland, at least in terms of defusing an immediate problem, in 1782–3. Then, British legislative authority was renounced in favour of the Dublin Parliament. Although compromises in the case of the American colonies were floated prior to 1778, it would have been difficult to win widespread support for them in America, and there was no consensus in Britain in favour of a compromise.

Chatham had certainly sought a settlement. Having discussed the situation with Franklin, on 1 February 1775 he introduced, a 'Provisional Act for Settling the Troubles in America', designed to pacify America by giving the Continental Congress that had met the previous year a role in devising a new constitutional and financial settlement. Chatham proposed that the colonies accept parliamentary sovereignty and the Crown's right to keep an army in America, but, in return, recent coercive British legislation was to be repealed. Parliament was to agree that taxes should not be raised other than with the approval of a provincial assembly, and the representative role of the Continental Congress was to be recognized.

This Bill was defeated. There was little sympathy in the political establishment for the Americans who, looking back to contention over credit and debt for victory (see pp. 86–7), were seen as ungrateful for the efforts made on their behalf during the Seven Years' War, and also as acting in an illegal manner. In addition, Chatham had done little to encourage support, either within or outside Parliament. Indeed, it was a measure of Franklin's lack of influence that he spent time with Chatham.

More generally, American hopes that their action might inspire renewal within Britain proved abortive. There was to be no second Glorious Revolution to save English liberties in the British Isles and North America. The Glorious Revolution was indeed the model for the Bill of Rights adopted by the First Continental Congress in 1774, like the Declaration of Independence, and they were both influenced by the English Declaration of Rights of 1689. Nor was there to be the more modest remedy of a change in the politics of Britain. The government's success in the 1774 election made the latter unlikely, while there was a more general political stability within the British Isles in the mid-1770s than was to be the case in the early 1780s.

Irrespective of this, Chatham's proposals were no longer acceptable to many colonists, for parliamentary authority was increasingly rejected in the Thirteen

Colonies. Yet there was also a widespread reluctance to turn to violence, and opinion in the Middle and Southern colonies was less radical than in New England. This was a point that was subsequently to receive insufficient attention, understandably so in terms of the public myth, but less helpfully for the historical record.

Given Chatham's speeches and his contacts with Franklin and other Americans, it is easy to appreciate both why he was seen as a champion of the colonists and why, after his death, it was claimed that, had his advice been followed, there would have been no war of independence. Chatham's position, however, was more complex. Although he pressed for conciliation and was prepared to envisage an abolition of the parliamentary taxation of America, Chatham was fixedly against American independence. The integrity of the British Empire, the political, strategic and economic interdependency of different parts that he saw so clearly, and that had led him to oppose concessions to France over the valuable Newfoundland fishery in peace negotiations in 1761, would be destroyed by American independence.

Chatham's views differed from those of the colonists in that they regarded immunity from parliamentary taxation as an inherent right, while he argued that it would have to be granted as a concession by a sovereign Parliament, in return for which Chatham envisaged a financial contribution from the colonies. Although, in 1766, he had distinguished between internal taxation and the external duties decreed by Parliament, such a distinction had been abolished by the Declaratory Act of 1766. Thus, in February 1775, Chatham pressed for the emendation of that Act in order to leave domestic taxation under the control of the colonists. In 1775, he described his

> whole system for America – which is, to secure to the colonies property and liberty, and to insure to the mother-country a due acknowledgement on the part of the colonies, of their subordination to the supreme legislative authority, and superintending power of the Parliament of Great Britain.[88]

As so often in Chatham's career, his own position was somewhat different to that generally attributed to him, in this case as a friend of America, although he would have seen no such incompatibility and would have regarded such friendship as entailing American membership in a strong and liberal British Empire. In light of the 1782–3 Irish settlement, Chatham's proposal for a permanent American legislature to exercise the powers of taxation renounced by the Westminster Parliament might appear prescient, but it was not politically viable in 1774–5. It would not have been easy to win widespread support for the proposal in America, still less for the preservation of parliamentary sovereignty and for the maintenance of a British Army there, but, more seriously, there was no consensus in favour of compromise in Britain.

Nor could Chatham create one. Aware of the tension in trans-Atlantic relations, the British government viewed the claims of the Continental Congress as an unacceptable challenge to parliamentary authority. Well-supported in Parliament, but keenly aware that a show of weakness towards the colonies might well alienate decisive elements of that support, the government decided to use force; although, at the same time, it hoped to assuage grievances, as indicated by the conciliatory propositions Lord North, the head of the ministry, put before Parliament on 20 February 1775. He proposed that, in return for a colony being willing to provide for its defence and civil government, it would be exempt from parliamentary taxation. Dismissed by Chatham as 'mere verbiage, a most puerile mockery', this was an offer too late, as it was incompatible with the position of the Continental Congress. Though presenting itself as a loyal body, the Congress claimed that the colonies should raise revenues as they thought appropriate, which was overthrowing Parliament's right to legislate.

The British government, in contrast, was determined to retain control of the constitutional position for Parliament and to reimpose order in America, a conviction that failed to address the danger of making the attempt, as well as the risks of failure. Although the issues were very different, the government did not show the flexibility it displayed over Québec. Yet, the Québec Act, unlike the demands of Congress, did not entail a challenge to the position of Parliament. Congress, anyway, formally rejected North's proposal in July 1775.

The emptiness of the imperial ethos for many Americans had been revealed in paranoia, and in symbolic and practical acts of defiance, at the same time, paradoxically, that the colonists were willing to fight to defend their vision of the Empire and of the rights of Englishmen.[89] In 1775, the spiral of violence ended in full-scale conflict, with the militarization of authority by the British government clashing with attempts by the colonists to defy the latter. The challenge posed by the Provincial Congress at Concord was unacceptable as it defied the Massachusetts Government Act.

Fighting began on 19 April, when the British tried to seize a cache of arms reported to be at Concord. This was 16 miles from Boston, past the village of Lexington, where the troops found about 70 militia drawn up in two lines. Heavily outnumbered, the militia began to disperse, but a shot rang out – it is not clear from whom – and the British opened fire, scattering the militia.

The shedding of blood outraged much of New England, and a substantial force, largely dependent on their own muskets, soon encircled Boston. Elsewhere in the Thirteen Colonies, British authority collapsed: due to the concentration of troops in Massachusetts, governors elsewhere were defenceless. The war would last far longer than either side anticipated.

5

Civil War, 1775–8

The image is clear and the message is obvious. Across a sun-kissed meadow, dappled with shade, lines of British soldiers, resplendent in red, move slowly forward, while brave Americans aim from behind trees and stone walls ready to blast these idiots to pieces. Frequently repeated on page and screen,[1] the image has one central message: one side, the American, represented the future in warfare, and one side, the American, was bound to prevail. Thus, the War of Independence (1775–83) is readily located in both political and military terms. In each, it apparently represents the triumph of modernity and the start of a new age: one of democracy and popular warfare. Before these forces, the *ancien régime*, the old order, was bound to crumble and its cause, that of the British Empire, and troops, the British Army, were doomed to lose.

Thus, the apparent political location of the struggle, in terms of the defining fight for freedom that supposedly ushered in the modern world, helps locate the conflict as the start of modern warfare, and considering the war in the latter light helps fix our understanding of the political dimension. Definition in terms of modernity also explains success, as most people adopt a teleological perspective (arguing that the course of developments was inevitable) and assume that the future is bound to prevail over the past. Moreover, this approach draws on eighteenth-century American assumptions of providential support for their virtuous strength.[2]

In making the war an apparently foregone conclusion, this approach, however, has several misleading consequences. First, it allows historians of the period to devote insufficient attention to the fighting and, instead, to focus on traditional (constitution-framing) and modish (gender, ethnicity, sexuality, discourse) topics, neglecting the central point: no victory, no independence, no constitution, no newish society. Second, making British defeat inevitable gravely underrates the American achievement. Third, any appearance of inevitability removes the sense of uncertainty in which contemporaries formulated options and made choices.

The war was a political as much as a military struggle, one in which it was necessary for the revolutionaries to convince themselves, and the British, that there was no alternative to independence. As a result, John Adams claimed that the war had been lost by the British before the fighting had begun. This was certainly true in New England, Adams' base, where there were few Loyalists, but was less the case elsewhere.

The politicization of much of the American public and the motivation of many of their troops were important aspects of modernity. However, there was little of the emphasis on large armed forces and the mass production of munitions that were to be such obvious aspects of the industrial warfare of the late nineteenth and early twentieth centuries.

Moreover, a popular fight for independence was scarcely unprecedented. Within the European world, it was possible to point to the Swiss and the Dutch, both of whom had overthrown Habsburg forces and created republics. Moreover, the history of Catalonia or Hungary over the previous 150 years offered ample demonstration of the precarious nature of authority. In the eighteenth century, the American war was less a new departure than a uniquely successful war in a series of unsuccessful popular risings within the British Empire, with those in Scotland in 1715 and 1745 and in Ireland in 1798 of particular importance. In this light, the American Revolution was significant not because it was a rebellion, but because, very unusually, it was successful and led to a new state; because it challenged the logic of colonialism; and because of the future importance of the United States.

This focuses attention not on the political causes of the rebellion, nor on the military consequences of popular warfare, but, instead, on the political and military factors that led to a successful outcome. Among them, it is important to stress America's geopolitical exceptionalism, as the first of the European overseas colonies to rebel, as well as issues that bridged politics and war. For example, the federal nature of the revolution ensured that there was no one single centre or region of power, control over which would lead to the suppression of the revolution.

Although only a minority of colonists wished for independence at the outbreak of fighting in April 1775, the strength of separatist feeling within this minority was such that compromise on terms acceptable to the British government appeared increasingly unlikely. Anything else, however, was unacceptable to the bulk of the British political nation, although there was a significant tranche of support for conciliation.[3] George III and the ministry were scarcely going to heed the call in the speech on conciliation by Edmund Burke, a prominent opposition parliamentarian, delivered in the House of Commons for 'magnanimity in politics', and, instead, they interpreted 'the greatness of that trust to which the order of Providence has called us' very differently. In response to the Olive Branch Petition, in which Congress declared a wish to remain in the Empire, but also underlined its conviction of the justness of its cause in the protection of constitutional liberties, George adopted the legalistic position of rejecting the petition because Congress had no legal status and, indeed, was composed of rebels.

This position greatly helped undermine American moderates who did not wish to move from resistance to independence. Many felt left with no alternative bar supporting the revolution. George also failed to appreciate the conflation of liberty and virtue that was important in American public culture. This conflation energized and moralized American views so that they could not simply be bargained away in political calculation, and made those who adopted different views appear a threat.

Virtue was also at stake for George III, as this was a struggle not only for the authority of a sovereign Parliament, but also against the political and moral challenges of disorder. In August 1775, a royal proclamation, which George pressed for, declared that his American subjects were 'engaged in open and avowed rebellion'. These views were also held by American Loyalists who became more vociferous in late 1775 in response both to the crisis and to the expression in Britain of support for the rebels.[4]

Whereas, prior to 1775, the colonists had tended to focus their hostility on ministers and Parliament, correctly believing them to be largely responsible for unwelcome legislation, there was now a major shift, so that George was seen by the Americans as the cause of their problems. There had been a breakdown of paternalism: George was seen as a bad father 'with the pretend title of FATHER OF HIS PEOPLE', in the words of Tom Paine's *Common Sense* (1776); while, in turn, George saw the colonists as 'rebellious children'.[5] These were both vivid points, although the extent to which American attitudes were affected by altering concepts of parenthood, emphasizing filial autonomy rather than paternal control, as well as by a changing, less Calvinistic, understanding of God,[6] is unclear.

In judging British policy, it is essential to avoid the traps of teleology, with their assumption that American independence was necessary and essential. That said, pre-war British fiscal policies were not only inappropriate in practical terms, resting as they did on a failure to understand American circumstances and attitudes, but also challenged the assumptions of politics, not so much on a British scale as on its imperial equivalent. By the Western standards of the time, British policies required some sort of consent, albeit that other empires did not accept the need for any form of parliamentary consent in their colonies. The colonial empires of the period were overseas extensions of composite states created by the addition of yet more pieces of territory, and this was particularly the case with British colonies that were dominated by settlers. Imperialism was continuous with composite monarchy, not therefore distinct from it and probably incompatible with it. Unless there was a States-General (federal parliament) covering all the territories of a monarch, the monarchs of composite states usually observed the right of estates (or parliaments) in component territories to assemble and legislate only within their own territory.

Crucially, the unifying institution in composite states was the Crown. The monarch ruled with the advice of separate estates or parliaments in each of his component territories. Thus, an assembly in one territory of a composite state claimed no authority over an assembly in another. The British Parliament was the first to do so when, with the Declaratory Act, it declared its sovereignty over the Irish Parliament in 1720. This claim was not pressed at the time, while the religious issue handicapped constitutional antagonism between Westminster and Dublin, as the Protestant Ascendancy that controlled the Irish Parliament could not call on support from the Catholic majority in Ireland. By the mid-eighteenth century, the British Parliament was working out a complicated theory of the unified sovereignty of the King-in-Parliament, in short the Westminster Parliament, over the Empire. This seemed the appropriate way to ensure that the reformulation of royal power in the Revolution Settlement that had followed the Glorious Revolution was protected (a reformulation in which this power was limited and expressed through Parliament); although this limitation was just as well defended by the idea of robust colonial assemblies, a point that was not appreciated in Westminster or Whitehall.

The British theory was unwelcome in North America. The Americans, in contrast, had no initial problem with royal sovereignty, but were clear that the King should tax them through their own assemblies, rather than through the Westminster Parliament. It seems insufficiently stressed that it was the latter that had everything to lose from this American formulation, and not the King who would have had an independent relationship with his colonies. Indeed, rebutting the claim by Charles James Fox, the opposition leader in the House of Commons, that the ministry was Tory and therefore authoritarian, Lord North, the First Lord of the Treasury, declared in the House of Commons on 26 October 1775 that the 'aim of Toryism was to increase the prerogative. That, in the present case, the administration contended for the right of Parliament, while the Americans talked of their belonging to the Crown.'[7]

Once rebellion had erupted in 1775, George III strongly advocated the normal eighteenth-century procedure of crushing it by force, although he totally failed to appreciate how many troops would be required. Before simply castigating him for inappropriate firmness, it is worth noting that it was by no means clear that the sort of retreat in the face of disaffection seen with Leopold II (r. 1790–2) in Hungary (a retreat that reversed the disruptive consequences of his brother and predecessor Joseph II's maladroit policies) would have made the outcome any different, although the prospect for such compromise might well have benefited from the disinclination of many Americans to opt for independence.

Yet conciliation posed problems, particularly if weakness on the part of George had been sensed by the determined revolutionary minority whom he confronted. After his political mistakes in the 1760s, George had clearly become aware of the calamitous dangers of failing to back his freely chosen ministers through thick and thin (although he still offered no such support to those he disliked). As in the continental European monarchies, anything else was an open incitement to a factional free-for-all. The baleful example of Louis XV of France was available for inspection. It rightly became a top priority not to be seen to wobble.

Moreover, conciliation was also advocated in Britain by those who were seen by George and the ministry as least reputable and reliable. For example, Joshua Toulmin's sermons in favour of conciliation, and later in open disagreement with the war, were preached from Unitarian pulpits. They appeared to align the colonists with religious dissenters in Britain who stood beyond the pale of the Toleration Act (as non-Trinitarians) and the Test Act.

Yet, conversely, wobbling in the sense of changing policy in the case of America might have accentuated the serious differences between the colonies and among the colonists, creating the basis for a popular loyalism, or, at least, for more successful negotiations. That the differences between the colonists were institutionalized in the contrasts between views in particular colonies created more possibilities for conciliation by George.

In assessing George and the ministry's policy toward America, it is important to note first that there had been previous clashes between royal authority and colonists, and also that George was not out of line with his royal contemporaries. The history of England's North American colonies in the seventeenth century had reflected the instability of the homeland. Rather than thinking primarily in terms of a tension between colonial autonomy and English authority, differing political positions spanned the Atlantic, with the overthrow of James II and VII accomplished not only in Britain in 1688-9, but also in the colonies.[8] Furthermore, prior to George III's reign, governors had clashed with assemblies. In part, this was because there was a strong sense of local rights and privileges that were seen as the necessary encapsulation of British liberties. Opposition to the power and pretensions of governors was widespread and frequent. If, therefore, British government was more intrusive and demanding from the Seven Years' War, this was not a case of totally new issues and attitudes playing a role or defining the situation.

Furthermore, there were not only tensions in British colonies. Louisiana, which had been transferred from France to Spain after the Seven Years' War, found the restrictions of an imperial trading system as unacceptable as Boston did. In October 1768, indeed, New Orleans rebelled against Spanish rule, after trade outside the Spanish imperial system or in non-Spanish ships was banned. Having expelled the Governor and his men, the Louisiana Superior Council appealed to Louis XV to restore French rule. Faced with the determination of their ally Spain to restore authority, the French, however, did not act, and, in August 1769, a Spanish force occupied New Orleans and executed the revolt's leaders.

More generally, Charles III of Spain (r. 1759–88) followed policies similar to those of George, and policies with which he also was closely identified. There was a long-standing tension in Spanish America between *peninsulares* (natives of Spain) and *criollos* (creoles, American-born descendants of Spanish settlers), and this was exacerbated by reforms. These reforms can be seen as pragmatic devices by officials concerned to maximize governmental revenues, but, as with Britain, this pragmatism was also an aspect of a search for economic benefit from Empire in the context of serious competition in the Atlantic world. Just as the British ministry was anxious to protect Empire, so Spain sought to strengthen it, not least in the aftermath of the shocking fall of Havana to the British in 1762.[9]

Charles' reforms generally ignored creole aspirations, both in economic regulation and in political matters. The former policy was motivated by a desire to help Spain, rather than its colonies, and also to exclude other colonial powers; a goal in which the British government followed established practice. Measures were taken to restrict foreign ships trading with Spanish colonies, a process explicitly seen as likely to strengthen Spain's control over its colonies. The role of creoles in government was also restricted, and, paralleling the Québec Act, administrative reorganization was designed to strengthen governmental control, with the establishment in 1787 of a viceroyalty of the Rio de la Plata and of a captaincy-general of Caracas.[10]

As with the British in North America, the issue of military force was seen as key. The deficiencies highlighted in the Seven Years' War led Charles III to send regular regiments for garrison duty in leading colonial centres and to set in train the raising of large forces of militia. Combined, these forces provided government with security to introduce changes, including new taxes, although there was also resistance.[11] A similar militarization of political authority was not to work for the British in Massachusetts, although the background in the 1770s was more charged than the situation across most of Spanish America, and, in British North America, there was also a more socially cohesive reaction against imperial authority. In part, this reflected the extent to which issues of ethnicity did not divide or challenge opposition in British North America as they did in Spanish North America and, indeed, the British West Indies. Concern about blacks, Native Americans and those of mixed race led to white support for royal government in Latin America.

Like Charles III of Spain, Sebastião, Marquês de Pombal, the chief minister of Portugal in 1750–77, sought to alter the relationship between the mother colony and its principal colony, Brazil. Aiming to derive more economic benefit for the state, Pombal also founded chartered companies to monopolize the trade of the Amazon region and north-east Brazil. This was a far more authoritarian position than that of the British over tea, but there were major contrasts in political culture, governmental power, and economic development between the Portuguese and British Empires.

To note that others matched elements of British policies without precipitating revolution, invites the response that the Spanish and Portuguese Empires in the New World were, in the face of revolution, to collapse by 1825. At the same time, revolution elsewhere challenges the tendency to search for an American exceptionalism of unique circumstances and lessens the charge that the British government was exceptionally foolish or wicked. It becomes more interesting to ask why the British New World Empire was the first to experience a major rebellion.

There, as later in the Spanish and Portuguese colonies, the attitude of the social elite was crucial. Across the American colonies, elite families had, from the outset, sought to exploit the resources of settled lands and 'wilderness', to control the institutions of local government, and to become representatives of the kingdom and the metropole, an always shifting combination.[12] The breakdown of this process in the Thirteen Colonies in the 1770s reflected a serious alienation, to which suspicion of royal and ministerial intentions contributed powerfully.

Two very different tendencies contributed to this breakdown. First, alongside a growing element of democratization in some American circles, an element that encouraged a rejection of the automatic acceptance of hierarchical inherited authority, there was also a willingness by many in the elite to accept elements of democratization, and, at the least, not to be alienated by them. Liberty did not have to be threatening; indeed far from it.

Secondly, especially in Virginia, there was a self-image of responsible patrician leadership, one that looked both to an image of Classical Rome, and to an ideal of British gentlemanly leadership. This self-image was also anti-authoritarian in content and ethos, and readily directed against what could be seen, first, as the abuses of the British system and, then, of the abuse represented by the British system. By the 1770s the colonists regarded the Glorious Revolution not only as their rightful inheritance, but also as one which Britain was obstructing.

However, once America became independent, the consequence of this self-image was a public politics of elite leadership different to that stemming from democratization. This patrician leadership was possible because, unlike the wealthy plantation owners of the West Indies, who tended to live in Britain and to remain part of its society, plantation owners in North America generally lived there, and thus became a key element in local politics.

The breakdown of allegiance to the British political system was symbolic as well as constitutional. On 9 July 1776, after the colonial assembly of New York gave its assent to the Declaration of Independence, the inhabitants of New York City pulled down a gilded equestrian statue of the King erected on Bowling Green in 1770 (its metal was to be used for cartridges),[13] while, more generally, the royal arms were taken down, and usually treated with contempt. The King's name was removed from governmental and legal documents, royal portraits were reversed or destroyed, and there were mock trials, executions and funerals of the King, each a potent rejection of his authority.

The Revolution was also to lead to the renaming of streets and buildings. Two famous instances were the changing of King Street in Boston to State Street, and the alteration of King's College in New York to Columbia. Fewer changes occurred in the South, not least because names and titles related generally to earlier royal Georges and to others. Georgetown went unchanged, as did Georgia. Prince and Duke Streets remained in Alexandria, Virginia. The name George also had a resonance of Washington, and could be associated with him.

The outbreak of fighting transformed the colonial relationship with Britain and, even more, the King. Britain could be seen as actively hostile, while George III could now be presented as using British forces to kill Americans, in short as a monarch of evil intent and action. Many refused to travel this road, and for others it was a hesitant process, but, alongside the habit of referring to the British troops as ministerial or parliamentary, rather than royal, a process that shunted aside the issue of the Crown, there were steadily stronger calls for a new order. To Tom Paine in *Common Sense* (1776), George was a 'hardened, sullen-tempered Pharaoh' and a 'royal brute', who composedly slept with American 'blood upon his soul'. This condemnation had an impact on American thought.

In March 1776, however, Congress was still unwilling to accept a motion by George Wythe and Richard Henry Lee that George, not the ministry, nor Parliament, be seen as 'the author of our miseries'. This only became possible due to the implications of George in effect branding the Americans as rebels and treating them accordingly.[14] British policies, including the ban on trade with the rebellious colonies, were indeed designed to hurt, while the government's attempts to recruit subsidy forces (the 'foreign mercenaries' of the Declaration of Independence) were associated directly with George, not least because he was Elector of Hanover and these troops were Germans, especially the Hessians who dominated attention.

Independence was also necessary if foreign alliances were to be made. This led Richard Henry Lee to move, on 7 June, that Congress declare independence, seek such alliances, and unite by adopting a constitution. Hesitation in the Middle Colonies caused delay, but the measure was finally passed on 2 July, although New York still abstained. The text of the Declaration of Independence was approved two days later. Much of it consisted of a lengthy criticism of George, and of him personally, rather than of the position of monarch, or the role of ministers. This was in part because the Americans had already, in their ideas, broken with Parliament, whereas, now, they were keen on breaking with George, as part of the transfer of political legitimacy.[15] It was also easier to personalize misgovernment as the acts of a tyrant, and thus to justify rejection, rather than to present pressure for a new system.

The Declaration was the destruction document of British North America and a key verdict on the state of Anglo–American relations. It also represented a powerful impulse for change, which takes on greater resonance if the Declaration is located not simply in American terms but also with reference to a broader-based process of development within both the British world[16] and the West as a whole. This process did not lead in a uniform or unilinear political direction, in North America, the British Isles,[17] nor the West as a whole, but it helps account for the wider significance of American aspirations and changes. According to the Declaration:

> The history of the present King of Great Britain is a history of unremitting injuries and usurpations, all having in direct object the establishment of an absolute tyranny over these States ...
>
> He has dissolved representative houses repeatedly, for opposing with manly firmness his invasions on the rights of the people ...
>
> He has endeavoured to prevent the population of these states; for that purpose obstructing the laws for naturalization of foreigners; refusing to pass others to encourage their migrations hither, and raising the conditions of new appropriations of lands ...
>
> He has excited domestic insurrections amongst us, and has endeavoured to bring on the inhabitants of our frontiers the merciless Indian savages, whose known rule of warfare, is an undistinguished destruction of all ages, sexes, and conditions.
>
> In every stage of these oppressions we have petitioned for redress in the most humble terms: our repeated petitions have been answered only by repeated injury. A prince whose character is thus marked by every act which may define a tyrant is unfit to be the ruler of a free people.

The extended criticism of George in the Declaration presented him as an active and threatening figure seeking to undermine liberty. While this attributed to him measures that had often in fact been taken by colonial governors, the attack on George helped personalize the war, but also reflected the strong role of loyalty to the sovereign in the American political culture of the age, and the powerful disillusionment with George that affected so many colonists in 1774–6. The listing of what Samuel Adams termed George's 'catalogue of crimes' was the indictment of a conspirator, who had misused his executive powers, as well as combining with Parliament to attack American liberties. The list also accused him of waging war in a cruel fashion, producing, by reiteration, at once, a black portrayal and a harsh indictment. In a tone resonant of a key American political discourse, some of the language was Biblical, making George akin to an Old Testament plague.[18] The Loyalist Thomas Hutchinson commented that the clauses were 'most wickedly presented to cast reproach upon the King'.[19] Indeed, the attack on the King's reputation was later to leave some colonists uncomfortable, John Adams claiming that it contained 'expressions which I would not have inserted, if I had drawn it up, particularly that which called the King tyrant'.[20] Nevertheless, the damage had been done.

It was not only monarchy that was rejected, but also the nature of British imperialism. Indeed, in July 1776, Benjamin Franklin offered a new prospectus of power, when writing of Britain:

> Her fondness for conquest as a warlike nation, her lust of dominion as an ambitious one, and her thirst for a gainful monopoly as a commercial one (none of them legitimate causes of war) will all join to hide from her eyes every view of her true interests; and continually goad her on in these ruinous distant expeditions, so destructive both of lives and treasure, that must prove as pernicious to her in the end as the Crusades were to most of the nations of Europe ... the true and sure means of extending and securing commerce is the goodness and cheapness of commodities and the profits of no trade can ever be equal to the expense of compelling it, and of holding it by fleets and armies.[21]

To an extent that was long overlooked, racial paranoia played a role in the unravelling of imperial links, for the developing crisis was fed by American anxieties about both Native and African Americans and by concern that each would turn to George III. In November 1774, James Madison, a prominent Virginian revolutionary and later President, warned:

> If America and Britain should come to a hostile rupture I am afraid an insurrection among the slaves may and will be promoted. In one of our counties lately a few of those unhappy wretches met together and chose a leader who was to conduct them when the English troops should arrive – which they foolishly thought would be very soon and by revolting to them they should be rewarded with their freedom. Their intentions were soon discovered and proper precautions taken to prevent the infection. It is prudent such attempts should be concealed as well as suppressed.

He returned to the theme the following June:

> It is imagined our Governor [John, 4th Earl of Dunmore] has been tampering with the slaves and that he has it in contemplation to make great use of them in case of a civil war in this province. To say the truth, that is the only part in which this colony is vulnerable; and if we should be subdued, we shall fall like Achilles by the hand of one that knows that secret.[22]

In 1775, Jeremiah Thomas, an African American ship's pilot who himself owned slaves, was sentenced to death in South Carolina for supplying arms to slaves and encouraging them to flee.[23] Later that year, Dunmore added African Americans and Loyalists to his forces, seizing the towns of Gosport and Norfolk. He issued a proclamation emancipating slaves who joined his army, creating an 'Ethiopian Regiment' of several hundred escaped slaves. Although Dunmore was defeated at Great Bridge on 9 December 1775, his actions, and even more anxiety about their possible consequences, fed white paranoia, notably, but not only, in Virginia. The black population of the Chesapeake had grown greatly, and its percentage of the overall population there had risen from about 13 in 1700 to 40 by 1750.[24] Such an increase fed concern, and arming slaves was a taboo.

This anxiety encouraged the harsh treatment of slaves who tried to flee. The first three to be captured attempting to join Dunmore in 1776, were publicly hanged, decapitated and quartered. The need for vigilance against slave rebellion was also an important theme in Georgia and South Carolina. Similarly, attacks by Cherokees in 1776 helped increase opposition to Britain in the South.

The war itself was the most traumatic episode in Anglo–American relations, and understandably so because it was a civil war in the Empire as well as a civil war in the Thirteen Colonies. Indeed, the combination of civil war with rebellion helps make recent comparisons of Britain in the War of Independence with the USA in Iraq from 2003, like earlier ones with the Vietnam War, rather unhelpful.[25] Unlike Iraq or Vietnam, the Thirteen Colonies were already part of the British Empire and had been settled in part by British colonists, and the war was a rebellion.

Until 1778, when France officially entered the war, the Americans fought alone. They had no formal allies, although France and Spain provided secret aid, especially of munitions and money, of which the Americans were short. The Americans also fought alone because Britain was not committed to any other war, which ensured that the undivided attention of the British state could be devoted to the USA. In light of Britain's success in the Seven Years' War, this was a formidable and fearful challenge. Indeed, it encouraged American critics of Britain to see the conflict as a meta-historical as well as a moral struggle, and both aspects lent themselves to Biblical imagery.

At a more mundane level, the war led to an increase in the information available in Britain on America, and thus serves as a reminder of the complexity of relations. The British knew more about America as they were losing it than they had done earlier. Thomas Jefferys, who had already published *A General Topography of North America and the West Indies* (1768), followed with *The American Atlas or, a Geographical Description of the Whole Continent of America* (1776).

Most of the news about America available in Britain came through the London press, but the extent of public interest was indicated by the greater variety of sources. In its issue of 24 November 1774, the *Cumberland Pacquet* stressed the particular quality of its American reporting: 'A respectable merchant in this town has favoured us with several American newspapers, and particularly the

Boston Gazette, Pennsylvania Journal, Massachusetts Gazette, and the *Virginia Gazette.*' The newspaper provided some examples. As another instance, the *Leeds Mercury* in late 1775 printed items derived from a letter received by a gentleman at Berwick from his friend at Boston (18 July), a letter from Boston to someone in Halifax, Yorkshire (1 August), a ship from Boston arriving at Liverpool (19 September), a letter from a soldier at Boston to his father in Chester (10 October), and a letter from Virginia to a correspondent at Whitehaven (24 October).

News about the war interacted with comment, in a debate that ranged from issues of morality to more specific political points. This debate was not restricted to the press. Other writers also joined the fray. Thomas Day, who, in *The Dying Negro* (1773), had criticized the American revolutionaries for supporting slavery, a theme he returned to in *Reflections on the Present State of England and the Independence of America* (1782), also attacked the war in his poems *The Devoted Legions* (1776) and *The Desolation of America* (1777).

At the level of formal politics in Britain, the opposition, which was led in the House of Lords by Charles, Marquess of Rockingham, the former Prime Minister, argued that Britain should concentrate on reconciliation with the Americans in order to prepare for war with the Bourbons. This was also Chatham's argument in the Lords in November and December 1777, and in his last parliamentary appearance on 7 April 1778. However, when the Americans formally allied with France in 1778, the situation became more complex for the opposition.

As Chapter 7 will suggest, the war was to have less traumatic consequences for relations between Britain and its former colonies than might have been anticipated, and thus reconciliation accepting American viewpoints might seem a viable option. At the time, however, the situation was very different. The British state had scant sympathy for rebellion, and government supporters were unwilling to share their opponents' ability to consider American views. Indeed, the outbreak of fighting led to an upsurge in anger that was directed at the Americans.

In part, this reflected frustration at the difficulty of defeating them. Although the British had extensive earlier experience of campaigning against the French in North America, American tactics were still able to pose major problems for them, especially when the Americans took advantage of the terrain. William Evelyn was part of the relief force sent to help the British column retreat from Concord and Lexington in April 1775:

> They [the British column] were attacked from the woods and houses on each side of the road and an increasing fire kept up on both sides for several hours, they [the Americans] still retiring through the wood whenever our men advanced upon them ... we were attacked on all sides from woods, orchards, stone walls, and from every house on the road side.

Subsequently blockaded by land in Boston, Evelyn felt that he was facing not only a rebellion, but also a novel kind of war. As a result of what he saw as a crisis in warmaking, a crisis resulting from the imperial breakdown, Evelyn felt that a new response was required:

> Five or six thousand men are not sufficient to reduce a country of 1500 miles extent, fortified by nature, and where every man from 15 to 50 is either a volunteer or able to carry arms ... some other mode must be adopted than gaining every little hill at the expense of a thousand Englishmen.

Evelyn, indeed, advocated total war, arguing that the sole way to win was by 'almost extirpating the present rebellious race'.[26] Despite much irritation on the part of officers, this was not the policy followed, although the Americans in arms could have been treated as traitors. Instead, however, of pursuing the harsh approach taken in Scotland in 1746, the British government chose to regard the struggle as a rebellion that was to be solved by an eventual return to loyalty requiring a measure of reconciliation. They were to be less forgiving in Ireland in 1798, but the rebels there, like the Scots in 1746, were allied to France in what was, for Britain, a bitter war of survival. In the War of American Independence, this was not the case until 1778, and, even then, there was not the fundamental threat to the British system posed by the Jacobite rising of 1745–6.

Yet, it was clear that an unprecedented military effort would be required. In June 1775, hopes that the rebellion would be swiftly quashed were crushed. On the night of 16 June, the revolutionaries marched to Breed's Hill on the Charlestown peninsula and began to fortify the position. It commanded the heights above Boston, although the subsequent battle was named after the more prominent hill behind Breed's Hill, Bunker Hill.

General Thomas Gage, the British Commander-in-Chief, decided, in response, on a landing at high tide on the afternoon of 17 June, followed by an attack on the American entrenchments. Once the forces had landed, however, Major-General William Howe, who had field command, moved ponderously. He spent about two hours deploying his men before launching a frontal attack on the American positions which had not been damaged to any significant extent by the British artillery. Such a deployment in disciplined order was the standard Western military method of the period, and was intended to overawe the opposition.

The Americans, nevertheless, waited until the advancing troops were almost upon them before shattering their first two attacks with heavy musket fire. Moreover, an attempt to turn the American flank was repelled. The Americans, however, were running short of ammunition, and a third British attack took the American redoubt. Yet, the exhausted British, harassed by sharpshooters, were unable to stop the Americans from retreating.

The British failure to win a striking success at Bunker Hill did not mean that the rebellion could not be defeated. The British after all had been defeated at Prestonpans in 1745 in the first battle caused by the Jacobite rising in Scotland of that year, but, having been defeated anew at Falkirk in 1746, had crushed the rising that year at Culloden. Nevertheless, Bunker Hill was still a major blow: British casualties were heavy, and they had been suffered without leading to a decisive victory. Instead, the battle induced caution in the British Army. Having lost the strategic initiative, so that their troops did no more than control the ground they stood on in Boston, the British were unable to prevent the rapid development and consolidation of the revolution. Moreover, as a result of Bunker Hill, which was seen as a failure, British operational and tactical capabilities were now also at issue. Gage wrote to the Secretary at War:

> These people show a spirit and conduct against us they never showed against the French, and everybody has judged of them from their former appearance and behaviour when joined with the King's forces in the last war [Seven Years' War, 1756–63] … They are now spirited up by a rage and enthusiasm as great as ever people were possessed of and you must proceed in earnest or give the business up. A small body acting in one spot will not avail, you must have large armies making diversions on different sides, to divide their force. The loss we have sustained is greater than we can bear. Small armies cannot afford such losses, especially when the advantage gained tends to little more than the gaining of a post.[27]

On the part of the Americans, Bunker Hill underlined the sense of betrayal by Britain, and the feeling that Britain had visited America with war. This appeared to justify the critique by American revolutionaries, and thus to make independence necessary. The last was crucial because, for both political and military reasons, it was important to win over the middle ground of American opinion. Again, this replicated the position in many civil wars.

This winning over the middle ground was significant if American independence was to be a viable option and, indeed, it took a year before independence was declared. In part, this declaration reflected a shifting in the middle ground. Options were reduced, because, by the summer of 1776, it was clear that the crisis was not going to be solved by a sort of armed demonstration on the part of the Americans that had been seen the previous year, as some had hoped. Crucially, having been driven from the Thirteen Colonies by the end of March 1776, the British struck back in force that summer, landing troops on Staten Island near New York from 3 July.

For the embryonic American state, the initial stages of the war reflected the difficulties of organizing a revolution, not least when there was a lack of certainty as to whether a revolution was desirable. The very determination to think for themselves and create their own arrangements, a drive that had led so many

Americans to defy their King, also posed serious problems. Institutionally, this determination led to tension in the new Continental Army, where many officers were elected and where there was a disinclination to accept the implications of the hierarchy of command. In September 1775, George Washington, the commander, had to confront, for example, the objections of the junior officers of the 2nd Connecticut Regiment to Ebenezer Huntington's appointment as a lieutenant because he thus superseded men of longer services. Washington's response was more in keeping with the ethos of European armies than those of New England town meetings:

> The decent representation of officers or even of common soldiers through the channel of their colonel, or other superior officers, I shall always encourage and attend to: But I must declare my disapprobation of this mode of associating and combining as subversive of all subordination, discipline and order … commissions should be ever the reward of merit not of age.

Washington believed that the army could be improved by reforming the officer corps; he saw 'gentlemen' officers as crucial to the discipline and subordination he believed necessary. Indeed, the Continental Army matched many of the socio-professional assumptions of the British Army.[28]

Washington's approach, however, was opposed to the marked particularism of much of American society which revealed itself, for example, in hostility to serving in the same unit with men from another colony. The views of Charles Lee were even more anathema to those opposed to discipline. A veteran of the Seven Years' War, in which he had served as a British officer, Lee, appointed 'Second Major General' by Congress in June 1775, advocated radical solutions amounting to a militarization of society and the creation of a national army under central control:

> 1st A solemn league and covenant defensive and offensive to be taken by every man in America, particularly by those in or near the seaport towns; all those who refuse, to have their estates confiscated for the public use, and their persons removed to the interior part of the country…. 4thly The regiments to be exchanged. Those who are raised in one province to serve in another rather than in their own.

Such notions reflected the longstanding importance of military organization in the politics of North America. They obviously conflicted with the profoundly local nature of American culture, a product of the separate and different governmental, political, social, religious, demographic and ethnic development of the colonies. Lee's ideas also clashed with the respect for the law and for individual and property rights that was central to this culture, although with the obvious exceptions of attitudes toward African and Native Americans. This respect compromised any idea of a total mobilization of national resources. Such a mobilization indeed was not to be achieved by legislation through a new national political system. Instead, the individual colonies in effect achieved independence first and then cooperated on their own terms through a federal structure.

Yet the Continental Army was also a powerful expression of federal identity and interest, while service in it was an individual commitment in which principle played a role.[29] Principle, however, could also underline the potent sense of local rights that was so important to the revolutionary cause, yet also a challenge to it. At the same time, the Loyalists who backed George III were also very much influenced by local concerns and grievances.[30]

Loyalism, however, was not to the fore in 1775. Instead, the revolutionaries took and used the initiative. Also eroding the middle ground, a mixture of popular zeal, the determination of the revolutionaries, and the weakness of their opponents, decided the fate of most of the colonies in 1775. Those who held contrary opinions were intimidated and Loyalist publications were attacked. The disorientating experience of the agencies of law and authority being taken over by those who were willing to connive at, or support, violence affected many who were unhappy about developments.

Meanwhile, on 26 October 1775, George III, opening a new session of Parliament, declared that it was necessary 'to put a speedy end to these disorders by the most decisive exertions'. The American decision to invade Canada further demonstrated the danger for Britain of failing to restore the Thirteen Colonies to royal authority. It could also be seen as changing the basis of the struggle as the result of:

> The commencing of an offensive war with the sovereign ... Opposition to government had hitherto been conducted on the apparent design, and avowed principle only, of supporting and defending certain rights and immunities of the people, which were supposed, or pretended, to be unjustly invaded. Opposition, or even resistance, in such a case ... is thought by many to be entirely consistent with the principles of the British constitution.[31]

This invasion was inconsistent with these principles, however the Glorious Revolution was understood. The attack on Canada also suggested that American action against the West Indies might follow, but disaffection with British rule was contained there, with support for change ebbing after the 1776 slave revolt in Jamaica. Moreover, despite the presence of American privateers, the revolutionaries lacked the naval lift to project power to the West Indies.

The invasion of Canada, like the later American attacks there in 1812–14, offered the prospect of a relationship between Britain and the USA, that would be far from benign. Conversely, Canada in British hands was seen as a strategic threat by the Americans, while it was hoped that the preponderantly French population of Québec would assist in overthrowing the small British garrison. This, however, was wishful thinking. Although the bulk of the population showed little support for George III, they accepted British rule with its backing for the position of the Catholic Church and the preservation of French culture. As a result, the invading Americans were forced to rely on their own efforts in Canada, which spelled major difficulties for a military that, lacking an institutional structure, was reliant on popular support. Available in New England, this was absent in Canada, which would have to be conquered.

Moreover, there was no organized and powerful American naval force capable of helping. Thus, in the now-hostile presence of British naval power, the Americans could not repeat earlier expeditions against (then French-held) Nova Scotia, Cape Breton Island or the St Lawrence. This was to be demonstrated in 1779 with the total failure of an amphibious expedition sent by Massachusetts against the British base at Castine on the coast of what is now Maine. Amphibious operations were about capability as well as opportunity, and this capability required infrastructure and training, in each of which the Americans were deficient.

Canada, however, was vulnerable to American attack overland, as the Seven Years' War had shown. The Lake Champlain axis was open to the Americans in 1775, not least because the peacetime deployment of the British Army had not prepared it for operational planning for war with a widespread American rebellion. Crown Point and Ticonderoga, the main British positions that blocked this axis, fell in May 1775. They had had a combined garrison of fewer than 60 men.

Later in the year, the main American invasion force, 2,000 strong under Richard Montgomery, advanced along that axis. It was delayed, however, for seven weeks besieging St Johns, a fort on the Richelieu river. This lengthy siege, in cold and wet conditions, demoralized Montgomery's force, already weakened by disease and threatened by the arrival of winter and the expiring of enlistments. The siege displayed the potential strength of the defensive, as the British did not surrender until they had only three days' provisions left, and also the extent to which plans could be readily overturned. After the fall of St Johns, Montgomery marched on Montréal. Outnumbered, the British Governor, Guy Carleton, fled to Québec, leaving Montréal to surrender on 12 November.

Meanwhile, another American force under Benedict Arnold had been sent across Maine to the St Lawrence. They were handicapped by vainglorious ignorance about the distance and terrain, poor maps, rain, food shortages, strong currents on the rivers, and rough trails across the intervening carrying places. Several hundred men turned back, and if the ability of Arnold to get through indicates that the terrain in non-cultivated parts of North America was not as impassable as might be suggested, the advance was a very debilitating one. Such operations played an important role in cultivating an American warrior-image of being at one with, and able to use, American terrain, although this was a delusion that was really only appropriate for Native Americans and a small number of frontier militiamen.

In 1775, the combined American force besieged Québec, but the British refused to sally out and risk defeat in the field, as the Americans had hoped. Bitter weather and terms of service due to end on 31 December led to an American attempt to storm the city, but this was defeated.

In 1776, the British government hoped that, by mounting what was then the largest transoceanic expedition ever sent out from the British Isles, it would be possible to overawe the Americans and drive them back into the political fold. Convinced that the Revolution was the work of a few miscreants who had rallied an armed rabble to their cause, they expected that the revolutionaries would be intimidated by the expeditionary force. Then the vast majority of Americans, who were loyal but cowed by the terroristic tactics of the Sons of Liberty and others of their ilk, would rise up, kick out the rebels, and restore loyal government in each colony.

Ignoring the advice of General Gage, the initial general British perception of the rebellion was more of a large-scale riot. The concept of a massive popular rebellion and what was tantamount to a nation in arms was alien to British ministers. Indeed, this was the first example of a large-scale transoceanic conflict fought between a European colonial power and subjects of European descent. It was also a major example of a revolutionary war, and became a struggle for independence in which the notion of the citizenry under arms played a crucial role. The new states[32] were accompanied by a new army that was more egalitarian and dynamic than any in Europe. Although many of the commanders of the leading American force, the Continental Army, were from the wealthier section of society, the social range of the American leadership was far greater than that in European armies, and discipline was different. The social composition of this army may have been similar to that of British regular troops, but this was an army of citizens, not subjects.[33]

Any stress on the difficulties confronting the British cannot detract from the immensity of the problems facing the revolutionaries. They were seeking to defeat a highly trained army backed by both the largest navy in the world and the strongest system of public finance in Europe. George III was supported by the Loyalists, about one-fifth of the population of the Thirteen Colonies, as well as by much of the population in nearby colonies: Canada, Nova Scotia, Newfoundland, West and East Florida, and the British West Indies. These provided the British with bases.

Manpower was a serious problem for both sides. This was the case for the Americans, not least because, as with the Confederacy during the Civil War, the conflict led to a dramatic decline in immigration, and thus in the supply of young men. The Continental Congress at first sought to create a broad-based army, with one-year terms of service: no one anticipated a long war. However, the British decision to send substantial reinforcements, the basis of Howe's army which seized New York in 1776, led Congress to vote to raise an army of 75,000 men. They were offered enlistments for the war, with the eventual reward of 100 acres and 20 dollars, or service for three years.

At first, voluntary enlistments sufficed, but eventually there had to be conscription, with drafts from the militia for a year's service. Thus, the states, which controlled the militia, played a major role in raising troops. Because men could avoid service by paying a fine or providing a substitute, the rank and file were largely drawn from the poorer sections of the community. They sought material benefits, bounties and wages, rather than glory. Moreover, there were never enough troops in the Continental Army and its size fluctuated greatly, causing Washington major problems. As a result, the soldiers, as well as the sea power, of France were crucial in helping bring victory in 1781.

There was a curious parallel in America with the situation in Britain. There also, despite impressments for the navy, there was an absence of support for conscription. Indeed, the very fact that many continental European states resorted to such a system established it as unacceptable in British and American eyes. Both lacked a regulatory regime and social system akin to those of Prussia or Russia and without them it was difficult to make a success of conscription or to control desertion. In 1780, when Britain was at war not only with the Americans but also with France, Spain, and the Indian Sultanate of Mysore, Charles Jenkinson, the Secretary at War, wrote to Amherst, now the Commander-in-Chief, that he did not see how the strength of the army could be maintained, but added:

> I am convinced that any plan of compulsion ... is not only contrary to the nature of the government of this country, but would create riots and disturbances which might require more men for the purpose of preserving the peace, than would be obtained by the plan itself ... besides that men who are procured in this way almost constantly desert, or at best make very indifferent soldiers.[34]

Instead, the conscription Britain used was to hire German troops raised by rulers such as Frederick II, Landgrave of Hesse-Cassel.

The decision to form a Continental Army was not simply a matter of military options: it was a political act. The army, a force that would not dissolve at the end of the year, even if individual terms of service came to an end, symbolized the united nature of the struggle by the Thirteen Colonies and was a vital move in the effort to win foreign recognition and support. It was not necessary to have such an army in order for individual colonies/states to assist each other militarily. Prior to the Revolution, military units had been deployed outside the boundaries of individual colonies: against Native Americans and French and Spanish forces. During the Revolution, militia units under the control of state governments were sent to assist other states, as indeed they were sent to the Continental Army. Yet, by having such an army, military decisions were in large part taken out of the ambit of state government. In theory, this made the planning of strategy easier, freeing generals in some measure from the direction of state governments and allowing them to consider clashing demands for action and assistance.

In practice, the creation of the army, although essential to the dissemination of a new notion of nationhood, did not free military operations from the views of state government, nor from the political disputes of the Continental Army. In addition, the army did not enjoy the support of a developed system for providing reinforcements and supplies, let alone the relatively sophisticated one that enabled the British armed forces to operate so far from their bases. The provision of men and supplies, instead, created major problems, preventing or hindering American operations, and producing serious strains in the relationship between the new national government and the states. Accounts, therefore, of how the militia served to suppress or inhibit Loyalist activity need to be complemented by an awareness of the extent to which local communities were not therefore disciplined to provide what was deemed necessary by Congress; indeed far from it.

The American supply system faced problems of inadequate overland transport, the inexperience of revolutionary leaders in logistical questions, the lack of an adequate central executive authority or centralized government machinery, the rivalries between the states, and the active defence of local interests. As a result, logistical support was sometimes (when vigorously managed) adequate, but, at other times, as a consequence of incompetence, inefficiency and selfishness, it was unsatisfactory. The commissary broke down almost completely in 1777–8. There were problems with personnel, transportation and financial resources and organization. The last was due to the governmental structure, the lack of an effective political organization and system of taxation, and the mismanagement of the resources that existed. The appointment of Robert Morris as Superintendent of Finance in 1781 was important for an improvement in American logistical effectiveness. Convinced that the system of procurement by purchasing commissaries was inefficient, Morris introduced a replacement focused on private contracting.[35]

The British anticipated in 1776 that one of their armies would clear Canada and then link up with another that would land in New York, exploiting naval strength and amphibious capability. This would cut off that hotbed of disaffection and sedition, New England, from the more loyal Middle and Southern colonies. This strategy was relatively sound had there been an energetic commander. The opposition was weak. Washington's army had dissolved in the late summer of 1775, and, having reassembled, dissolved again that winter outside Boston.

In military terms, the successful quelling of the rebellion required rapidity of movement, flexibility of action and boldness of execution. 1776, indeed, was a year of British attacks: the Southern expedition that culminated in the unsuccessful strike at Charleston; the relief of Québec and the subsequent clearing of Canada; and operations in the New York area. The last two were significant achievements, but neither was as conclusive as had been hoped. Defeats were inflicted on the Americans and territory was gained, but there was no decisive blow.

Politically, indeed, the year was bad for the British. American resolve stiffened and independence was declared on 4 July 1776, a measure that made it possible for some, for example prominent Lutherans, who argued that they owed loyalty to duly constituted authority to switch to the revolutionary cause. Congress slowly became better prepared to wage war, a Board of War and Ordnance being instituted on 12 June. The revolutionaries also strengthened their position at state level. The militia was used to consolidate the new revolutionary establishment and to harry or intimidate its opponents. In Pennsylvania, a new constitution destroyed the political ascendancy of the Quakers, many of whom were loyal to George. The principal Loyalist initiative, a rising in North Carolina, was defeated by the North Carolina militia at the Battle of Moore's Creek Bridge on 27 February 1776.

Meanwhile, after the failure of the attack on Québec at the end of 1775, the Americans continued their siege, although they had little prospect of success, and their force was affected by expiring enlistments, a shortage of provisions, powder and money, and a lack of support from the local population. Without hard cash, the Americans were forced to issue a proclamation declaring that those who would not receive their paper currency as an equivalent were enemies, a measure that lost them Canadian support, of which they had little to begin with. The American army in Canada was also greatly affected by smallpox, lessening the chance of an effective attack on Québec,[36] although, later in the war, Washington's great care to limit smallpox, not least by encouraging inoculation, was important to the effectiveness of his forces, especially in 1780–1.[37]

When the St Lawrence ice broke in May 1776, a British relieving force reached Québec. The Americans were defeated the following month at Trois Rivières, which broke their will to remain in Canada. This ended the best American chance to conquer Canada. Fresh attempts were to be suggested, not least by Canadian émigrés, such as Moses Hazen, but invasion plans were not followed through for a variety of reasons, including the logistical difficulties of operating in this largely forested region, a lack of French support, and, crucially, more pressing opportunities and problems in the Thirteen Colonies. Militarily, indeed, the Americans benefited from being driven from Canada. Extended lines of communication and supply, and the commitment of manpower required, would have bled the Continental Army dry. Without Canada, the Americans maintained their advantage of interior lines, and this was important in responding to the British offensives in 1776 and 1777.

An attempt in the summer of 1776 to negotiate with the Americans failed, and, on 22 August, the British made an unopposed landing on Long Island. Against his better judgement, Washington allowed political considerations to dictate his operations and sought to hold New York, despite the British ability to employ their navy in order to land troops at will. On 27 August, the Americans were heavily defeated at the Battle of Long Island, and, in the aftermath, Washington was lucky to be able to withdraw his troops from Brooklyn across the East River. Whether the British commanders, the Howe brothers, deliberately let Washington retreat, or simply lacked the necessary vigour to move the fleet into the East River, is unclear.

The Battle of Long Island exemplifies the extent to which it is misleading to exaggerate the war's novelty in terms of battlefield operations. It was essentially fought in terms that would have been familiar to those who had been engaged in the Seven Years' War, and the British could cope, albeit with difficulties. On their side, Captain William Congreve recorded:

> I found the enemy numerous and supported by 6-pounders [cannon]. However, by plying them smartly with grapeshot their guns were soon drawn off but the riflemen being covered by trees and large stones had very much the advantage of us, who were upon the open ground ... [had] not the light infantry of the Guards ... come up in time I believe we should all have been cut off.[38]

Both the Americans and the British fought in a more open order, with more significant gaps, than was the norm in Europe, because the general absence of cavalry made the infantry less vulnerable to attack, while the enclosed nature of much of the terrain encouraged developments that reflected the topography. Heavily encumbered regular units, manoeuvring and fighting in their accustomed formations, were vulnerable in the face of entrenched positions. The terrain of much of America was appropriate for such defences. Narrow valley routes were flanked by dense woodland, deep rivers often had few crossing points, and in New England the omnipresent stone walls created ready-made defences. These regular units were unsuited to the heavily wooded and hilly terrain of the Canadian frontier, and were also not ideal for the vast expanses of the South.

Artillery and fortifications played a smaller role than in conflict in Western Europe. Compared to war in Europe, both sides were lightly gunned. The Americans did not inherit a significant artillery park; while, for both sides, the distances of America and the nature of communications discouraged a reliance on cannon, which were relatively slow to move. As a result, although cannon played a role in battles such as Monmouth Court House (1778), these clashes were not characterized by the efficient exchanges of concentrated and sustained artillery fire seen in Europe.

As more generally with transoceanic operations, the force–distance relationship was different: here, relatively small armies operated across great distances in a war in which there were no real fronts. Moreover, Bunker Hill had shown the hazards of frontal assaults on American positions. Indeed, heavy British casualties in that battle helped to account for Gage's subsequent caution in the face of steadily more-extensive American entrenchments. They were also responsible for Howe's caution, for Howe had commanded the actual assaults.

Yet this did not make the Americans invulnerable. The struggle between offence and defence is a constant theme in military history, endlessly replayed and, at the same time, difficult to evaluate as a number of factors are involved in capability and success. Improvements in firepower gave the defence a greater advantage in the eighteenth century, but the situation was more complex than this general trend. Secondly, there were means to counteract defensive positions, ranging from the 'counter' fire of artillery, to manoeuvre warfare, especially movements round the flanks or flank attacks. Thirdly, frontal attacks could still be successful, as the British were to show at the Battle of Guilford Court House (1781). The vulnerability of the Americans in positional warfare had been demonstrated from 1776. Their forces were outflanked at the battles of Long Island and Brandywine (11 September 1777). Moreover, major fortified American positions could be captured, as at Fort Washington (1776) and Charleston (1780).

This threw light on the strategic choice faced by Americans. Charles Lee, a former officer in the British Army, had served in North America and Portugal before transferring to the Polish army, which had to confront the greater strength of Russia. He pressed for a strategy centred on irregular warfare, especially the avoidance of position warfare (the location of units in order to protect particular positions) and battle. The British would have found it difficult to identify targets had such a strategy been followed, but it was not, except in 1781 after American defeats in the South.

In contrast, Washington wanted a regular army that could provide America with legitimacy. He stressed drill and discipline. This preference was not simply a matter of Washington's opinion. Over 10,000 Americans had served as regulars in the mid-century wars against the Bourbons. Many others were familiar with the methods of European armies, especially the British Army, through reading, observation or discussion.

The state of fortifications ensured an important contrast between warfare in North America and Europe. The Thirteen Colonies had a somewhat demilitarized character as existing fortifications were concentrated facing Native Americans rather than being scattered across the more populated coastal littoral in which most of the conflict took place. This put a premium on battle, rather than siege, although so also did the extent to which American forces were not prepared for major sieges. The war did not centre on episodes comparable in scale to British operations against Québec in 1759 or Havana in 1762.

Yet this argument has to be employed with care. Fortified positions still played a major role in the conflict. This was true both with sieges, such as Québec in 1775, Fort Washington in 1776, the Delaware River defence network in 1777, Savannah in 1779, Charleston in 1780 and Yorktown in 1781, and also with positions that were not besieged but that helped to define operational possibilities, for example the role of the British occupation of New York from 1776 on the conflict in the Middle Colonies.

Much of the American operational dynamic, indeed strategy, in the war was determined by their repeatedly proven inability to defend their own fortified positions and by their shifting ability to confront the British in defended, forti-fied positions. The American sieges of Boston and Québec in 1775 were made possible by the unpreparedness of Britain for war. When subsequently incapable of threatening a fortified British force, the Americans tried to choose battlefields with great care. The great achievement of Washington (and the French) at Yorktown in 1781 was the capability of laying effective siege to a British Army, but this arose from the most unusual opportunity provided by the assistance of the French fleet and French siege guns. Moreover, Cornwallis was in a vulnerable position.

Washington was a believer in position warfare, although he was also willing to use the militia as partisans. Washington was not a military genius, but his character and background were very useful. He had learned the value of mobility and irregular warfare in the Seven Years' War. The major role of the American militia certainly created a problem for the British. This was true, both in operational terms, for example by restricting the range of the British supply gatherers, and in the political context of the conflict, especially in harrying Loyalists, the large number of Americans who supported continued allegiance to the British Crown. This harrying helped give the Americans strategic depth. The militia could also provide at least temporary reinforcements for the Continental Army. It helped to ensure that the British were outnumbered, and thus limited their effectiveness as an occupation force. At the outset of the Revolution, the militia overcame royal governors and defeated supporting Loyalists. Thus, in December 1775, the Earl of Dunmore, the last royal Governor of Virginia, was defeated by Virginia militia at Great Bridge; Josiah Martin, his North Carolina counterpart, followed two months later at Moore's Creek Bridge.

Yet Washington's correspondence shows that there was no major capability gap in favour of the revolutionaries. The American cause was greatly handicapped by the problems of creating an effective war machine. This was not due to poverty, as the colonists were relatively affluent, but to the problem of mobilizing and directing resources. The anti-authoritarian character of the Revolution and the absence of national institutions made it difficult to create a viable national military system. Indeed, much of Washington's correspondence is an account of organization and improvisation under pressure. For example, in early 1777, after Washington had defeated the British at Trenton, his army was still in a troublesome situation. Although in a protective position at Morristown, it was badly affected by desertion, expiring enlistments and supply problems. There were difficult negotiations over the militia, as seen, for example, in his letter to the Pennsylvania Council of Safety on 29 January: 'If some mode is not adopted for obliging the officers of the militia to return the arms and accoutrements that are lent to them, we shall be in the greatest want of them when the regular regiments are raised.' On 3 February, he wrote to Jeremiah Wadsworth: 'The present unsettled state of the Commissary's department in this quarter makes me fearful that unless some measures are fallen upon to reconcile the jarring interests of those who act, or pretend to act ... that the army will in a little while want supplies of every kind.'

That spring, Washington was similarly affected by a high desertion rate and also handicapped by unhelpful state authorities; and there were reiterated signs of weakness. Brigadier-General George Clinton wrote from Fort Montgomery on 1 May, 'The garrisons of this and the other fortresses in this neighbourhood being already rather weak considering their importance and their defenceless situation on the land side where we are now busily employed in erecting proper works.' Major-General Horatio Gates added his contribution of gloom from Albany on 30 May: the garrison at Ticonderoga had a 'shameful deficiency' and 'artillerists are likewise much wanted'.[39] These problems did not disappear. In 1780, Nathanael Greene resigned as Quartermaster General because of his anger with politicians and with their responsibility for his failure to meet the logistical demands of the Continental Army.

Another British attempt to negotiate led, on 11 September 1776, to the sole meeting between officially appointed representatives of the two sides before the final negotiations. In a reprise of Franklin's earlier point about Parliament lacking the ability to understand the need to be flexible about its constitutional position, the Declaration of Independence proved to be the stumbling block. Admiral Howe declared that it prevented him from negotiating and that he could not acknowledge Congress as it was not recognized by the King. Against this, the American delegates stressed the importance of independence, Edward Rutledge of South Carolina arguing that Britain would receive greater advantages by an alliance with an independent America than she had hitherto done from the colonies. His perspicacious observation underlined the emptiness of the British negotiating position. As with most states dealing with rebellions, it was difficult to put aside past relationships and the constitutional perspective, and the British government did not rise to this challenge.

On 15 September 1776, British troops landed on Manhattan and, on 16 November, they captured Fort Washington at its northern end. The size of the surrendering American force, 2,818 men, was not to be surpassed until the fall of Charleston in 1780. The American position was in severe difficulties. The British advanced into New Jersey, reaching Trenton on 8 December. Also in early December, Newport, Rhode Island was seized, falling without resistance to an amphibious force. The British were hopeful that many Americans would accept the offer of pardon made on 30 November, and their press carried reports of the strength of American Loyalism.

Conversely, although Washington had been reinforced by Pennsylvania militia and the Philadelphia Associators, a volunteer force, the inadequate response of the New Jersey militia was discouraging, while acute supply problems were being exacerbated by widespread demoralization. Congress itself adjourned from Philadelphia to Baltimore.

As an ugly side in relations, however, and one that reflected the stress arising from the conflict, many British and German troops perceived Americans as rebels, and pillaging and rape were rampant, especially in northern New Jersey. As a result, some Americans who had hitherto been lukewarm towards the revolutionaries turned against Britain.

British hopes, moreover, were overturned by Washington's successful riposte, which was a key episode in the Revolution. After a difficult night crossing of the icy Delaware River, a well-executed surprise Christmas attack on the Hessian outpost at Trenton led to the surrender of its garrison. Washington followed up with a victory at Princeton on 3 January. Richard Henry Lee wrote to Washington on 27 February:

> I really think that when the history of this winter's campaign comes to be understood, the world will wonder at its success on our part. With a force rather inferior to the enemy in point of numbers, and chiefly militia too, opposed to the best disciplined troops of Europe; to keep these latter pent up, harassed, and distressed – But more surprising still, to lessen their numbers some thousands by the sword and captivity![40]

Although Washington was a Fabian commander who understood the need for a defensive strategy, and the value of conceding space in order to preserve his forces, he could also take the offensive. This had a military value, helping to throw the British off balance, but was also important in maintaining political support for the Revolution. Far from feeling that time was on his side, Washington wished to exhaust the British before America grew too weary and weak to continue. For example, during the war of attrition in New Jersey in January–May 1777, the frequent and devastating attacks by American forces on British outposts and foraging parties demonstrated their capability. Washington's increasing employment of light infantry enhanced American strength, as did British delay in mobilizing the Loyalists.

As a result of Trenton, hopes of an easy and rapid British advance on Philadelphia had been quashed. Indeed, most of New Jersey was abandoned by the British and they adopted a defensive posture. This put the British in a worse situation for the start of the 1777 campaigning season, and also indicated their difficulty in defining an appropriate strategy. The reviving effect the victories of Trenton and Princeton had on Washington's army, Congress, and the Revolution as a whole (prefiguring Robert E. Lee's successes in 1862 from the Peninsula campaign on), was never fully appreciated by the British. These victories spoiled the Howes' conciliatory efforts, their offer of pardon. The battles around New York had suggested that American forces could not face regulars with confidence, but the operations in New Jersey had revealed British vulnerability when in units of less than army size. It seemed reasonable to predict that Howe would be able to seize Philadelphia in 1777, but the prospect of conquering America with his army was remote. Moreover, the retreat across New Jersey dismayed the Loyalists, and discouraged those who were considering embracing Loyalism.

The year 1777 was to be the one in which British generals mismanaged the war, while the Americans fought with more success than the previous year. It marked arguably the last real chance the British had, if indeed one had ever existed, to conquer America. 1777 was the last year in which the British fought only the revolutionaries and did not have to worry about French naval power.

The rebels had already sought the assistance of France, finding her ready to provide financial and military assistance, but unwilling to commit herself publicly. Charles Gravier, Comte de Vergennes, the Foreign Minister from 1774 to 1787, hoped that the British would lose America and, therefore, that a colonial balance of power, lost in the Seven Years' War, would be restored, enabling the two powers to cooperate in limiting the influence of Austria, Prussia and Russia within Europe.[11] Indeed, in March 1777, Vergennes, whose formative years had been as envoy at Constantinople, wrote of the need for Anglo–American cooperation against Russian measures to weaken the Ottoman (Turkish) empire.[42] Alongside concern about the cost of war with Britain on the part of some French ministers, others were more interested in the simple idea of weakening Britain.

Yet the French move to war was hesitant. It was affected by the course of the conflict in North America and by the state of French preparations. The French were unsure that any other European power would provide support, particularly Spain, which controlled the third largest navy, but, as expenditure on the French navy increased, so it became more plausible to think of war. Tension over French aid to the rebels – specifically, allowing their privateers to use French ports – led

Vergennes to press Louis XVI in the summer of 1777 for French entry into the war. As yet, however, the situation did not seem propitious.

This is a reminder of the need to set American developments in their wider international context, which is a key theme of this book. That might appear questionable if the American Revolution is seen as a successful rejection of the *ancien régime* and one that exposed the limited resources the latter could deploy in such circumstances, and, to a certain extent, this is a reasonable view. At the same time, the Revolution was not only a civil war within the British Empire but also a struggle within the European international system. Indeed, from the outset, American leaders understood the need to win international support.

Given Britain's defeat of France and Spain in the Seven Years' War, the situation was not propitious for the Americans. Moreover, Vergennes' predecessor, Emmanuel, Duc d'Aiguillon, French Foreign Minister from June 1771 to June 1774, had thought it necessary to seek good relations with Britain, and David, Viscount Stormont, the British envoy in Paris, reported in 1774: 'I cannot easily bring myself to believe that the Duke will hastily renounce his pacific plan and … engage France in a war with Great Britain for which she certainly is not sufficiently prepared, and to which the nation in general, and the French King [Louis XV] in particular seem very averse.'[43] The path from this to war was uncertain, and this is a reminder of the multiple uncertainties of the crisis: not only the breakdown in Anglo–American relations, but also of their Anglo–French counterparts, as well as the course of the conflict itself.

In 1777, the British mounted two attacks in America, but these were uncoordinated. Operating in conjunction with each other, Howe and Burgoyne might have been able to wreck the American armies, to gain total control of the Hudson valley, to separate New England from the Middle and Southern states, and to initiate a state-by-state pacification of New England, while the coast was controlled by the navy, which was scarcely hindered by America's weak naval effort. Operating, however, as two roving columns, and commanded by two lacklustre generals, with no overall unity of command and no clearly defined master strategy or guidance from London, the two armies could not have achieved the potential success that was hoped for, even had the American forces been defeated. Even well-planned and well-coordinated operations fail, but the absence of unity of command was certainly felt in the British planning.

Howe and Burgoyne acted with a complete lack of coordination; but, in addition, the situation challenged Eurocentric military thinking, based as it was on a well-known topography with roads, strategic rivers and cities. In part, this thinking was irrelevant in the New World, for, although the cities were crucial to the economy, the campaigning repeatedly showed that the Americans could and would fight on even when the British controlled them.

There was also a political dimension. Without reliable popular support, the British commanders were obliged both to obtain the bulk of their supplies from Britain and to employ much of their army in garrison duty, an obligation made more necessary by the need to protect supply bases and the crucial trans-shipment points. Sir Henry Clinton, Howe's replacement as the Commander-in-Chief in North America, argued in 1778, 'provisions … we should never have less than six months in advance', and, as the French had joined the Americans, 'always twelve … and if we lose one fleet of supply, adieu'.[44] Thus, only a part of the army was available for operations, while the supply of new posts, such as New York (1776) and Newport (1776), forced them to deploy still more of the troops as garrison units. This helps to account for the stress on a decisive battle, because it was only by destroying the American field armies that troops could be freed from garrison duty in order to extend the range of British control. Such a battle also offered a way to make use of the effectiveness of the British troops.[45]

America, even during the Revolutionary War, was a continental power. A maritime state, such as Britain, could raid, blockade, and even occupy strategic points, such as New York or Charleston, but the issue was not going to be settled until a British Army was put ashore that could destroy the Continental Army, as happened to the Confederacy during the American Civil War. Fleets with small armies could not do this kind of thing. Military need, moreover, arose from political circumstances. The problem in the American War of Independence was to get the Americans to consent to rule by London. Any policy or strategy which did not destroy Washington's army, and conquer or intimidate the country, forcing consent on the Americans, would not have worked.

By stressing the British need for decisive victory, a greater emphasis can be placed on American skill and determination in avoiding such a defeat. Much can doubtless be ascribed to British indecision, and to generals who were insufficiently prepared to take risks, such as Howe, or who were too reckless, such as Burgoyne (in 1777) and Cornwallis (in 1781), but there were major engagements, and in these, after the campaign of 1776, whatever the fate of parts of the army, the main Continental Army was not routed. In part, this was because the British were unable to exploit battlefield advantages, because of deficiencies on their part, principally caution, fatigue and the absence of cavalry, but also due to skilful American withdrawals and the toll inflicted in battle by the Americans, most obviously at Bunker Hill and Guilford Court House.

Burgoyne's advance south from Canada was mistaken, not least because his force was outnumbered and lacked adequate supplies. The need to cut a route through a wilderness on part of the advance was symptomatic of what appeared to be a clear contrast between the two societies, although this contrast was less pronounced than it appeared. Once he had reached the Hudson, Burgoyne was unable to replenish his supplies or to win local support. He was also faced by a growing American force, including reinforcements sent by Washington. Unable to obtain sufficient supplies to remain on the upper Hudson, Burgoyne had the choice of advancing or retiring. Optimism, overconfidence, and conceit led him to the former, his army crossing the Hudson on a bridge of rafts on 13 and 14 September.

A defence can be made of his conduct until this point. All war involves risk and not to have pressed on, having taken Ticonderoga so easily, and when in command of one of the only three British forces able to mount an offensive, would have been to make no contribution to what appeared likely to be a decisive campaign. Burgoyne, however, also underrated the risks of advancing, not least because he was well aware of his lack of accurate information.

On 19 September 1777, Burgoyne approached the American position, fortified by breastworks and redoubts, at Freeman's Farm, a heavily wooded area on the western side of the Hudson River. The advance was a disaster with the British losing heavily to American riflemen. On 7 October, after a fresh defeat, British morale collapsed. A planned retreat was blocked by the Americans, and the British surrendered at Saratoga on 17 October. The British had suffered from underestimating their opponents. Burgoyne's approach to forest operations had been insufficiently flexible, the heavy baggage train a particular mistake, while the army had too few light infantry and discovered that reliance on Native Americans was foolish. Most of the fighting on the American side was done by men detached from Washington's army, but they were enabled to stand and fight because of the large number of militia who had rallied to their support, rapidly creating an effective field army.

Victory at Saratoga raised the morale of the Revolutionaries, offsetting the effect of the loss of Philadelphia on 26 September. It also ensured that, thereafter, British forces based in Canada would be no more than a modest diversion to the American war effort. In the longer term, the strategic situation had altered greatly. The prospect of a successful British advance into the Hudson Valley or New England had largely disappeared.

American resilience also encouraged French intervention, and that was to alter the war totally. On 4 December 1777, the news of Saratoga reached Paris. Two days later, the American commissioners were asked to resubmit their proposal for an alliance with France, a measure that, by acknowledging rebels against the British Crown, would make war with Britain inevitable. The news of Washington's (partly successful) counter-attack at Germantown on 4 October also affected French opinion. It showed that, despite the loss of Philadelphia, Washington was still able to attack. Saratoga also led to British interest in reconciliation with the Americans, but this was now too late.

Meanwhile, the development of American privateering had completed the transformation of Anglo–American commercial relations. Alongside a breakdown of the complex web of trade, demand, supply and credit, a breakdown bemoaned in both countries, for example by the Taunton clothmen, had come active animosity. British concern was shown at the highest level. In 1777, George III wrote to John Robinson, Secretary to the Treasury:

> I trust the different vessels that hover round the island will be put on their guard particularly to protect Liverpool, Whitehaven, the Clyde, and even Bristol, for I do suspect that the rebel [American] vessels which have been assembling at Nantes and Bordeaux mean some stroke of that kind which would undoubtedly occasion much discontent among the merchants.[46]

American privateering indeed hit British shipping and trade. This was particularly true of Bristol. Yet the British naval blockade of the American colonies, though far from complete, was more effective than American privateering and greatly weakened the American economy. In March 1777, the King had also indicated his support for economic warfare against America. He had 'suggested that a few vessels stationed on the coast of Virginia' might be able to control the tobacco trade from the Chesapeake.[47] Indeed, with the supply cut, leaf prices rose ten fold in Europe.[48]

Thanks to Washington's caution and the fighting skills and spirit of the American soldiers, there had been no decisive British victory in 1777. The quality of the American soldiers had been complemented by enough leadership under pressure and tactical flexibility to create a formidable military challenge to the British by the Hudson. The terrain, Burgoyne's folly, and American numerical superiority had brought the Americans a clear victory there. Near Philadelphia, the outcome had been less happy for the Americans, but they had fought well enough at Germantown to deny Howe what he needed, a clearly successful conclusion to the Pennsylvania campaign, one that could not only justify his strategy, but also convince opinion in America, Britain and the continent that Britain was winning and would triumph.

6

France and America Win, 1778–83

The entry of France into the conflict followed on from the signing on 6 February 1778 of a treaty of alliance and another of amity and commerce between France and the United States. France acknowledged her new treaty of commerce with the Americans on 13 March 1778. This was a deliberate challenge to George III, who could not accept the recognition of American independence, although Anglo–French hostilities did not begin until 16 June. The French Foreign Minister, Vergennes, sought war in order to humble Britain's colonial and maritime position, and thus restore France's international influence. The Franco–American alliance completely altered the war for the British and the Americans, pushed naval considerations to the forefront, and brought a shift of geographical focus to encompass the West Indies, and even India. The war in North America took second place for the British, below the struggle with France, which itself centred on the security of home waters.

From 1778, Britain lacked the initiative overall. There were individual advances, such as those that came to comprise the Southern Strategy, but, on the whole, Britain's opponents were able to take the initiative in North America, the West Indies and the Indian Ocean, and this caused major problems for British force-availability. Once the British lacked naval dominance and the initiative, they found that troops had to be spread out on defensive duties, and it was therefore difficult to take units from garrisons in order to assemble an expeditionary force. Furthermore, losing the initiative exposed the weaknesses of British preparations. Being pushed onto the defensive did not necessarily lead to failure. Indeed both Québec and Gibraltar successively defied attack during the War of American Independence, by the Americans and Spaniards respectively; but on other occasions the situation was less favourable.

The shift in British strategy was marked most clearly in the North American colonies by the fact that new units of British troops largely stopped coming. Within North America itself, the struggle widened when Spain entered the war in 1779, leading to the Gulf Coast becoming a sphere of hostilities. Furthermore, the arrival of a French expeditionary force in Newport, Rhode Island in 1780 altered the situation.

The Franco–American alliance also encouraged the British sense of the Americans as different. To rebel against authority was scarcely separate from

British political tradition, especially in light of the Glorious Revolution. Allying with the French, however, *was* different, and recalled, instead, Jacobite treason. Thus, an alienation from the Americans developed to match that among the latter. A sense of the British as alien and hostile had been the response to the British use of force in 1775.[1]

Even before French entry into the war appeared inevitable, it was already clear that a major change was required in British military policy. The plans of 1777 had clearly failed, not only at Saratoga, but also in Pennsylvania, where the British position was now exposed to an increasingly impressive American army, which had displayed its vigour in attacking at Germantown. This was more significant than the extent of land under control: at the beginning of 1778, the British, indeed, controlled more of America than they had done at any stage since the beginning of the Revolution. The fall of Philadelphia, however, had not been followed by an explosion of Loyalist military activity, and the presence of Howe and much of the army near the city suggested that it could only be retained if such large forces were deployed that Britain's offensive capability elsewhere would be drastically reduced.

Such a strategy could have worked only if American morale and resistance had collapsed after the fall of major cities or if there had been a Loyalist resurgence capable of taking over the defence of such cities, but neither had occurred. Although Loyalist troops could be brave, there had been insufficient time to raise and train a substantial army of them.

Moreover, after the loss of Philadelphia, the Continental Army under Washington camped at Valley Forge. As over previous winters, Washington's army largely dissolved in the winter of 1777–8, leaving only a hardcore of officers and men who were, by now, attaining the status of veterans; learning war through war. They had an arduous time, cold and short of supplies, but it was important for the training of the Continentals so that they could confront the British on the battlefield without having to rely on defensive positions or on surprise.

Under the self-styled Baron von Steuben, a German soldier of fortune, the Continentals were drilled in bayonet practice and in battlefield manoeuvres. Steuben reworked Fredrickian drill (the drill of the Prussian army under Frederick the Great) to fit American needs. Unlike Prussian practice, he was prepared to explain manoeuvres, and to answer questions. The manpower problems of the Continental Army meant that it had to be largely recreated in order to put any sort of force in the field that spring. Washington was unwilling to see militiamen as a substitute for regular troops, but faced the American ideological–political preference for militia over a trained army.

Yet the degree to which, despite this preference, the army represented a new political identity and social practice helped to sustain its cohesion and, thus, the continuation of the revolutionary cause. The winter of 1777–8 was a key instance of the extent to which the Continental Army, although demoralized and poorly paid, clothed and fed, confined the scope of the British military presence and operations in the Middle Colonies/states, by its very presence. The subsequent immobility and defensive posture of the bulk of the British forces in 1778–81 owed much to the French naval threat and to the caution of Sir Henry Clinton, Howe's successor as Commander-in-Chief, but it was also a consequence of Washington's crucial ability to keep the Continental Army in the field and undefeated.

The British government had responded to the failure of the 1777 campaign by reviving the attempt to negotiate, last made through the Howes, in 1776. In February 1778, Parliament agreed to renounce the right to tax America except for the regulation of trade, and a commission, headed by Frederick, 5th Earl of Carlisle, was appointed to negotiate the end of the war. It was to be allowed to address the revolutionaries 'by any style or title which may describe them', a concession not made in 1776, and to accept, as part of the peace settlement, the withdrawal of all British forces from the colonies; but 'open and avowed independence' was unacceptable. The concessions offered were radical, representing the complete recasting of the imperial system, and they were accepted gloomily by Parliament and grudgingly by George III. Charles, 1st Earl Camden, an opposition peer, pointed out that 'ministers who had all along contended for unconditional submission' were now forced to consider 'plans of conciliation'.[2]

The offer of concessions interacted with the debate within Britain about the war that had existed from the outset, a debate that carried forward pre-war differences. Opinion was sharply divided. This was seen not only in Parliament, but also in the press. Aside from the London press, the provincial newspapers took contrasting views. Newspapers such as the *Cambridge Chronicle*, *Leeds Mercury* and *Newcastle Chronicle* supported the Americans. Others, for example the *Newark and Nottingham Journal* and the *Newcastle Courant*, were Loyalist.[3] New papers founded during the conflict tended to take sides: the *Nottingham Gazette*, launched in 1780, backed the Americans.

Although, however, a conciliatory policy on the part of Britain might indeed win friends, it was not going to impress the revolutionary leaders, other than as a sign of weakness. Also, if such a policy failed as a basis for negotiation, it could only encourage a Loyalist upsurge in America if supported by a significant military presence.

The dispatch of the Peace Commissioners in 1778 marked a new stage in the conflict. The ministry, and more crucially George III, had been forced to accept both that the war would be ended by negotiation – that a war of conquest, a decisive victory followed by an American collapse, was unlikely – and that the imperial relationship would be substantially altered. The ministry, thereafter, still hoped to wear down American resistance, leading to American acceptance of terms similar to those offered by the Carlisle Commission, or, alternatively, to lure the Southern and Middle Colonies back to their old allegiance. Yet although there was still a determination to keep America in the Empire, not least in order to separate her from France, this was now a lesser priority than the new war with France. A desire for revenge, a hope of gain, a sense of the intractability of the American conflict and an awareness of the greater strategic and commercial importance of the West Indies, not least to French as well as British power, led to a shift of British attention towards the Caribbean.

The arrival of a French fleet in American waters in July 1778 reflected the British failure to keep the French warships in European waters. This fleet, based on the Mediterranean port of Toulon, was able to sail to America and threaten New York because British naval strength was concentrated on defending home waters, where it failed to destroy the French Atlantic fleet (based at Brest) off Ushant in July 1778. The French threatened British naval control of North American waters, and thereby challenged the application of British resources and the articulation of the British imperial system.

The more serious nature of the military challenge increased the pressure on British leaders. They had no additional resources. Moreover, the customary problems of poor communications in the age of sail, and the consequences both for command and control and for transport and supply, were accentuated by the scale of the war and the unpredictable interconnections between different spheres, most obviously naval operations in the Caribbean and off North America.

In the face of the new strategic situation, the British had already abandoned Philadelphia, fighting off an American attempt to block their retreat across New Jersey to the sea, in an indecisive battle at Monmouth Court House (28 June), a clash that demonstrated Washington's willingness to attack. That December, however, in a determined effort to strike back and to take advantage of local possibilities, a British amphibious force captured Savannah, opening a new front in the South. This was helped by the strength of Loyalism in Georgia and by the extent to which Britain remained in control of neighbouring East Florida. West Florida, in contrast, was overrun in 1779–81 by Spanish forces after Spain followed its ally France and entered the war in 1779.

The American position, however, was not without severe difficulties. Washington's army had serious weaknesses. Poor pay and inadequate supplies continued to hit enlistments and many units were below strength. Nevertheless, in the winter of 1778–9, Washington was able to keep the largest American force-in-being of any winter of the war thanks to improvements in the supply system the previous year. This was a development doubtless helped by the abandonment of inland offensive operations by the British, as such operations might have threatened the newly created American system of magazines along the main lines of communications. Yet the extension of the war to the South created new problems for the Americans, as it was necessary to sustain and support the struggle there, while the logistical situation for the Continental Army the following winter was far less promising.[4]

The basis for a united American response had been set by the policies of Congress, not least the draft of a confederation that Congress presented to the states in November 1777. Article 13 decreed that:

> Every state shall abide by the determinations of the united states in Congress assembled, on all questions which by this Confederation are submitted to them. And the Articles of the Confederation shall be inviolably observed by every state, and the union shall be perpetual; nor shall any alteration at any time hereafter be made in any of them; unless such alteration be agreed to in a Congress of the united states, and be afterwards confirmed by the legislatures of every state.

Yet the Articles of Confederation were not accepted by all the states until March 1781.

Despite the problems the American forces faced, there was a growing confidence on the American side about the likely military outcome of the war, a confidence which can be seen in the letters of Delegates to Congress. This owed much to international recognition. Because the French alliance was followed by Spain joining France, the British were outnumbered at sea and under particular pressure in the Caribbean and the Mediterranean. As an aspect of this pressure, the French and Americans cooperated in 1779 in order to attack Savannah, but the British successfully resisted the siege. The difficulty of Britain's position was further increased by war in India with the Marathas, who, in 1779, forced a surrounded British Army to surrender at Wadgaon. In 1780, the range of Britain's opponents further increased, to include the Dutch, as well as Haidar Ali, ruler of Mysore in southern India. In 1779, Lord Herbert remarked 'Eighteen years ago the World at our feet, but alas! now we die at the feet of the world.'[5]

The Americans, of course, had no comparable range of commitments, but, aside from the British, were also concerned about the Native Americans. Initially, many of the latter had tried to remain neutral, but trade with whites and the length of the struggle led them to commit themselves. Most backed the British, who did not seek their lands. Native American pressure on the American backcountry in New York and Pennsylvania, especially in 1778, led to a brutal response, particularly with the scorched earth devastation that John Sullivan visited on the Iroquois lands in 1779. He destroyed many villages and 160,000 bushels of corn, causing much suffering. Furthermore, thanks to careful reconnaissance, Sullivan's army was able to avoid ambush. Yet despite the devastation Sullivan had not established any permanent bases, and, in 1780, the Iroquois returned to the attack. Indeed, the Native Americans maintained the initiative at the close of the war, defeating the Americans in Kentucky and on the shores of Lake Erie in 1782.[6]

The Native Americans, however, were distant from the principal theatres of operation, and not in a position to advance towards them. Instead, in response to Britain's problems, Loyalist support was increasingly seen as an option to be tried, if not as a panacea for Britain's manpower problems. The policy, although designed in large part to serve military ends, was itself dependent on the creation of secure areas through military means. From 1779, there was a duality: the securing and protection of areas within which civil government could develop, and a war of movement. This duality, and the contradictions it posed, were linked to what has been fairly seen as the slow and hesitant manner in which the British moved to implement a fully fledged Southern strategy between 1778 and 1780.

The British stress on Loyalist support, in turn, focused attention on the activities of the American militia, which became more important as the war in the South became more significant. With their role in irregular warfare and political surveillance, intimidation and control, the militia was best suited to limit Loyalist support. Furthermore, the militia was well placed to seize what Nathanael Greene called 'all their little outposts':[7] the British positions that offered an appearance of control in the hinterlands of the well-fortified posts.

Operating as a 'Home Guard' that could turn to guerrilla action, the militia therefore counteracted the consequences of British success in field operations in the South. It is too easy, indeed, to concentrate on the campaigns of the major armies and to lose sight of the degree to which local struggles, generally between Loyalists and revolutionary militia, although sometimes also with the participation of regulars, affected the context within which these campaigns were conducted, not least by influencing the supply of provisions.

Despite the role of the militia, 1779 was a year of disappointment for the American revolutionaries. Washington appeared to be able to do little more than avoid battle and wait for the French. This was a strategy that left the initiative for most of the year with the British, but it was also sound. Resting on the defensive, Washington wished to avoid battle, and was able to do so while continuing to challenge the British position in the Middle States. He was also affected by serious problems. Indeed, on 22 May, Washington sent a circular to the states referring to the weakness of his army, as well as increasingly dramatic currency depreciation, and lethargy and disaffection among the population. That year, there was relatively little conflict in the Middle Colonies. British amphibious raids inflicted serious damage, but a bold night attack led to the capture of the British position at Stony Point on the Hudson on 15 July. In the face of a British advance, however, Washington ordered Stony Point's works destroyed and the position abandoned.

Most of the campaigning in 1779, instead, was in the South. The British arrival at Savannah led to an upsurge of Loyalist activity, but this was contained by the militia at Kettle Creek on 14 February. The British regulars, under

General Augustine Prevost, nevertheless, invaded South Carolina and marched on Charleston. Summoning the town, he was offered its occupation by John Rutledge, Governor of South Carolina, in return for a guarantee of the neutrality of the harbour and the rest of the state for the remainder of the war. These proposals scarcely implied a bellicose spirit, and suggest that, whatever American claims about their determination, negotiation from a position of strength was not a policy without hope for Britain.

Prevost, however, foolishly insisted on unconditional surrender, and then had to withdraw on the approach of a relief force under Benjamin Lincoln. In September 1779, Lincoln advanced to besiege Savannah in conjunction with a French amphibious force. After bombardment had failed to obtain surrender, a storming attack was launched on the morning of 9 October. Thanks, however, to a deserter, the British were forewarned, the attacking columns did not coordinate their operations, and, despite the bravery of the South Carolina Continentals and the French, they were repulsed with heavy losses.

The British attack on Charleston was the only major planned operation of 1780 that was executed and, as a result, the siege and its consequences have dominated the military history of the year. Had, however, any of the major blows intended further north been attempted, for example Washington's plans for a Franco–American attack on New York, the war then would not have had such a pronounced Southern orientation.

The absence of major engagements in the Middle Colonies in 1779 and 1780 should not be taken to indicate a disinclination to fight, but the manpower situation in both armies was a testimony to the strains they were suffering. The British had lost one army at Saratoga, and now had other pressing worldwide commitments, while the Americans were finding it increasingly difficult to sustain a major army. As a result, both sought new support: the British looked to the Loyalists, and their opponents to France intervening in America rather than the West Indies. The war therefore became a curious interplay of cautious moves and bold aspirations, as increasingly exhausted participants played for stakes that had been made higher as a consequence of the new factor of the intervention of French naval power, and in an atmosphere that the changing arithmetic of naval strength helped to make volatile for both sides.

For Britain's enemies, 1780 was also a year of disappointment. The French expeditionary force which arrived in Newport achieved nothing, while Washington was unable to shake British control of New York. Although not a particularly good field general, Washington, nevertheless, was an excellent leader and an able strategist. Following the disasters of 1776, he recognized that, for many, his army was the Revolution. Thereafter, he did not take risks unless success was all but guaranteed. Yet his troops were increasingly demoralized and some units were to mutiny early in the new year.

The British still controlled the sea, and, if their impact in the interior was limited, they revealed at Charleston and around the Chesapeake in 1780, an ability to use their amphibious forces to considerable effect, taking the initiative, harrying their opponents and disrupting the American economy. Nevertheless, this achievement was precarious due to the strength of the French navy, and British generals continued anxiously to scan the ocean.

The surrender of Charleston on 12 May 1780 was followed by the speedy spread of British control over most of Tidewater, South Carolina. On 5 June, more than 200 of the more prominent citizens of Charleston congratulated the British commanders on the restoration of the political connection with the Crown. A loyal address came from Georgetown the following month, while several of the leading politicians of the state returned to Charleston to accept British rule. This appeared to be a vindication of the British policy of combining military force with a conciliatory policy, offering a new imperial relationship that granted most of the American demands made at the outbreak of the war. It is scarcely surprising that Northern politicians, such as Ezekiel Cornell of Rhode Island, came to doubt the determination of their Southern counterparts.

British hopes of pacification through conciliation, however, were to be compromised by the attitude of Clinton, the British Commander-in-Chief. He was opposed to ending the rule of military law, and foolishly refused to accept the apathetic and neutral sentiments of much of the Southern population, instead insisting that they pledge themselves to provide active support. This aroused hostility. Those on parole were released but required to take an oath to support British measures; if they refused, they were to be treated as rebels. The logic of the British strategy in the South, a symbiosis of reconciliation and military superiority, was undermined by such steps. Many felt themselves no longer bound by their parole. This British failure matched a more general inability, seen also in the Middle Colonies, to devise an effective strategy for waging political warfare.[8]

The military situation, however, still seemed propitious for the British, and, on 16 August 1780, Charles, 2nd Earl Cornwallis heavily defeated Horatio Gates at Camden. This left North Carolina exposed to British attack. Cornwallis's victory underlines British military proficiency in the South, a proficiency that is often overlooked due to eventual failure. Earlier successes at Savannah and Charleston were also significant in revealing flexibility, mobility and fighting quality.

Yet the task of consolidation was far from easy. Cornwallis, whom Clinton had left in command in the South, faced the familiar problems of insufficient troops and precarious supplies, while uncertainty over local support was a worrying and unpredictable exacerbating factor. Cornwallis found the Loyalist militia lacking in subordination, loyalty and morale. He came to the conclusion that he should conquer North Carolina in order to cover South Carolina and Georgia.

Believing that it would be useful to advance, Cornwallis was delayed by sick troops, the enervating summer heat and partisan attacks on his supply lines. The British Army uniform was ill-suited for the high humidity and deadly heat of fever-ridden coastal Carolina. A supporting Loyalist force was destroyed at King's Mountain on 7 October, while Revolutionary partisans helped launch a vicious and confused local war in South Carolina. Far from the British bringing a new peaceful order, they had brought chaos. The Loyalists found that British military control was insufficiently extensive to provide protection, while British officers were increasingly frustrated by their limited control over their supply lines.

By the end of 1780, it was clear that the optimism inspired in Britain by the fall of Charleston, and the surrender of the largest American force to capitulate during the war, had to be qualified by a realization that this would not mean an uncontested triumph in the Carolinas. British hopes of a successful war in the South, sustained by Loyalist troops and by supplies from securely held areas, were dashed.

Alongside that of geographical scale, the political dimension helped ensure that the American war and Western European *ancien régime* warfare seemed sufficiently different that the former appeared to have little to teach the latter. The difference in force–space ratios meant major contrasts in staff work, logistics and operational concepts, while strategy was fundamentally affected by the politics of widespread commitment to independence on the part of the revolutionaries. This was also true operationally, in the case of the major contribution made by the militia, not least in partisan warfare.

This contribution undermined the Southern strategy adopted by the British in 1780–1, as it proved impossible to consolidate the British position in the Carolinas. Moreover, in that relatively sparsely populated region, supplies were harder to obtain and, aside from the ports, there were fewer places that it was crucial to hold, and therefore less opportunity for the positional warfare, that the British sought to force on the Americans.

Mastery in the South had slipped from British hands, although it did not come into American keeping. Instead, it was a true civil war with all the awfulness such a war entails. It was more and more tempting for the British to feel that, if only operations were extended farther north, and consequently American supplies cut and their regular forces driven back, that this would lead to the settlement of the South. This attitude, combined with the feeling that something had to be done, and that it would be best to leave South Carolina and its debilitating environment, led Cornwallis to look north, although before he is blamed for unsound judgement it is worth bearing in mind that the South had been invaded as a stage on the route to a denouement in the Middle Colonies, and not as part of a separate war.

In many respects, the fate of the war after 1778 depended on which side would make the best use of temporary naval superiority to secure a permanent advantage in the war on land. The close of 1780 saw the central themes of the 1781 campaign already clear: the need for Franco–American cooperation if a major blow was to be struck against the British; Cornwallis's problems in the South; and the crucial role of naval power. The contrasting results of the campaigns of 1780 and 1781 indicate that these circumstances and problems made nothing inevitable, which encourages the consideration of counterfactuals.

Thanks to Cornwallis's surrender at Yorktown on 19 October, 1781 was to witness the last real campaign of the war in America. Until then, however, the war had not been as disastrous as had been feared and anticipated by some British participants and observers. Despite the anxieties expressed in 1778, French entry did not oblige the British to abandon New York, nor had it led to another attack on Canada, nor to the permanent postponing of operations in the South. Similarly, the British position did not collapse outside America. Thanks to her well-established system of public credit, which was far better than that of France, Britain was able to finance massive expenditure on the war, substantially by borrowing. This enabled Britain to increase its naval strength faster than its opponents, so that in 1782 general naval superiority was established over France and Spain. In addition, Lord North's government won the general election of 1780, in part thanks to the reaction against scenes of anarchy in London and elsewhere during the anti-Catholic Gordon Riots. At that point also the war seemed to be going well, Charleston having fallen. The election results meant that a negotiated end of the war was unlikely unless the military situation altered greatly, and this was appreciated by Americans.

In the early 1780s, there was an upsurge of radicalism in the British Isles. In some respects, this paralleled aspects of popular activism in North America. There, the revolution, and the civil war it entailed, provided the occasion for the politicization of groups that had not hitherto played a significant role. In Britain and Ireland, the crisis of the early 1780s came close to doing the same, and contemporaries noted parallels, not least wondering whether the Volunteer movement in Ireland or the Yorkshire Association in Britain might lead to a new politics. Yet, partly due to the lessons in conciliation learned from failure in North America, there was no breakdown in public order in the British Isles and nothing to match American developments. The avoidance of violence was the key element. Crucially, the war with the Americans could go on.

At the beginning of 1781, British control in inland South Carolina and Georgia was obviously limited, but Gates' heavy defeat at Camden suggested that the Americans would not be able to operate successfully in army size, as opposed to partisan groups, unless Cornwallis left the region. He had been able to advance unchallenged to Charlotte. Moreover, the Chesapeake was clearly open to British amphibious attack. Washington's hopes of an advance on New York continued to be fruitless, and, as yet, scant lasting benefit had been obtained from French military intervention. At the same time, the American army was poorly supplied, still affected by recruitment problems and, in the winter of 1780–1, its morale was very poor. The correspondence of Delegates to Congress continued to be full of the crippling financial problem that the new state faced. It was therefore reasonable for British generals to hope that they would make some progress in the campaign of 1781, although the expectation that something could, and, therefore, should, be achieved was in large part responsible for the disaster that was to ensue.

Finding the pacification of the South an increasingly intractable task, and with his army weakened by his costly victory in a hard-fought battle at Guilford Court House (15 March 1781), Cornwallis advanced north. He faced a choice in April 1781: either moving south to help hold South Carolina, or marching to the Chesapeake in order to seek the decisive battle in Virginia and to cover the Carolinas. Cornwallis preferred the latter option, because South Carolina had been tried and found wanting as a field of operations: provisions lacking, the rivers difficult to cross, and the Loyalists disappointing because of poor handling, lack of support, and too many defeats and broken British promises. Indeed, Cornwallis's correspondence and his move to Virginia, leaving the Carolinas unpacified and Georgia threatened, suggest that he was a broken man. On 13 May, he crossed the Roanoke on his way north.

Cornwallis's invasion of Virginia led to demoralization and chaos among the Americans, but he rapidly abandoned his ill-conceived plan for conquering the state, in part because of the lack of Loyalist support. In June 1781, Washington, on his part, shelved his plan for a joint American–French attack on New York when surprise was lost; but Cornwallis not only discarded the idea of offensive possibilities, but also fortified a position on the Chesapeake, a foolish decision. Yorktown was seen as a potential naval base, but it was low-lying, unfortified and commanded no ground.

At this point, the war in America was far from over, although it was apparent that neither the British Southern strategy nor the advance into Virginia had brought the anticipated gains. Nevertheless, in the South, as earlier around New York, the British had shown that they could gain and hold important points and defeat American forces. Furthermore, the economic burden of the struggle was becoming more punishing for the Americans.

Given the weak state of the armies of Washington and Greene, and French concern with the West Indies, it is probable that Clinton and Cornwallis could have preserved their positions and waited on the defensive while Britain pursued its maritime war against France and Spain outside America. This would not have brought victory, but might have resulted in negotiations with the Bourbons and the consequent collapse of the anti-British coalition. Such a scenario was a threat to the Americans, and one of which they were aware. Conversely, although a different balance of naval power and advantage would have led to a successful British withdrawal from Yorktown, this would not have resulted in British victory. Instead, having fought their way to impasse in the Middle Colonies and the South, the British would have had to evacuate Virginia.

Yet French intervention in the war turned one important type of American success (avoiding being defeated) into another very different type of success (defeating Britain). In 1781, Britain's opponents saw an opportunity and grasped it. Franco–American cooperation, especially between Jean, Comte de Rochambeau and Washington, was crucial to the British failure, as was the insufficient and belated response of the British navy. The French fleet anchored off the Chesapeake on 30 August, and the landing of French troops provided vital support for a siege of Yorktown. Moreover, on 5 September, the French beat back a British naval attack off the Virginia Capes. The British fleet was outnumbered in this battle and did not press its attack hard. As a result of the battle, the Chesapeake remained blocked.

Cornwallis was besieged in Yorktown from the night of 28–9 September. Supported, from 6 October, by more and heavier artillery, the American–French siege pressed on, with British casualties mounting. On 17 October 1781, Johann Conrad Döhla, a member of the Ansbach-Bayreuth forces in Cornwallis's army, recorded:

> At daybreak the enemy bombardment resumed, more terribly strong than ever before. They fired from all positions without let-up. Our command, which was in the Hornwork, could hardly tolerate the enemy bombs, howitzers and cannon-balls any longer. There was nothing to be seen but bombs and cannonballs raining down on our entire line.

Under heavy pressure, Cornwallis surrendered on 19 October. This was the biggest humiliation of British military power until the surrender of Singapore to the Japanese in 1942. Had a better site been chosen, then Cornwallis might have resisted to better effect, while the Franco–American plan was not without its faults; but the British had failed to transfer sufficient ships from the West Indies in order to counter French naval movements. This mishandling of the naval dimension was crucial to British failure and underlines the oceanic theme in early American history.

The war had revealed serious faults in the British military system, including the problems posed by the absence of a large enough army. The limited forces at their disposal affected the strategic plans and tactical moves of the generals. The forces operating in the field were often quite small, and thus especially vulnerable to casualties. There were also serious problems in cooperation between army and navy, as well as issues in coordination in both land and sea operations that raise questions about both the calibre of the military leadership and the ability of the military system to execute plans. The Yorktown debacle exemplified this. The need Britain faced to confront a number of challenges around the world placed considerable burdens on the ability to control and allocate resources, and raised issues of strategic understanding and of the accurate assessment of threats, all of which were exacerbated by poor communications.

Defeat at Yorktown did not necessarily mean the end of the war. The British still held Charleston, Savannah and New York; and had substantial forces in America, while the Americans remained dependent on a France that had its own agenda. Washington appreciated that his success at Yorktown was largely due to French assistance, and hoped to persuade the French admiral, François-Joseph, Comte de Grasse, to cooperate in an attack on Charleston or Wilmington, North Carolina. In the event, Grasse thought it more important to sail directly for the West Indies, where France had its own territorial interests. The following April, Grasse was to be soundly defeated by Admiral George Rodney off the Iles des Saintes south of Guadeloupe. This helped thwart the prospect for the joint operations against New York that Washington sought in 1782. Further south, British troops were to be increasingly hemmed in around Charleston and Savannah, but they were secure in both cities.

Lord George Germain, the Secretary of State, responded to the news of Yorktown by producing a plan for fighting on, holding onto existing positions, mounting amphibious expeditions along the coast, regaining Rhode Island if possible, and exploiting Loyalist support in the lower counties of the Delaware. Germain argued that, by retaining New York, Charleston and Savannah, British trade would be secured and bases maintained from which counter-operations could be mounted in the Caribbean.

Such ideas, however, were no longer politically viable, whatever their military chances. Willingness to battle on in America was disappearing and there was increasing pressure in Britain for a change of ministry, while the government faced growing pressure from its supporters for a change of policy. On 8 December 1781, the Cabinet decided to send only replacements, not new units, to America. The country gentlemen who usually backed the government in the House of Commons were no longer willing to continue supporting the cost of an unsuccessful war. On 7 February 1782, the ministry's majority in the Commons fell to only 22 on a motion of censure. On 22 February, an address against continuing the American war was only narrowly blocked and, on the 27th, the ministry was defeated on the issue. The motion encapsulated the opposition view:

that the further prosecution of offensive warfare on the continent of North America, for the purpose of reducing the revolted colonies to obedience by force, will be the means of weakening the efforts of this country against her European enemies, tends under the present circumstances dangerously to increase the mutual enmity, so fatal to the interests both of Great Britain and America, and, by preventing an happy reconciliation with that country, to frustrate the earnest desire graciously expressed by His Majesty to restore the blessings of public tranquillity.

George III, however, was determined to fight on in order to save the Empire, leading to criticism that he was ready to see Britain become a much weaker power rather than yield American independence.[9] George, indeed, saw the latter as the end of Empire, and was not prepared to concede that peace could be obtained only by yielding. Pressed to respond to the views of the Commons, George sought, in early 1782, to create a new ministry. He also wished to attempt, by agreements with the individual American states, to detach the Americans from France, provided that the American states remained separate from each other.[10] This, though, was unrealistic[11] and so, now, were George's assumptions about his ability to create a viable ministry able to persuade the Commons to back his policies. Instead, the ministry of Lord North resigned on 20 March, and George was forced to turn to the detested opposition.

On 27 March 1782, the government of the Marquess of Rockingham took office pledged to peace. A new political wind blew. The American Department was abolished. On 22 April, William, 2nd Earl of Shelburne, the new Secretary of State for Home and Colonial Affairs, notified the commander in Canada that the ministry had decided to abandon offensive action as well as any measures suggesting an intention of regaining America by force.[12] Washington, in turn, had a plan for a French-supported invasion of Canada, but the French were unwilling to back him. This was wise as it would have proved difficult to move from force projection to seizing the positions necessary to secure control, particularly in the face of an undefeated British fleet which would have been able to challenge maritime routes of supply.

The British, meanwhile, decided to withdraw from their remaining bases in the Thirteen Colonies, in order to focus on the war with France in the West Indies. On 11 July 1782, Savannah was evacuated to the dismay of the Loyalists. The Americans were in no state to take Charleston and New York, although they were able to limit foraging by their garrisons. The cities were finally evacuated on 18 December 1782 and 25 November 1783 respectively, tasks complicated and delayed by the tremendous administrative and transportation burdens that were faced.

The British withdrawal was particularly welcome from the American perspective, because the grave challenges facing American unity and, indeed, military effectiveness had not ceased with the victory at Yorktown. Aside from tension from the French, there were important divisions, not least between those primarily attached to the Continental cause and those who thought largely in terms of the individual states. In turn, the latter were divided in their particular interest, so that, by the spring of 1783, there was talk of New England and New York meeting to discuss matters of common concern.

The sickly Rockingham died swiftly in July 1782, to be replaced by Shelburne. As linked goals, Shelburne hoped to divide the opposing international coalition, which, in truth was riven by distrust, and, instead, to create a new and harmonious Anglo–American relationship. The negotiations were conducted in Paris, leading to the Peace of Versailles, signed on 3 September 1783. Shelburne's offer of generous peace terms ensured that the Anglo–American preliminaries had already been agreed on 30 November 1782.[13] The British proved more intractable to the French, let alone the Spaniards and, even more, the Dutch. Indeed, the major British territorial loss was to the Americans, not the Bourbons. Nevertheless, France received Tobago, Senegal, and concessions in the Newfoundland fisheries, as well as the return of St Lucia, while Spain obtained Minorca and East and West Florida. The latter was to be important to the USA, as it ensured that Britain did not retain a presence to both north and south. Had that been the case, it would have been far more difficult to move to eventual good relations.

In the negotiations between Britain and the Americans, the fate of the lands between the Appalachians and the Mississippi proved to be more contentious than American independence. Competing British, Spanish and American claims were decided in America's favour, because neither of the other powers was as determined, Shelburne hoping for concessions elsewhere. America, in turn, only agreed to recommend to the individual states that the Loyalists be treated fairly, an undertaking that was scant compensation for their service and that anyway was widely ignored.

The Native Americans were also badly let down. Most had fought on the British side, although they were divided, and their politics often factionalized. The Native Americans maintained the pressure on the Americans in New York, on the upper Ohio and in Kentucky until the end of the war. Sovereignty over their land was, however, transferred to the new nation in the 1783 peace treaty. This transfer linked pre-war tensions to post-war developments, ensuring that the pressure of American expansion on the Native Americans would be unrestrained.

There was no British commitment to the African Americans comparable to that to their Native American allies, but the African Americans did not benefit from the American victory. Indeed, there had been claims, for example in the diaries of Hessian soldiers, of American hypocrisy in fighting for freedom while maintaining slavery. When, for example, an American detachment, under Captain James Willing, which had travelled from Pittsburgh via the Ohio and Mississippi Rivers, raided Natchez and nearby settlements in early 1778 they seized slaves whom they subsequently sold in New Orleans.[14]

During the war, the slave issue remained one that exacerbated relations between Americans and Britain, because the British were seen as ready to arm and free slaves. General Prevost, indeed, armed 200 African Americans at the time of the American–French siege of Savannah in 1779, a step that was criticized by the Americans.[15] When the British threatened Charleston in May 1779, a large number of slaves fled to their camp in search of promised freedom, and, during the city's siege in 1780, the British encouraged slaves belonging to revolutionaries to run away. The slaves of Loyalists were returned to their masters on condition they were not penalized, but the slaves of revolutionaries were to work on sequestered estates or perform other designated tasks, in return for which they would receive their freedom at the end of the war. Although inexperienced in the use of firearms, African Americans acted with success as irregulars, fighting on the eastern shore of the Chesapeake alongside Loyalist partisans.

Towards the end of the war, there was increased British interest in the idea of African American troops. In January 1782, Dunmore supported John Cruden's proposal to arm 10,000, who would receive their freedom. Two months later, the British commanders at Charleston proposed raising a regiment.[16] Yet there was no employment of African Americans for military purposes on any scale. To have done so would have greatly complicated the British position in the South, where there was a need to mobilize Loyalist support, and would also have affected opinion in the West Indies.

Indeed, looking ahead, it is unclear how, had the British succeeded in America, the imperial bond could have survived the challenge posed by the rise in Britain of support for the end of the slave trade, legislation for which passed Parliament in 1807, and subsequently for emancipation of slaves across the Empire. This indeed raises the question whether, had the rejection of British rule occurred later, American freedom would have been asserted, at least in the South, in terms of the continued ability to import and keep slaves. At a more immediate level, in 1783 British commanders refused to return slaves to their masters as part of the peace, leading to complaints from American negotiators.

This dimension of the war was to be neglected in American memorialization, part of a process by which the African American role in national history was minimized or misrepresented, a process that was also to be seen after the Civil War, notably as an aspect of reconciliation with, and integration of, the former Confederacy. Militarily, a more serious flaw in the American account of the War of Independence was the underrating of the role of France. This was doubly so, first in so far as French land and naval operations in and off America were concerned and, secondly and more comprehensively, in terms of a neglect of the global dimensions of the Anglo–Bourbon struggle. As a result, the role of the latter in both British warmaking and diplomacy was forgotten.

As far as America itself was concerned, there was a tendency to underrate the Continental Army and, instead, to exaggerate the role of the militia. More serious from the political dimension was the extent to which, as so often with public history, whereas the future was clear, the past required rewriting. If the future was an independent republic with continental ambitions, then both Loyalists and Native Americans appeared redundant and unworthy of attention. History, instead, was an account of the path by which a people had created themselves and been revived in independence.

In contrast, it is not necessary to agree with Loyalist propaganda in order to note that, at the very least, Loyalism offered an alternative approach. 'The savage insolence of a continental mob' complained of by the pamphleteer Joseph Plymley, in his *An Appeal to the Unprejudiced; or, a Vindication of the Measures of Government, with Respect to America* (Oxford, 1776), was indeed much in evidence during the conflict, as Loyalists were intimidated, and worse. This process continued after the war as they were written out of history. Such a writing-out had an obvious effect not only on the coverage of the war, but also of that of the earlier history of Anglo-America. Its British dimension was treated as an anachronism that was bound to be discarded, and, in more specific terms, the central theme was of growing disunity, culminating in revolution. As this book has suggested, this was not the case.

From that also stems the conclusion that the war might have had a different outcome. It is commonplace to cite John Adams to the effect that the revolution was made first in men's heads, but, aside from the fact that the remark was made years later, when the tendency to discern a pattern was all too easy, there were other examples both in the British world and further afield, of such revolutions failing. The comparison with Poland in the early 1790s is particularly instructive because there, as in the Thirteen Colonies, there was a broad-based, constitutional basis for political renewal and independence, whereas in Scotland in 1745-6 and Ireland in 1798 the movements were far more sectional.

Yet that simply serves to underline the extent to which the American Revolution was also, like those movements, a civil war. As such, the process of post-war forgetfulness was an important aspect of the application of nationalism to history, one in which history was seen to make nationalism necessary and inevitable. The speedy success of America as a rapidly growing independent state also helped vindicate the process. To draw attention to contingencies and victims, to the strengths as well as the weaknesses of Anglo-America, Loyalists, Native Americans and African Americans, thus seemed redundant. This largely remains the case, and the commonplace contrast between public and academic history is still amply on display.[17]

In the event, the American Revolution split the unity of the English-speaking world. America, inhabited by an independent people of extraordinary vitality, was to be the most dynamic of the independent states in the western hemisphere, the first and foremost of the decolonized countries, the people that were best placed to take advantage of the potent combination of a European legacy, independence and the opportunities for expansion and growth that were to play an increasingly important role in the new world created from 1776. America was also to ensure that aspects of British culture, society and ideology, albeit in altered forms, were to enjoy great influence, outside and after the span of British Empire. Yet to contemporaries the signs of British defeat, decline and division appeared clear. American independence seemed both cause and consequence of this failure.

7

After the Revolution

The New World is now opening scenes and subjects for great political speculation, wherein the interests of Europe may be deeply concerned ... It shall be the object of the *Oracle* to report the rising consequence of the American states, whenever circumstances may challenge the attention of statesmen, or the contemplation of a politician. We have assurances of constant communication with persons high in confidence, and of the most unimpeachable integrity.

Oracle, London newspaper, 11 June 1789, printing a speech to Congress
by Washington

The Revolution shattered the unity of the English-speaking world and the British Empire, creating a new state that was a potent rejection of the latter. This was understood by contemporaries, not least American revolutionaries, and served them as a demonstration of the success and importance of their struggle. The war was also a very costly one, and the sense of loss emphasized the importance of the struggle. Although American fatalities in battle amounted to about 6,000, the number of probable deaths in service was over 25,000, as a result of casualties in camp and among prisoners. This was 0.9 per cent of the population in 1780, compared to near 1.6 per cent for the Civil War, 0.12 per cent for World War One, and 0.28 per cent for World War Two.[1]

At the same time, there were strong elements of continuity between the British world and the new state. If what had started as a rejection by the colonists of allegedly authoritarian novelty on the part of British government, had become a new state pledged to new principles, both, nevertheless, represented aspirations voiced within the British world. Indeed, there was a continuity between earlier debates over the location and sharing of sovereignty of power and those in the new state.[2] Furthermore, as with other revolutions, in constructing the new, there had been borrowings from the old. The extent to which this made possible an easing of tension in Anglo–American relations is unclear, not least because a shared background had been a condition of the recent civil war within the Empire. Moreover, revolution, war and independence ensured that common institutions, such as the Church of England and Freemasonry, went in different directions, with distinctive practices and systems of control, as well as particular rites. America's Methodists organized as a distinctive body in 1784. Greater national self-confidence, as well as a greater institutional density, lessened the appeal to Americans of education in Britain and also encouraged a stronger sense of intellectual autonomy.

There was also a strong sense of continuity in terms of the apparent and real challenge posed by Britain. It might appear in a modern retrospect that the 1760s marked a turning point between the collapse of French power in North America and the rise of American dominance on the continent,[3] but to Americans in the early republican period it was Britain's continued power that appeared more obvious and threatening. This was very much a strand in American politics and public consciousness until the mid nineteenth century and it was particularly strong until the War of 1812. This conflict, which finished in 1815,[4] was the last war fought between the two powers. It also therefore represents what can be seen as the close of the stage in their relations that had become dominant in the late eighteenth century, that of rivalry born of distrust and a breakdown in relations. Whether within or outside the Empire, there was a continuity.

If this set a key political theme, it was not the only one. There was also an extrapolation of the tension within American politics onto the issue of Britain, with the corollary that cooperation with Britain or, at least, not competing with it, became an acceptable (albeit also divisive) position within American political discourse. This was related to, but separate from, the argument that there were prudential reasons why better relations with Britain should be pursued. This prudential argument owed something to anxiety about British intentions – in short the continuation of the wartime alignment of debate, but much to the extent to which this alignment no longer appeared so salient. This owed something to the extent to which Britain no longer appeared a threat in some eyes and to certain interests, especially influential ones within New England. In practice, the British system of government was largely unchanged, but this was less of a challenge once the American colonies were outside the Empire.[5]

Instead, it was the American constitution that was the issue. The contentious debates, if not bitter disputes, that accompanied the framing of the Constitution and then its implementation, were aspects of the difficulty in devising a widely accepted political practice once the shock of war had ended. Some of these problems could be discussed in terms of the British challenge, but this expedient was not open in most cases.

The collapse of another aspect of the wartime alignment was also significant in that France rapidly ceased to be seen as an ally. Instead, it was considered by many in America as a threat. As with Britain, this threat could be considered in prudential terms, but also owed much to ideology. Prior to 1789, this could be located in terms of the traditional hostility to French absolutism and Catholicism within the British world, a hostility that owed much to the extent to which France was the other against which this world was defined. From 1789, in contrast,

France moved rapidly in a more radical direction that posed challenges to American political suppositions. There was a degree of shared enthusiasm looking back to French support for American independence. Thus, after Benjamin Franklin's death in 1790, the French National Assembly voted to honour him with official mourning. Nevertheless, the progress of the Revolution was unwelcome. This was a matter not only of political and social suppositions, but also of the rejection of Christianity that was officially sponsored by revolutionary France.

Initially, the balance of hostility from 1783 had been toward Britain. The War of Independence had left many issues unsettled, and suspicion remained, not least over British encouragement of Native American hostility in the Old North-West. If that support was exaggerated,[6] it nevertheless seemed a real prospect. That Britain retained seven posts there in territory allocated to the USA in the peace, including Detroit, Niagara, Oswego and Fort Mackinac, added to the tension, not least because the American presence in much of the region was limited.

In turn, the British argued that the Americans were failing to fulfil the peace terms, particularly the restoration of Loyalist property and the settlement of pre-war debts. The British delay in sending an envoy was also an issue. In 1785, William Miles, a hustling, would-be influencer of British policy, informed William Pitt the Younger:

> I have met a Mr Bingham ... a native of America.... He speaks in the highest terms of admiration of Sir James Harris and laments that a minister of his manners and capacity has not been sent to America. He assured me that the people of property and weight in the United States wish very much for a cordial and permanent reconciliation with Great Britain and that all ranks of people were dissatisfied at the appointment of a man for Consul General who was universally reprobated and detested ... He also assured me that unless some measures were speedily adopted by government, that resolutions would be taken by all the provinces, fatal to our commerce with America.[7]

George Hammond, the first British Minister Plenipotentiary to the United States, however, was not to arrive in Philadelphia until October 1791. He found that the suspicions, indeed hostility, towards British policy of Jefferson, then Secretary of State, hindered the progress of negotiations.[8] Early British envoys were not terribly sympathetic to American political culture, but many of their complaints echoed those of earlier foreign commentators on British politics, for they focused on the difficulties created by both public discussion and governmental change. In 1796, the disclosure of diplomatic papers relating to Anglo–American relations became an issue in the House of Representatives.[9] It took time for American political practice and theory to define a response to the conduct and contents of international relations. Thus, as a result of the Longchamps affair in 1784, in which a French diplomat was attacked, the Supreme Court was given jurisdiction over international law, and the authority of the individual states subordinated.[10]

Britain was having to come to terms with the problems of decolonization, and to define a diplomacy with a newly independent state, as she had not done before. George III had been pleased to be away from London when the humiliating peace that acknowledged American independence was proclaimed in 1783, but he struck an appropriate note of wise and honest courtesy, on 1 June 1785, when he received John Adams as the first American envoy to the Court of St James's. A delighted Adams recorded George as saying:

> I have done nothing by the late contest but what I thought myself indispensably bound to do, by the duty which I owed to my people … I was the last to consent to the separation; but the separation having been made, and having become inevitable, I have always said, as I say now, that I would be the first to meet the friendship of the United States as an independent power… let the circumstances of language, religion, and blood have their natural and full effect.[11]

Not everything, however, was so benign. The following March, Jefferson, on a visit from his embassy in Paris, was received by George. There are no detailed contemporary accounts of the meeting, although in his autobiography, written 35 years later, Jefferson was very critical. Claiming that he had been ungraciously received, Jefferson added 'I saw, at once, that the ulcerations in the narrow mind of that mulish being [George III] left nothing to be expected on the subject of my attendance.'[12] Ironically, the two men in fact had much in common, from an interest in architecture and applied science, to a disdain for luxury.

Relations with America, however, did not bulk large in British governmental concern, and unsurprisingly so, as there were far more contentious issues with other European states. Indeed, Britain, which saw a major post-war recovery in stability and prosperity, came near to war with France in 1787, France and Spain in 1790, and Russia in 1791. It was also at war with France from 1793 until 1802 and 1803 to 1814, and in 1815. These wars included France's allies, which, as a result of French military successes, swelled to include the Dutch and, until 1808, Spain. In 1800, Spain was obliged to cede Louisiana to France, reversing the transfer of power in 1763.

Moreover, although the independence of the USA was of great importance in the long term, it had little immediate consequence for European power politics. America did not develop as a major naval power until the late nineteenth century, and the Americans did not see their revolution as for export throughout the European world. Instead, within the USA, there was a powerful sense of American exceptionalism: of a culture and society separate from those of Europe.[13] This disengagement was further encouraged by the turmoil of the French revolutionary period.[14] The sense of distance helped ease relations with

European powers, although it also fostered a degree of unreality in responding to their policies.

On the British side, George III himself, from 1783, devoted little attention to the USA, although, indirectly, he played a role thanks to his personal commitment to the many Loyalists who had fled America, and whose claims to compensation were largely ignored there. In the peace treaty, the American government only agreed to recommend to the individual states that the Loyalists be treated fairly. In practice, their claims were generally neglected. Although some returned to the USA, and others had taken refuge in Bermuda and Britain, many Loyalists had fled to the British colonies in what is now Canada, and George supported schemes to provide them with land there.[15]

This was envisaged as a very different society to that in the USA. An Act of Parliament of 1791 gave the Church of England a considerable amount of land in Upper Canada (now Ontario), in order to provide for its clergy, and also the colleges that would sustain its local position. A hereditary aristocracy was also seen as a way to safeguard loyalty. Names affirmed loyalty. The colony of New Brunswick, created in 1784, had, among its counties, Kings, Queens and Charlotte, and its capital at Fredericton. In the St Lawrence Valley in Québec after the war, Loyalists settled in newly surveyed townships that included Charlottesburg, Osnabruck, Williamsburg, Edwardsburg, Augusta, Kingston, Fredericksburg and Adolphustown.

In the USA, in contrast, aside from anger towards and suspicion of Britain, a political practice and national culture different from, and often in opposition to, that of the former mother country was developing; although such a contrast had already preceded independence, with rival stereotypes of England as the home of aristocratic gentlemen and America as that of men of the people.[16] The search in the new nation for a new identity, or, at least, a new source of authentication, however, aroused worries. In 1813, for example, John Jay, former Secretary of State, expressed his concern to Noah Webster, the compiler of the *American Dictionary of the English Language* (1828), that his work would 'impair' the sameness of the language in the two countries. To underline the complexity in relations, however, British traditions also influenced the new national culture.[17]

Moreover, America had cut free from the French alliance which had been so threatening to Britain. The *Public Advertiser*, a prominent London newspaper, had carried a letter from a 'Bostonian' (newspaper letters were pseudonymous), in its issue of 15 January 1783, claiming that 'the French and our States [the USA] will rear such a navy in America, that England will not hold an inch of territory on the face of the Earth in a very few years'. However, despite the rhetoric of shared struggle and common goals, the French found the Americans unwilling to help, ungrateful, and opposed to accepting a commercial relationship on French terms. French officials thought the Americans self-interested and unprepared to translate declarations of gratitude into action, and this at a time when the financial burdens of her intervention were felt all too keenly. Indeed, these burdens helped contribute to the political crisis that led to the French Revolution. No lasting political or economic entente had been created between America and France as a result of wartime cooperation. Cultural links remained weak, although French-language newspapers were produced: the Philadelphia-based *Courier de l'Amérique* in 1784 and the *Courier de Boston* in 1789.

Peace, indeed, allowed British competitors to re-establish their commercial position, and caused a precipitate decline in Franco-American trade. British trade, in contrast, boomed, and – combined with the negative balance of trade between France and the United States – this ensured that trade with America moved French capital into the British economy. American success in overcoming French efforts to keep them out of the trade of the French West Indies (principally Martinique, Guadeloupe and Saint Dominique) was an added cause of tension, while the Americans also competed in traditional French markets, such as the Ottoman (Turkish) Empire. Moreover, French officials complained about indifference on the part of American political leaders to their commercial aspirations. A consular convention signed in 1783 was not ratified by the Americans for five years and, in contrast to Britain, the Americans did not respond positively to French approaches for a trade treaty.[18] An Anglo–French trade treaty was signed in 1786, although it did not prevent the two powers from coming close to conflict in the Dutch Crisis of 1787, nor from going to war in 1793.

Commercial links between Britain and America revived strongly after the War of Independence. In defiance of traditional mercantilist assumptions, which linked commerce to politically controlled markets, American trade with Britain rose greatly after independence. America was populous, lacked the range of British industrial production and was short of liquidity, and thus still needed access to Britain's credit (often generously supplied). This was fortunate for Britain as she also faced growing export problems in American markets. The continued influence of Britain on the eastern seaboard led to New York being described by the French envoy, Louis-Guillaume Otto, in July 1790, as more like a suburb of London than an American town.[19]

Nevertheless, although there had been a willingness on the part of Britain to concede or shelve contentious issues in order to bring the War of American Independence to a close, and (successfully) to divide the opposing coalition of the Americans, France, Spain and the Dutch, there were limits to the British willingness to make compromises. Sensitivity over the protectionist trading system of the British Empire led, in March 1782, to the failure of an 'American Intercourse Bill' designed, at least for a while, to give American ships the right to carry American goods to British possessions, and also to export from them, and both at the preferential tariffs of British-owned goods in British ships. Instead, protectionist principles were entrenched by Orders of Council of May and July 1782 which, respectively, allowed free access to Britain for American raw materials only, and banned American ships from carrying goods from the British colonies in the West Indies to America. This blocked what had been a major trade route prior to the Revolution. The Revolution had divided not only British North America, but also the British New World, with its close links between North America and the West Indies.

This ban was unpopular among Britain's West Indies colonists, but the active lobbying of Parliament against it in 1783–5, both by the Society of West Indies Merchants and Planters in London, and from the West Indies, was unsuccessful. Instead, the ban on American ships carrying goods from the West Indies was strengthened by an Act in 1788, and Charles, Lord Hawkesbury, from 1796 1st Earl of Liverpool, the President of the Board of Trade from 1786 to 1804, was a keen advocate of banning American trade with the West Indies.[20] Liverpool, whose son, the 2nd Earl, was to be Prime Minister throughout the War of 1812, was also angered by American restrictions on British shipping, and saw the limitations on American trade in part in political terms: 'Our West Indies islands will never be safe if the subjects of the United States are allowed to have a free intercourse with them, and to import, among other articles, their democratical principles'.[21]

Liverpool also saw shipping as crucial. In 1797, he responded to the argument that imposing a tonnage duty on American shipping might damage Britain's role as an *entrepôt* for rice and tobacco, both of which were exported from America. He claimed, instead, that imposing a duty would be an appropriate response to American duties on British ships, as Britain had lost this trade since America became independent, and that 'the extent of our navigation is to be preferred in general to the extent of our commerce, for on the first depends the security of everything'.[22] This looked toward British action against American shipping in the 1800s, particularly the impressment (forcible recruitment) of sailors. The British were uninterested in claims that these sailors were no longer British subjects because they had become American nationals. Thus, part of the rivalry was over what was seen as an arrogant British contempt for American sovereignty, which became a major issue in 1806–7. Moreover, British trade policy hit America hard, for British conquests, during the French revolutionary and Napoleonic wars, of the colonies of other states, of France, and her allies, Spain, the Dutch and Denmark, ended the right of the Americans to trade there.

Americans were worried about British intentions on their borders. Concern about Britain sponsoring Vermont separatism was significant.[23] In 1790, war between Britain and Spain seemed a possibility in the Nootka Sound Crisis, which arose as a result of competing territorial claims on the Atlantic coast of what is now British Columbia. As a result, the British approached the USA for support, their agent in New York holding informal talks with Alexander Hamilton, but there was no agreement. This might have been a serious issue for the USA, as the Spanish colonies of East and West Florida and Louisiana were vulnerable to British attack, not least because Spain's ally France was in the throes of revolutionary chaos. Indeed, this prevented the French from fulfilling their promise of staging a major naval armament in support of Spain. British interest in an attack on New Orleans was particularly serious as this was seen as crucial to the future of the Mississippi valley. In the event, Spain backed down and there was no war. The possibility of Britain relaunching its career as a power on the Gulf shore was therefore cut short, but this underlined the extent to which there was no certainty over North American geopolitics.

Anglo–American relations continued uneasy in the early 1790s, in particular as conflict between the USA and the Native Americans in the North-West, which had continued through the 1780s, flared up. American forces did badly in 1790–1, especially in a defeat at the Wabash River on 4 November 1791, but political and military developments changed the situation. Combined with Anglo–American negotiations in London that led in 1794 to Jay's Treaty, the British failure to fulfil Native American hopes helped lead to a transformation in relations in 1794–6. Defeated at Fallen Timbers by a well-prepared Anthony Wayne on 20 August 1794, the Natives of the North-West settled with the Americans on the latter's terms by the Treaty of Greenville of 1795. The following year, the British returned their seven bases in the North-West.[24] This resolution of the immediate crisis sat alongside bold American assumptions about the destined extent of their country.

These assumptions were not simply a matter of frontier enthusiasts. Instead, they were pushed at the highest level by Jefferson, who became President after the bitterly contested election of 1800. Although he had idealistic notions about Native Americans, these were subordinated to his determined support for territorial expansion. For Jefferson, this meant not only sovereignty, but also the acquisition of Native lands and the expulsion of the Native Americans. Whereas during the colonial period the concept of discovery had not been seen as entailing the transfer of land-ownership from the Natives, Jefferson took a very different view, and employed this to support the exploration of, and beyond, the lands acquired in 1803 by the Louisiana Purchase, not least in supporting the Lewis and Clark expedition.[25] His vision was a bleak one and it needs emphasis in any account of Anglo–American history. In 1812, Jefferson observed to John Adams that some Native Americans were becoming agricultural settlers in his terms, a process he saw as beneficial as far as competition with Britain was concerned:

> On those who have made any progress, English seductions will have no effect. But the backward will yield and be thrown further back. These will relapse into barbarism and

misery ... and we shall be obliged to drive them, with the beasts of the forest into the strong mountains.[26]

Earlier, in place of hostility towards Britain, the focus for America in the late 1790s became animosity with France. In 1798–1800, in the Quasi War, France sank or captured over 300 American merchantmen, in response to the American part in maintaining British trade routes. Opposed to this, France did not accept that neutral ships (among which American merchantmen were very important) could carry British goods, and thus sought to match Britain's blockade of trade with France.[27] Even Liverpool warmed to the Americans as a result, seeing the crisis as an opportunity to reknit relations, with the British navy playing a key role:

> They must depend on our fleet for the general protection of their commerce, and this circumstance will tend, I think, to unite the two countries in a closer bond of union: their armed vessels however will afford us a considerable degree of assistance in destroying the small French privateers.[28]

Such an argument looked toward the language used about German submarines prior to America's entry into war against Germany in 1917 and 1941. In practice, during the Quasi War, there was considerable naval cooperation between Britain and the USA against French attacks on trade. This underlined a general theme of the book, that external pressures drove, and drive, Britain and America together at times, and that the absence of such pressures allowed them to drift apart or even to resume old antagonisms.

The late 1790s were a high point in friendly political relations between Britain and the USA, but, as a background, there had been a rapid post-war improvement in commercial relations between Britain and its former colonies. Pre-war networks were rapidly reconstructed, a process helped by the extent to which French merchants had not been able to replace them during the war. The uncertainty of the pre-revolutionary and, even more, revolutionary, years in France exacerbated this situation. If there were important improvements within the American transport system, for example the Philadelphia–Lancaster turnpike, and regular stagecoach services, including a one-day service between the two leading cities, Philadelphia and New York, this system served both to help integrate the new state and to make it more convenient for international trade.

France had become a stronger force in North America in the early 1800s. In 1800, Spain was bullied into the Treaty of San Ildefonso, by which it ceded Louisiana to France. In 1802, peace with Britain enabled the French to make a major attempt to regain Haiti. Yet the tide turned in 1803. French military failure in Haiti reflected both local opposition and the resumption of war with Britain in 1803. Any resumption made New Orleans an obvious target for British attack and that year Napoleon sold the Louisiana Territory to the USA, thus giving the USA control over the Mississippi and rule, as far as Western powers were concerned, over the lands to the Rockies.

French diplomacy was also hit by the resumption of war. General Bernadotte was appointed envoy to the USA in January 1803, but was unable to assume that duty. Instead, he commanded I Corps of the *Grande Armée* in the Ulm-Austerlitz campaign of 1805. Nevertheless, France remained a key presence in Anglo–American relations, not least because the economic blockade and impressments of sailors that so angered American politicians in the run-up to the War of 1812 seemed necessary to the British in order to strengthen them against the French challenge. The Americans were not sufficiently mindful of the extent to which Britain was involved in a life-and-death struggle with France. This reprised the situation in the mid-eighteenth century, but did so in a far more bitter fashion. To the British, American policies helped Napoleon, and, indeed, the latter deliberately manipulated the situation in order to exacerbate Anglo–American relations.

Moreover, Anglo–American relations were affected by the extent to which American politicians came to view the contest between Britain and France as an extension of their own divisions.[29] Although many American 'War Hawks' might make the case, the War of 1812 was no second stage of the War of American Independence. By 1812, indeed, the complex play of interests that had affected Anglo–American relations in the decades prior to 1775, and indeed, albeit differently, during the war itself, had given way to a situation in which both diversity and interplay were expressed through different governmental structures and with reference to political cultures that bore the stamp of the recent conflict, at once civil war and war for empire. However much there were continuities in interest and concern, the history of Anglo–America had been transformed.

8

Conclusions

Relations between Britain and the USA have been both troubled and close over the last two and a quarter centuries.[1] It is tempting to trace both or either to their relationship in the eighteenth century, not least the American Revolution. This, however, is only of limited value because of the role of the circumstances of particular situations, especially the apparent threat posed by third parties. Indeed, as so often was, and is, the case with bilateral relations, these relations can only be understood in a multilateral context. Over the last century, the two powers have been closest when challenged by another, whether Germany or the Soviet Union, and, conversely, most apart, as in the 1890s, 1900s, 1920s and 1930s, when no such threat seemed imminent. Current discussion of relations in part hinges on the question of how far terrorism and/or states such as Iran pose a common threat.

The eighteenth century can be discussed in these terms, with external challenges presented as driving the colonists to seek British support. Thus, France, Spain and the Native Americans, differently challenging at particular junctures and for specific colonies, combined to encourage a sense of menace. This had strategic and economic dimensions, but was also meta-historical in that the religious 'other' that these forces represented was presented as engaged in a life-and-death struggle with Protestant English liberties. Both souls and liberties were at risk, and, depending on the commentator, either might be emphasized.

Moreover, whereas, in Europe, there were reasons why Britain allied with one major Catholic state against another, in particular fighting alongside Austria against France in 1689–97, 1702–13 and 1743–8, this was not really a factor in North America, although, in 1719–20, Britain was allied with France and both were at war with Spain. As a result, there was a short-lived military cooperation against East Florida. The rarity of such action alongside a Catholic state ensured that, to adopt a moral view, the compromises that reality, or looked at differently, corruption, entailed in Europe were kept at a distance in North America. This moral perspective on power politics provided a parallel to the continued vitality in the colonies of Country Whig attitudes on domestic politics with their theme of corruption.

From this perspective, the American Revolution owed much to the ending of one meta-historical challenge, the external threat to the liberty of the colonies from France, a challenge that bound Britain and colonies together, and its replacement by a more serious, because apparently more insistent, one, the domestic threat. In one respect, this anxiety repeated the concern about a domestic (or at least imperial) threat that had already occurred twice during the seventeenth century, first in the Civil War, and then in response to James II. That theme of repetition, indeed, is an instructive reminder of the limitations of teleological and linear accounts of change. To note differences in the particular episodes raises the question whether an earlier crisis of the length of that in the early 1770s might not have thrown up a similar response.

A similar response, however, was unlikely. Aside from the extent to which the experience of the years since the Glorious Revolution of 1688–9 had created a different political atmosphere in the colonies with contrasting norms, as a result, for example, of the decline of proprietorial control, there was also major demographic and economic growth there. These changes did not inherently threaten the demise of trans-Atlantic links. Indeed, in many respects, these links became closer in the decades and, particularly decade, prior to the American Revolution of 1775–83, not least with immigration at a particularly high level. The growth of the American economy, or rather economies, meant more imperial integration with Britain, but, as this book indicates, this was not solely a matter of functional convenience. Instead, there were cultural factors, in the broadest sense, that encouraged colonists to look to Britain. These included multiple religious links, as well as a commitment to a British identity that was seen as encompassing the colonies within an empire of liberty.

It was the failure of these integrative hopes that provided much of the dynamic for the resort to violence, but it was a failure that cannot be sought solely in developments in the colonies. Instead, the British government played a key role, not only with specific policies, but also by a tone and style of rule that colonial commentators were able to typecast, however misleadingly, as authoritarian if not tyrannical. A mutual dynamic, in which contrasting negative images were built up, was fed enough provocative actions on both sides to ensure that the threshold to large-scale violence was crossed even though there was no wish to do so on the part of most of those involved, let alone on that of less engaged contemporaries.

There is an understandable wish to believe that great events have great causes, and the heroic mode of public history frequently strikes that note. American independence was a great event, indeed a key episode in the history of the modern world. Yet great causes are less obviously in sight. Moreover, as this book has indicated, the history of the period cannot be accurately written without due recognition of the fate of victims, principally but not only, African and Native Americans.

Notes

Notes to Introduction: Seventeenth-Century Background

1   *Henry VIII*, V, iii.
2   D.B. Quinn (ed.), *The Roanoke Voyages, 1584–1590* (2 vols, London, 1955); K.O. Kupperman, *Roanoke: The Abandoned Colony* (Savage, Maryland, 1984).
3   Kupperman, 'Apathy and death in early Jamestown', *Journal of American History*, 66 (1979), 24–42.
4   S. Mallios, *The Deadly Politics of Giving: Exchange and Violence at Ajacan, Roanoke, and Jamestown* (Tuscaloosa, Alabama, 2006).
5   As it was Mothers' Day, he also urged listeners to remember to telephone their mothers.
6   K. MacMillan, *Sovereignty and Possession in the English New World. The Legal Foundations of Empire, 1576–1640* (Cambridge, 2006), p. 207.
7   N. Salisbury, *Manitou and Providence: Indians, Europeans, and the Making of New England, 1500–1643* (New York, 1980).
8   H.C. Porter, *The Inconstant Savage: England and the North American Indian, 1500–1660* (Cambridge, 1979).
9   J.F. Martin, *Profits in the Wilderness: Entrepreneurs and the Founding of New England Towns in the Seventeenth Century* (Chapel Hill, North Carolina, 1991).
10 W. Cronon, *Changes in the Land: Indians, Colonists, and the Ecology of New England* (New York, 1983).
11 D.H. Sacks, *The Widening Gate. Bristol and the Atlantic Economy, 1450–1700* (Berkeley, California, 1991).
12 N.E.S. Griffith and J.G. Reid, 'New evidence on New Scotland, 1629', *William and Mary Quarterly*, 3rd ser., 39 (1992), 492–508.
13 The lack of roads also affected European forces.
14 P.M. Malone, 'Changing military technology among the Indians of southern New England, 1600–77', *American Quarterly*, 25 (1973), 48–63; M.L. Brown, *Firearms in Colonial America: The Impact on History and Technology* (Washington, 1980); B. Given, 'The Iroquois and native firearms', in B.A. Cox (ed.), *Native Peoples, Native Lands. Canadian Indians, Inuit and Metis* (Ottawa, 1987), pp. 3–13; D. Delage, *Bitter Fast: Amerindians and Europeans in Northeastern North America, 1600–64* (Vancouver, 1993).
15 J. Kepler, 'Estimates of the volume of direct shipments of tobacco and sugar from the chief English plantations to European markets, 1620–69', *Journal of European Economic History*, 28 (1999), 155–72.

16   G. Rommelse, *The Second Anglo-Dutch War, 1665–1667* (Hilversum, 2006), p. 103.

17   M.K. Geiter, *William Penn* (Harlow, 2000).

18   E.S. Morgan, 'The first American boom: Virginia 1618 to 1630', *William and Mary Quarterly*, 3rd ser., 28 (1971), 169–98, esp. 197.

19   R. Menard, 'The tobacco industry in the Chesapeake colonies, 1617–1730: an interpretation', *Research in Economic History*, 5 (1980), 109–77, esp. 153–5.

20   A. Games, *Migration and the Origins of the English Atlantic World* (Cambridge, Massachusetts, 1999).

21   W.E. Washburn, 'The moral and legal justifications for dispossessing the Indians', in J.M. Smith (ed.), *Seventeenth-Century America: Essays in Colonial History* (Chapel Hill, North Carolina, 1959), pp. 24–32; B. Arneil, *John Locke and America* (Oxford, 1996); S. Banner, *How the Indians Lost Their Land: Law and Power on the Frontier* (Cambridge, Massachusetts, 2005).

22   J.D. Drake, *King Philip's War: Civil War in New England, 1675–1676* (Amherst, Massachusetts, 1999), p. 198.

23   J. Black, *The Curse of History* (London, 2008) pp. 186–8.

24   P.M. Malone, *The Skulking Way of War. Technology and Tactics among the New England Indians* (Baltimore, Maryland, 1993).

25   J.A. Sainsbury, 'Indian labor in early Rhode Island', *New England Quarterly*, 48 (1975), 378–93.

26   R. Menard, 'From Servants to Slaves: The Transformation of the Chesapeake Labor System', *Southern Studies*, 16 (1977), 355–90, esp. 389.

27   A. Gallay, *The Indian Slave Trade: the Rise of the English Empire in the American South, 1670–1717* (New Haven, Connecticut, 2002).

28   R. McColley, 'Slavery in Virginia, 1619–1660: A Reexamination', in R.H. Abzug and S.E. Maizlish (eds), *New Perspectives on Race and Slavery in America* (Lexington, Kentucky, 1986), pp. 11–24.

29   A.T. Vaughan, 'The Origins Debate: Slavery and Racism in Seventeenth-Century Virginia', *Virginia Magazine of History and Biography*, 97 (1989), 353.

30   For the sake of clarity, this is referred to by its later name of Charleston.

31   R.S. Dunn, 'The English Sugar Islands and the Founding of South Carolina', *South Carolina Historical Magazine*, 72 (1971), 81–93.

32   R.C. Nash, 'South Carolina and the Atlantic economy in the late seventeenth and eighteenth centuries', *Economic History Review*, 45 (1992), 677–702.

33   W.E. Washburn, *The Governor and the Rebel: A History of Bacon's Rebellion in Virginia* (Chapel Hill, North Carolina, 1957); S.S. Webb, *1676: The End of American Independence* (New York, 1984).

34   R.H. Balmer, *A Perfect Babel of Confusion: Dutch Religion and English Culture in the Middle Colonies* (Oxford, 1989).

35   R. Bliss, *Revolution and Empire: English Politics and the American Colonies in the Seventeenth Century* (Manchester, 1990).

36   D.S. Lovejoy, *The Glorious Revolution in America* (New York, 1972).

37   H.A. Johnson, 'The rule of law in the realm and the province of New York: prelude to the American Revolution', *History*, 91 (2006), 22.

38   P. Boyer and S. Nissenbaum, *The Salem Witchcraft Papers* (3 vols, New York, 1977);
     B. Rosenthal, *Salem Story. Reading the Witch Trials of 1692* (Cambridge, 1993);
     M.B. Norton, *In the Devil's Snare: The Salem Witchcraft Crisis of 1692* (New York, 2002).

39   E.W. Baker and J.G. Reid, *The New England Knight. Enrichment, Advancement and the Life
     of Sir William Phips, 1651–1695* (Toronto, 1998); K.A.J. McLay, 'Wellsprings of a "World
     War": An Early English Attempt to Conquer Canada during King William's War 1688–97',
     Journal of Emperial and Commonwealth History, 34 (2006), pp. 155–75.

40   J. Parmenter, 'After the mourning wars: the Iroquois as allies in colonial North American
     campaigns, 1676–1760', *William and Mary Quarterly*, 3rd ser., 64 (2007), 39–82;
     G. Harvard, *The Great Peace of Montreal of 1701: French-Native Diplomacy in the
     Seventeenth Century* (Montreal, 2001).

41   W.E. Lee, 'Fortify, fight, or flee: Tuscarora and Cherokee defensive warfare and military
     culture adaptation', *Journal of Military History*, 68 (2004), 768–9.

42   J. Axtell, *Beyond 1492: Encounters in Colonial North America* (New York, 1992), p. 239;
     D.K. Richter, *The Ordeal of the Longhouse: The Peoples of the Iroquois League in the Era of
     European Colonization* (Chapel Hill, North Carolina, 1992).

43   L.V. Eid, '"A kind of running fight": Indian battlefield tactics in the late eighteenth century',
     Western Pennsylvania Historical Magazine, 71 (1988), 171; A. Hirsch, 'The collision of
     military cultures in seventeenth-century New England', *Journal of American History*,
     74 (1987–8), 1187–212.

44   N. Canny, 'England's New World and the Old, 1480s–1630s', in N. Canny (ed.), *The Oxford
     History of the British Empire*: I, *The Origins of Empire* (Oxford, 1998), pp. 148–69.

Notes to Chapter 1: The Growth of British North America, 1700–38

1   J.A. Sweet, 'Bearing feathers of the eagle: Tomochichi's trip to England', *Georgia Historical
     Quarterly*, 86 (2002), 339–71 and *Negotiating for Georgia. British-Creek Relations in the
     Trustee Era, 1733–1752* (Athens, Georgia, 2005), pp. 48–50.

2   E.J. Graham, *A Maritime History of Scotland, 1650–1790* (East Linton, 2002), pp. 14–18.

3   C.A. Whatley, 'Taking stock: Scotland at the end of the seventeenth century', in T.C. Smout
     (ed.), *Anglo-Scottish Relations from 1603 to 1900* (Oxford, 2005), pp. 122–4.

4   Whatley, *The Scots and the Union* (Edinburgh, 2006), p. 360; J. Price, 'The rise of Glasgow
     in the Chesapeake tobacco trade, 1707–1775', *William and Mary Quarterly*, 3rd ser., 11
     (1954), 179–99.

5   AE. CP. Ang. 451 fol. 481, 455 fol. 5.

6   J.F. Bosher, *Business and Religion in the Age of New France, 1600–1760* (Toronto, 1994).

7   C.A. Brasslaux, 'The image of Louisiana and the failure of voluntary French emigration,
     1683–1731', and G.R. Conrad, 'Immigration force: a French attempt to populate Louisiana,
     1717–20', both in *Proceedings of the Fourth Annual Meeting of the French Colonial Historical
     Society* (1979).

8   J.N. Biraben, 'Le peuplement du Canada français', *Annales de démographie historique* (Paris,
     1966), 104–39 ; J. Dupâquier (ed.), *Histoire de la Population Française*. II: *De la Renaissance
     à 1789* (Paris, 1988), pp. 125–7.

9 P.N. Moogk, 'Reluctant exiles: the problems of colonisation in French North America', *William and Mary Quarterly*, 46 (1989), 463–505.

10 W.A. McDougall, *Freedom Just Around The Corner. A New American History, 1585–1828* (New York, 2004), pp. 120–1.

11 M.S. Wokeck, *Trade in Strangers: The Beginnings of Mass Migration to North America* (University Park, Pennsylvania, 1999).

12 A.B. Benson (ed.), *Peter Kalm's Travels in North America: The English Version of 1770* (New York, 1987).

13 R.H. Balmer, *A Perfect Babel of Confusion: Dutch Religion and English Culture in the Middle Colonies* (Oxford, 1989).

14 Wokeck, 'German and Irish immigration to Colonial Philadelphia', in S.E. Klepp (ed.), *The Demographic History of the Philadelphia Region, 1600–1800* (Philadelphia, 1989), pp. 128–43.

15 A.R. Ekirch, *Bound for America: The Transportation of British Convicts to the Colonies, 1718–1775* (Oxford, 1987); D.M. Hockedy, 'Bound for a New World: emigration of indentured servants via Liverpool to America and the West Indies, 1697–1707', *Transactions of the Historic Society of Lancashire and Cheshire*, 144 (1995), 124–5.

16 D. Richardson, 'Slave exports from West and West-Central Africa, 1700–1810', *Journal of African History*, 30 (1989), 10.

17 J. Coughtry, *The Notorious Triangle: Rhode Island and the African Slave Trade, 1700–1807* (Philadelphia, Pennsylvania, 1981); A. Jones, 'The Rhode Island slave trade: a trading advantage in Africa', *Slavery and Abolition*, 2 (1981), 225–44.

18 P.D. Morgan, *Slave Counterpoint: Black Culture in the Eighteenth-Century Chesapeake and Lowcountry* (Chapel Hill, North Carolina, 1998).

19 W.D. Piersen, *Black Yankees: The Development of an Afro-American Subculture in Eighteenth-Century New England* (Amherst, Massachusetts, 1988).

20 M.L.M. Kay and L.L. Cary, *Slavery in North Carolina, 1748–1775* (Chapel Hill, North Carolina, 1995).

21 D.W. Cohen and J.P. Greene (eds), *Neither Slave Nor Free: The Freedmen of African Descent in the Slave Societies of the New World* (Baltimore, Maryland, 1972).

22 P. Wood, *Black Majority: Negroes in Colonial South Carolina from 1670 through the Stono Rebellion* (New York, 1974).

23 J. Pritchard, *In Search of Empire: The French in the Americas, 1670–1730* (Cambridge, 2003).

24 J.C. Rule, 'Jérôme Phélypeaux, Comte de Pontchartrain, and the establishment of Louisiana', in J.F. McDermott (ed.), *Frenchmen and French Ways in the Mississippi Valley* (Urbana, Illinois, 1969), pp. 179–97.

25 M. Giraud, *A History of Louisiana.* I: *The Reign of Louis XIV, 1688–1715* (Baton Rouge, Louisiana, 1974), pp. 39–41, 45, 214, 218–21, 329, 353, and II: *Years of Transition, 1715–1717* (Baton Rouge, Louisiana, 1993), pp. 107–9, 155–6, 175; J. Higginbotham, *Old Mobile. Fort Louis de la Louisiane, 1702–1711* (Mobile, Alabama, 1977).

26 W.E. Lee, 'Subjects, clients, allies or mercenaries?: the British use of Irish and Indian military power, 1500–1800.' I would like to thank Wayne Lee for giving me a copy of this paper.

27   C.W. Arnade, *The Siege of St Augustine in 1702* (Gainesville, Florida, 1959).

28   J.H. Hann, *Apalachee: the Land between the Rivers* (Gainesville, Florida, 1988), pp. 264–83.

29   R.I. Melvoin, *New England Outpost: War and Society in Colonial Deerfield* (New York, 1989); E. Haefeli and K. Sweeney (eds), *Captive Histories: English, French and Native Narratives of the 1704 Deerfield Raid* (Amherst, Massachusetts, 2006).

30   Dudley to Marlborough, 28 Dec. 1703, 29 Sept. 1706, BL. Add. 61306 fol. 144, 61310 fol. 82.

31   B.T. McCully, 'Catastrophe in the wilderness: new light on the Canada expedition of 1709', *William and Mary Quarterly*, 3rd ser., 11 (1954), 441–6.

32   J.D. Alsop, 'Samuel Vetch's "Canada Survey'd: the formation of a colonial strategy, 1706–1710', *Acadiensis*, 12 (1982), 39–58.

33   J.G. Reid, M. Basque, E. Mancke et al., *The 'Conquest' of Acadia, 1710 : Imperial, Colonial, and Aboriginal Constructions* (Toronto, 2004).

34   T.C. Parramore, 'With Tuscarora Jack on the back path to Bath', *North Carolina Historical Review*, 64 (1987), 115–38.

35   S.J. Oatis, *Colonial Complex: South Carolina's Frontiers in the Era of the Yamasee War, 1680–1730* (Lincoln, Nebraska, 2004).

36   P. Earle, *The Pirate Wars* (London, 2003).

37   R.W. Van Alstyne, *The Rising American Empire* (Oxford, 1960), pp. 13–14.

38   J.S. McLennan, *Louisbourg from its Foundation to its Fall, 1713–1758* (Sydney, 1957); F.J. Thorpe, *Remparts Lointains: La politique française des travaux publics à Terre Neuve et à l'île Royale, 1695–1758* (Ottawa, 1980).

39   Louis XV to M de St Ovide, 10 May 1735, Paris, Archives Nationales, Archives de la Marine, B 63.

40   L.J. Burpee (ed.), *Journals and Letters of Pierre Gaultier de Varennes de la Vérendrye and his Sons* (Toronto, 1927).

41   *London Evening Post*, 8 Jan. (OS), 5 Feb. (OS) 1737; Chammorel, French Chargé des Affaires, to Dubois, French Foreign Minister, 21 Jan. 1723, AE. CP. Ang. 344.

42   Horatio Walpole, envoy in Paris, to Thomas, Duke of Newcastle, Secretary of State for the Southern Department, 10 July 1728, James, Earl Waldegrave, envoy in Paris, to Chauvelin, French Foreign Minister, 13 June, Waldegrave to Newcastle, 27 June 1732, BL. Add. 32756, 32777 fols 283–6.

43   K. Morrison, 'Sebastien Rasle and Norridgewock, 1724', *Maine Historical Quarterly*, 14 (1974), 76–97; C.G. Calloway, 'Gray Lock's war', *Vermont History*, 55 (1987), 212–27.

44   M.S. Arnold, *Colonial Arkansas, 1686–1804* (Fayetteville, Arkansas, 1991), pp. 99–106.

45   M. Giraud, *A History of French Louisiana. V. The Company of the Indies, 1723–1731* (Baton Rouge, Louisiana, 1991), pp. 404, 419.

46   J. Price, 'The economic growth of the Chesapeake and the European market, 1697–1775', *Journal of Economic History*, 24 (1964), 496–511.

47   C.E. Clark, *The Public Prints: The Newspaper in Anglo-American Culture* (Oxford, 1994).

48   E. Wolf II, *The Book Culture of a Colonial American City. Philadelphia Books, Bookmen, and Booksellers* (Oxford, 1988).

49   R.R. Johnson, *Adjustment to Empire: The New England Colonies, 1675–1715* (New Brunswick, New Jersey, 1981).

50 BL. Stowe Mss 246 fol. 214.

51 Dudley to Lord Chancellor Cowper, Hertford, County Record Office, Panshanger papers, D/EP F144.

52 A.G. Olson, *Anglo-American Politics, 1660–1775: The Relationship Between Parties in England and Colonial America* (Oxford, 1973).

53 R.L. Sickinger, 'Regulation or ruination: Parliament's consistent pattern of mercantilist regulation of the English textile trade, 1660–1800', *Parliamentary History*, 19 (2000), 211–32.

54 M.E. Newell, *From Dependency to Independence: Economic Revolution in Colonial New England* (Ithaca, New York, 1988).

55 N. Zahedieh, 'London and the colonial consumer in the late seventeenth century', *Economic History Review*, 47 (1994), 239–61; B. Arneil, 'Trade, plantation, and property: John Locke and the economic defence of colonialism', *Journal of the History of Ideas*, 55 (1994), 591–609; S.D. Smith, 'The market for manufactures in the thirteen continental colonies, 1698–1776', *Economic History Review*, 51 (1998), 676–708.

56 Board of Trade to George I, 24 July (OS) 1724, London, National Archives (hereafter NA). SP. 35/50 fols 206–12.

57 J. Price, *Capital and Credit in British Overseas Trade: The View from the Chesapeake, 1700–1776* (Cambridge, Massachusetts, 1980).

58 Board of Trade to Thomas, Duke of Newcastle, 9 Feb. (OS) 1728, C(H) Mss. 86/12/2.

59 J. Horn, *Adapting to a New World. English Society in the Seventeenth-Century Chesapeake* (Chapel Hill, North Carolina, 1994); A. Kulikoff, *Tobacco and Slaves: The Development of Southern Cultures in the Chesapeake, 1680–1800* (Chapel Hill, North Carolina, 1986).

60 T.H. Breen, 'An empire of goods: the anglicization of colonial America, 1690–1776', *Journal of British Studies*, 25 (1986), 467–99; R.L. Bushman, *The Refinement of America: Persons, Houses, Cities* (New York, 1992).

61 Dudley to Marlborough, 28 Dec. 1703, BL. Add. 61306 fol. 144.

62 I.R. Christie, *Crisis of Empire. Great Britain and the American Colonies, 1754–1783* (New York, 1966), pp. 20–1.

63 J.P. Greene, *The Quest for Power: The Lower Houses of Assembly in the Southern Royal Colonies, 1689–1776* (Chapel Hill, North Carolina, 1963).

64 J.R. Pole, 'Historians and the problem of early American democracy', *American Historical Review*, 67 (1962), 626–46.

65 P.U. Bonomi, *A Factious People: Politics and Society in Colonial New York* (New York, 1971) and *Under the Cope of Heaven: Religion, Society, and Politics in Colonial America* (Oxford, 1986).

66 R. Middleton, *Colonial America. A History, 1565–1776* (3rd edn, Oxford, 2002), p. 363.

67 CUL. C(H) Mss. 84/75.

68 I.K. Steele, *The English Atlantic, 1675–1740: An Exploration of Communication and Community* (New York, 1986).

69 A.L. Hatfield, 'Mariners, merchants, and colonists in seventeenth-century English America', in Mancke and Shammas (eds), *The Creation of the British Atlantic World* (Baltimore, Maryland, 2005), p. 159.

Notes to Chapter 2: *Imperial Rivalries, 1739–53*

1 J.T. Lanning, *The Diplomatic History of Georgia: A Study of the Epoch of Jenkins' Ear* (Chapel Hill, North Carolina, 1936).

2 I.K. Steele, *Warpaths. Invasions of North America* (Oxford, 1994), p. 174.

3 L.E. Ivers, *British Drums on the Southern Frontier: the Military Colonization of Georgia* (Chapel Hill, North Carolina, 1974); P. Spalding, *Oglethorpe in America* (Chicago, Illinois, 1977).

4 J.A. Sweet, *Negotiating for Georgia: British-Creek Relations in the Trustee Era, 1733–1752* (Athens, Georgia, 2005), p. 144.

5 J.J. Tepaske, *The Governorship of Spanish Florida, 1700–1765* (Durham, North Carolina, 1964).

6 Stewart to John, 2nd Earl of Stair, 10 Sept. 1741, New Haven, Connecticut, Beinecke Library, Osborn Shelves, Stair Letters, no. 70.

7 W. Barr and G. Williams (eds), *Voyages to Hudson Bay in Search of a North-West Passage, 1741–1747* (London, 1995).

8 K.E. Braund, *Deerskins and Duffels: The Creek Indian Trade with Anglo-America, 1685–1815* (Lincoln, Nebraska, 1993); C.G. Calloway, *New Worlds for All: Indians, Europeans, and the Remaking of Early America* (Baltimore, Maryland, 1997).

9 J. Gwyn, *An Admiral for America. Sir Peter Warren, Vice Admiral of the Red, 1703–1752* (Gainesville, Florida, 2004), p. 111.

10 M. Mimmler, *Der Einfluss Interessen in Nordamerika auf die Strategie und Diplomatie Grossbritanniens während des 18. Jahrhunderts* (Hildesheim, 1983). A failure to note such work is a serious flaw with M. Peters, 'Early Hanoverian consciousness: Empire or Europe?' *English Historical Review*, 122 (2007), 632–68.

11 D. Milobar, 'Aboriginal peoples and the British press, 1720–1763', in S. Taylor, R. Connors and C. Jones (eds), *Hanoverian Britain and Empire* (Woodbridge, 1998), p. 68.

12 Paris, Archives Nationales, Archives de la Marine, B^7 359.

13 J.M. Sosin, 'Louisbourg and the peace of Aix-la-Chapelle, 1748', *William and Mary Quarterly*, 3rd ser., 14 (1957), 516–35.

14 R.L. Merritt, *Symbols of American Community, 1735–1775* (New Haven, Connecticut, 1966).

15 D. Armitage, *The Ideological Origins of the British Empire* (Cambridge, 2000); E.H. Gould, 'Entangled histories, entangled worlds: the English-speaking Atlantic as a Spanish periphery', *American Historical Review* (2007), 770–1.

16 R. Strong, *Anglicanism and the British Empire, c. 1700–1850* (Oxford, 2007), p. 71.

17 Vernon to Sir Francis Dashwood, 29 July (OS) 1749, Oxford, Bodleian Library, MS D.D.Dashwood B11/12/6.

18 *Calendar of State Papers Colonial Series 1728–9*, p. 66; Board of Trade memorandum, 20 Mar. (OS) 1728, CUL. C(H) Mss. 84/17; Edward Finch, envoy in Stockholm, to William, Earl of Harrington, Secretary of State for the Northern Department, NA. SP. 95/84 fol. 146.

19 K. Hautala, *European and American Tar in the English Market during the Eighteenth Century and Early Nineteenth Century* (Helsinki, 1963).

20 C. Swanson, *Predators and Prizes: American Privateering and Imperial Warfare, 1739–1748* (Columbia, South Carolina, 1991).

21 L. Neal, *The Rise of Financial Capitalism: International Capital Markets in the Age of Reason* (Cambridge, 1990).

22 Holdernesse to Robert Keith, envoy in Vienna, 21 June 1756, NA. SP. 80/197 fol. 179.

23 *Reflections*, pp. 17–18.

24 Joseph to Philip Yorke, 19 Aug. 1750, BL. Add. 35363 fol. 277.

25 Puysieulx to Marquis de Mirepoix, envoy in London, 12 Dec. 1750, Paris, Ministère des Relations Extérieures, Correspondance Politique Angleterre (hereafter CP.Ang.) AE. CP. Ang. 429 fol. 315.

26 AE. CP. Ang. 429 fol. 15.

27 W. Eccles, 'The fur trade and eighteenth-century Imperialism', *William and Mary Quarterly*, 3rd ser., 40 (1983), 341–62.

28 A. Reese, *Europäische Hegemonie und France d'outre mer. Koloniale Fragen in der französischen Aussenpolitik, 1700–1763* (Stuttgart, 1988); C.J. Balesi, *The Time of the French in the Heart of North America, 1673–1818* (Chicago, 1991).

29 Walpole to Dinwiddie, 15 July 1754, San Marino, California, Huntington Library, HM. 9406.

30 L.W. Labaree (ed.), *The Papers of Benjamin Franklin* (New Haven, Connecticut, 1959–), IV, 227–34.

31 D.W. Meinig, *The Shaping of America. A Geographical Perspective on 500 Years of History*. I. *Atlantic America, 1492–1800* (New Haven, Connecticut, 1986), p. 154.

32 M.L.M. Kay and L.L. Cary, *Slavery in North Carolina, 1748–1775* (Chapel Hill, North Carolina, 1995), pp. 17–19.

33 J.M. Johnson, *Militiamen, Rangers, and Redcoats. The Military in Georgia, 1754–1776* (Macon, Georgia, 1992), p. 75.

34 D.W. Galenson, *White Servitude in Colonial America: An Economic Analysis* (Cambridge, 1981).

35 P. Griffin, *The People with No Name: Ireland's Ulster Scots, America's Scots Irish, and the Creation of a British Atlantic World, 1689–1764* (Princeton, New Jersey, 2001).

36 W. Holton, *Forced Founders: Indians, Debtors, Slaves, and the Making of the American Revolution in Virginia* (Chapel Hill, North Carolina, 1999).

37 P. Thompson, *Rum Punch and Revolution: Taverngoing and Public Life in Eighteenth-Century Philadelphia* (Philadelphia, Pennsylvania, 1999).

38 W.A. McDougall, *Freedom Just Around the Corner. A New American History, 1585–1828* (New York, 2004), pp. 175–85.

39 R. White, *The Middle Ground: Indians, Empires and Republics in the Great Lakes Region, 1650–1815* (Cambridge, 1991); E. Hinderaker, *Elusive Empires: Constructing Colonialism in the Ohio Valley, 1673–1800* (Cambridge, 1997); F. Cooper and A.L. Stoler, *Tensions of Empire: Colonial Cultures in a Bourgeois World* (Berkeley, California, 1997); K. DuVal, *The Native Ground: Indians and Colonists in the Heart of the Continent* (Philadelphia, Pennsylvania, 2006).

40 M. Mullin, *Africa in America: Slave Acculturation and Resistance in the American South and the British Caribbean, 1736–1831* (Urbana, Illinois, 1994).

41 J.R. Hertzler, 'Slavery in the yearly sermons before the Georgia Trustees', *Georgia Historical Quarterly*, 59 (1975), 118–26.

42 M.A. Stewart, *'What Nature Suffers to Groe': Life, Labor, and Landscape on the Georgia Coast, 1680–1920* (Athens, Georgia, 1996).

43   J.M. Murrin, '1776: the countercyclical revolution', in M.A. Morrison and M. Zook (eds), *Revolutionary Currents. Nation Building in the Transatlantic World* (Lanham, Maryland, 2004), p. 70.

Notes to Chapter 3: The Defeat of France, 1754–60

1   W.W. Abbot, 'George Washington, the West, and the Union', *Indiana Magazine of History*, 84 (1988), 3–14.
2   R. Marton, 'Confrontation at the Monongahela: climax of the French drive into the Upper Ohio region', *Pennsylvania History*, 37 (1970), 133–50.
3   A.G. Olson, 'The British Government and Colonial Union, 1754', *William and Mary Quarterly*, 3rd ser., 27 (1960), 22–34.
4   T.R. Clayton, 'The Duke of Newcastle, the Earl of Halifax, and the American origins of the Seven Years' War', *Historical Journal*, 24 (1981), 590.
5   BL. Add. 32736 fol. 515.
6   Newcastle to Horatio Walpole, 14 May, 29 June, Cabinet minute, 26 June 1754, BL. Add. 32735 fols 269, 597, 33029 fol. 124.
7   John Thomlinson, London merchant and colonial agent for New Hampshire, to John, Earl Granville, Lord President of the Council, 13 Dec. 1756, in S. Pargellis (ed.), *Military Affairs in North America, 1748–1765* (New York, 1936), pp. 257–8; Anon., *A Letter from a Merchant* (London, 1757), p. 25.
8   Rouillé to Boutel, French agent in charge in Mirepoix's absence, AE. CP. Ang. 437 fols 296–7.
9   Rouillé to Mirepoix, 3 Feb. 1755, AE. CP. Ang. 438 fol. 80.
10 D.S. Graham, 'The planning of the Beauséjour operation and the approaches to war in 1755', *New England Quarterly*, 41 (1968), 551–66.
11 C.M. Hand, *The Siege of Fort Beauséjour, 1755* (Fredericton, 2004).
12 G. Plank, *An Unsettled Conquest: The British Campaign against the Peoples of Acadia* (Philadelphia, Pennsylvania, 2004).
13 T. Keppel, *The Life of Augustus, Viscount Keppel* (2 vols, London, 1842) I, pp. 209–21; Sackville to Sir Robert Wilmot, 6 Aug. 1755, Derby, Public Library, Catton Collection WH 3448; Delancey to Sir Thomas Robinson, Secretary of State, 7 Aug. 1755, BL. Add. 32858 fol. 25; M.C. Ward, '"The European Method of Warring is not practiced here": The failure of British military policy in the Ohio Valley, 1755–1759', *War in History*, 4 (1997), 247–63.
14 O. Rochereau, 'Louisbourg, 1713–1758, ou l'échec d'un grand projet', *Revue Historique des Armées*, 222 (2001), 70.
15 Huntington Library, San Marino, California, Loudoun papers, nos 2765A, 2764A.
16 I.K. Steele, *Betrayals. Fort William Henry and the 'Massacre'* (New York, 1990).
17 K.J. Banks, *Chasing Empire Across the Sea. Communications and the State in the French Atlantic, 1713–1763* (Montreal, 2002), pp. 200–2.
18 G.S. Kimball (ed.), *Correspondence of William Pitt when Secretary of State with Colonial Governors and Military and Naval Commissioners in America* (2 vols, London, 1906), I, 143.
19 Pitt to Abercromby, 30 Dec. 1757, Kimball, I, 143–9.
20 BL. Add. 45662 fols 6–7.

21   John Calcraft to Lieutenant Colonel Hale, 27 Aug. 1758, BL. Add. 17494 fol. 17.

22   M. Ward, *Breaking the Backcountry. The Seven Years' War in Virginia and Pennsylvania, 1754–1763* (Pittsburgh, 2003).

23   Richard Rush to John Adams, 25 Sept. 1813, Philadelphia, Historical Society of Pennsylvania, AM. 1352.

24   Pargellis, *Military Affairs in North America, 1748–1765*, pp. xviii–xxi.

25   BL. Add. 45662 fols 33–4.

26   Journal, possibly by Henry Fletcher, Providence, Rhode Island, John Carter Brown Library, Codex Eng. 41.

27   BL. Add. 45662 fol. 40.

28   M.C. Ward, *The Battle for Quebec, 1759* (Stroud, 2005), p. 229; BL. Add. 45662 fol. 41.

29   S. Brumwell, *Redcoats: The British Soldier and War in the Americas, 1755–1763* (Cambridge, 2002); R. Middleton, *Amherst and the Conquest of Canada* (London, 2003).

30   BL. Add. 45662 fol. 43.

31   W.J. Eccles, 'The role of the American colonies in eighteenth-century French foreign policy', in *Atti del I Congresso Internazionale di Storia Americana* (Genoa, 1978), pp. 165, 171.

32   G. Chet, *Conquering the American Wilderness. The Triumph of European Warfare in the Colonial Northeast* (Amherst, Massachusetts, 2003), p. 141.

33   George Ross to Brigadier John Forbes, 11 Mar. 1758, Edinburgh, Scottish Record Office, GD 45/2/20/10.

34   I have benefited from discussing this topic with Jeremy Gregory.

35   D.C. Jones, 'A Glorious Work in the World'. *Welsh Methodism and the International Evangelical Revival, 1735–50* (Cardiff, 2004).

36   F. Lambert, *Pedlar in Divinity: George Whitefield and the Transatlantic Revivals, 1737–1770* (Princeton, New Jersey, 1994).

37   R.W. Pointer, *Protestant Pluralism and the New York Experience: A Study of Eighteenth-Century Religious Diversity* (Bloomington, Indiana, 1988); S. Schwartz, 'A Mixed Multitude': *The Struggle for Toleration in Colonial Pennsylvania* (New York, 1988).

38   J.P. Greene, *Pursuits of Happiness. The Social Development of Early Modern British Colonies and the Formation of American Culture* (Chapel Hill, North Carolina, 1988).

39   T.P. Thornton, *Cultivating Gentlemen: The Meaning of Country Life Among the Boston Elite, 1785–1860* (New Haven, Connecticut, 1989).

40   W. Craven, *Colonial American Portraiture* (Cambridge, 1987).

41   S. Brumwell, *Paths of Glory. The Life and Death of General James Wolfe* (London, 2006), pp. 295–6.

42   F. Anderson, *Crucible of War: The Seven Years' War and the Fate of Empire in British North America, 1754–1766* (New York, 2000).

43   N.L. York, *Turning the World Upside Down. The War of American Independence and the Problem of Empire* (Westport, Connecticut, 2003), p. 41.

44   Maggs Bros Ltd, *Autograph Letters and Historical Documents*, catalogue no. 1410 (London, 2007), no. 73.

Notes to Chapter 4: Gathering Crisis, 1760–74

1   M.A Noll, 'British and French North America to 1765', in S.J. Brown and T. Tackett (eds), *The Cambridge History of Christianity. VII. Enlightenment, Reawakening and Revolution, 1660–1815* (Cambridge, 2006), p. 403.

2   G.M. Day, 'Rogers' raid in Indian tradition', *Historical New Hampshire*, 17 (1962), 3–17; C.G. Calloway, *The Western Abenakis of Vermont, 1600–1800* (Norman, Oklahoma, 1990), pp. 174–80.

3   Leland to Charles Hotham, 28 Apr. 1760, Hull, University Library, DDHo/4/11(60).

4   J. Grenier, *The First Way of War. American War Making on the Frontier* (New York, 2005), p. 143.

5   R.L. Meriwether, *The Expansion of South Carolina, 1729–1765* (Kingsport, Tennessee, 1940), pp. 213–40; D.H. Corkran, *The Cherokee Frontier: Conflict and Survival, 1740–1762* (Norman, Oklahoma, 1962); T. Hatley, *The Dividing Paths: Cherokees and South Carolinians through the Era of Revolution* (New York, 1993); J. Oliphant, *Peace and War on the Anglo-Cherokee Frontier, 1756–63* (Baton Rouge, Louisiana, 2001).

6   Bull to General Amherst, 15 Apr. 1761, NA. CO. 51/61 fol. 277.

7   M. Ward, *Breaking the Backcountry: The Seven Years' War in Virginia and Pennsylvania, 1754–1765* (Pittsburgh, Pennsylvania, 2003), p. 253.

8   D.H. Kent and B. Knollenberg, 'Communications', and Knollenberg, 'General Amherst and germ warfare', *Mississippi Valley Historical Review*, 41 (1954–5), 454–89, 762–3.

9   Edward Sedgwick, Under Secretary, to Edward Weston, former Under Secretary, 17 Jan 1765, BL. Add. 57928, fols 23–4.

10 G.E. Dowd, *War under Heaven: Pontiac, the Indian Nations, and the British Empire* (Baltimore, Maryland, 2002).

11 P.M. Malone, *The Skulking Way of War. Technology and Tactics among the New England Indians* (Baltimore, 1993), p. 128.

12 G. Plank, *An Unsettled Conquest. The British Campaign Against the Peoples of Acadia* (Philadelphia, Pennsylvania, 2001), p. 163.

13 A. Smith, 'Lectures on Jurisprudence 1762–63', note in *An Inquiry into the Nature and Causes of the Wealth of Nations* (1776; Oxford, 1976), p. 692, fn. 9.

14 R. Middleton, *Pontiac's War* (New York, 2007), p. 201.

15 L. Vorsey, *The Indian Boundary in the Southern Colonies, 1763–1775* (Chapel Hill, North Carolina, 1966), pp. 162–4.

16 M.N. McConnell, *Army and Empire. British Soldiers on the American Frontier, 1758–1775* (Lincoln, Nebraska, 2004), p. 147.

17 D.H. Usner, *Indians, Settlers and Slaves in a Frontier Exchange Economy. The Lower Mississippi Valley before 1783* (Chapel Hill, North Carolina, 1992).

18 R.H. Brown, 'The De Brahm Charts of the Atlantic Ocean, 1772–1776', *Geographical Review*, 28 (1938), pp. 124–32.

19 R.R. Rea, 'Urban problems and responses in British Pensacola', *Gulf Coast Historical Review*, 3 (1987), 56.

20 J.H. Franklin and L. Schweninger, *Runaway Slaves: Rebels on the Plantation* (New York, 1999).

21 J.E. Chaplin, *An Anxious Pursuit. Agricultural Innovation and Modernity in the Lower South, 1730–1815* (Chapel Hill, North Carolina, 1993).

22 D. Armitage and M.J. Braddick (eds), *The British Atlantic World, 1500–1800* (Basingstoke, 2002), p. 247; E. Mancke and C. Shammas (eds), *The Creation of the British Atlantic World* (Baltimore, Maryland, 2005).

23 A.R. Ekirch, 'The North Carolina regulators on liberty and corruption, 1766–1771', *Perspectives in American History*, 6 (1977–8), 199–256; M. Kars, *Breaking Loose Together: The Regulator Rebellion in Pre-Revolutionary North Carolina* (Chapel Hill, North Carolina, 2002).

24 A.H. Tillson, 'The localist roots of backcountry loyalism: an examination of popular political culture in Virginia's New River Valley', *Journal of Southern History*, 54 (1988), 387.

25 J. Gommans, *Mughal Warfare: Imperial Frontiers and Highroads to Empire, 1500–1700* (London, 2002).

26 D.W. Conroy, *The Public House: Drink and the Revolution of Authority in Colonial Massachusetts* (Chapel Hill, North Carolina, 1995).

27 Yorke to Edward Weston, 25 Oct. 1763, BL. Add. 58213 fol. 308.

28 J.C.D. Clark, *The Language of Liberty, 1660–1832: Political Discourse and Social Dynamics in the Anglo-American World* (Cambridge, 1994); P.M. Doll, *Revolution, Religion, and National Identity: Imperial Anglicanism in British North America, 1745–1795* (Madison, New Jersey, 2000).

29 W.C. Ford (ed.), *Journals of the Continental Congress, 1774–1789*, I (Washington, 1904), p. 76.

30 D.C. Lord and R.M. Calhoon, 'The removal of the Massachusetts general court from Boston, 1769–1772', *Journal of American History*, 55 (1969), 735–55; B. Bailyn, *The Ordeal of Thomas Hutchinson* (Cambridge, Massachusetts, 1974).

31 D.R. Coquillette and N.L. York (eds), *Portrait of a Patriot. The Major Political and Legal Papers of Josiah Quincy Junior* (Boston, Massachusetts, 2005), p. 64.

32 G. Newman, *The Rise of English Nationalism: A Cultural History, 1740–1830* (London, 1987).

33 J.M. Price, 'Tobacco use and tobacco taxation. A battle of interests in Early Modern Europe', in J. Goodman, P.E. Lovejoy and A. Sherratt (eds), *Consuming Habits. Global and Historical Perspectives on How Cultures Define Drugs* (2nd edn, Abingdon, 2007), p. 167.

34 T.H. Breen, *Tobacco Culture: The Mentality of the Great Tidewater Planters on the Eve of the Revolution* (Princeton, New Jersey, 1985); T.R. Thompson, 'Personal indebtedness and the American revolution in Maryland', *Maryland Historical Magazine*, 73 (1978), 13–29; B.A. Ragsdale, 'George Washington, the British tobacco trade, and economic opportunity in pre-revolutionary Virginia', *Virginia Magazine of History and Biography*, 97 (1989), 133–62.

35 J. Komlos, *Nutrition and Economic Development in the Eighteenth-Century Habsburg Monarchy: An Anthropometric History* (Princeton, 1989).

36 K.L. Sokoloff and G.C. Villaflor, 'The early achievement of modern stature in America', *Social Science History*, 6 (1982), 453–81.

37 J.P. Greene, *Pursuits of Happiness: The Social Development of Early Modern British Colonies*

and the Formation of American Culture (Chapel Hill, North Carolina, 1988) and *The Intellectual Construction of America. Exceptionalism and Identity from 1492 to 1800* (Chapel Hill, North Carolina, 1993); K.O. Kupperman (ed.), *America in European Consciousness, 1493–1750* (Chapel Hill, North Carolina, 1995).

38 F. Jennings, *The Creation of America. Through Revolution to Empire* (Cambridge, 2000), p. 314.

39 P.J. Marshall, 'The Thirteen Colonies in the Seven Years' War. The view from London' in J. Flavell and S. Conway (eds), *Britain and America Go to War. The Impact of War and Warfare in Anglo-America, 1754–1815* (Gainesville, Florida, 2004), pp. 85–8.

40 Bedford to Bute, 16 Nov. 1762, Mount Stuart, papers of John, 3rd Earl of Bute, manuscripts, from Cardiff Public Library, 5/162.

41 J. Bullion, 'The ten thousand in America. More light on the decision on the American army, 1762–1763', *William and Mary Quarterly*, 3rd ser., 43 (1986), 646–57, esp. pp. 651–2, and 'Security and economy: the Bute administration's plans for the American army and revenue, 1762–1763', ibid., 45 (1988), 499–509, esp. 507.

42 Grenville to Waller, 29 Sept. 1763, Huntington Library, San Marino, California, Stowe papers, 7 vol. 1; J. Bullion, *A Great and Necessary Measure: George Grenville and the Genesis of the Stamp Act, 1763–1765* (Columbia, Missouri, 1982).

43 J.J. McCusker and R.R. Menard, *The Economy of British America, 1607–1789* (Chapel Hill, North Carolina, 1991).

44 *The Atlas of Pennsylvania* (Philadelphia, Pennsylvania, 1989), p. 81.

45 C.M. Carver, *American Regional Dialects: A Word Geography* (Ann Arbor, Michigan, 1987).

46 B.S. Schlenther, 'Colonial America's "un-royal society": organized Enlightenment as a handmaid to revolution', *British Journal for Eighteenth-Century Studies*, 11 (1988), 22–3.

47 B. Daniels, 'Economic development in colonial and revolutionary Connecticut: an overview', *William and Mary Quarterly*, 3rd ser., 37 (1980), 429–50; W.B. Rothenberg, 'The market and Massachusetts farmers, 1750–1855', *Journal of Economic History*, 41 (1981), 283–314.

48 P.D.G. Thomas, *George III. King and Politicians, 1760–1770* (Manchester, 2002), p. 105.

49 Sedgwick to Weston, 14 Feb. 1765, BL. Add. 57928 fol. 49.

50 General Henry Conway to Charles, 2nd Marquess of Rockingham, 10 Oct., Governor Thomas Boone of New York to Rockingham, 8 Nov. 1765, Sheffield, Archives, Wentworth Woodhouse papers, R1–502, 522.

51 Newcastle to Rockingham, 22 Oct. 1765, WW. R1–511.

52 Sedgwick to Weston, 24 Dec. 1765, BL. Add. 57928 fol. 180.

53 P. Langford, *The First Rockingham Administration, 1765–1766* (Oxford, 1973), pp. 108–98; P.D.G. Thomas, *British Politics and the Stamp Act Crisis. The First Phase of the American Revolution, 1763–1767* (Oxford, 1975), pp. 154–252.

54 Sedgwick to Weston, 15 June 1767, BL. Add. 57928 fol. 224.

55 A. Goodwin, 'Wood's halfpence', *English Historical Review*, 51 (1936), 647–74.

56 L.B. Namier and J. Brooke, *Charles Townshend* (London, 1964), pp. 158–72; Thomas, *Stamp Act Crisis*, pp. 287–95, and *The Townshend Duties Crisis. The Second Phase of the American Revolution, 1767–1773* (Oxford, 1987), pp. 18–36.

57   A.G. Olson, *Making the Empire Work: London and American Interest Groups, 1690–1790* (Cambridge, Massachusetts, 1992).

58   S.F. Duff, 'The case against the King: the *Virginia Gazette* indict George III', *William and Mary Quarterly*, 3rd ser., 6 (1949), 383–97; P. Maier, 'John Wilkes and American disillusionment with Britain', ibid., 20 (1963), 373–95.

59   Gage to Viscount Barrington, 2 Sept. 1772, 18 July 1774, BL. Add. 73550.

60   A.M. Schlesinger, *Prelude to Independence. The Newspaper War on Britain, 1764–1776* (New York, 1958), p. 311.

61   J.E. Crowley, *The Invention of Comfort: Sensibilities and Design in Early Modern Britain and Early America* (Baltimore, Maryland, 2000).

62   H.V. Bowen, *Revenue and Reform. The Indian Problem in British Politics, 1757–1773* (Cambridge, 1991).

63   Thomas, *The Townshend Duties Crisis.*

64   P.J. Marshall, *The Making and Unmaking of Empires: Britain, India, and America, c. 1750–1783* (Oxford, 2005), e.g. p. 378.

65   G.B. Nash, *The Urban Crucible: Social Change, Political Consciousness, and the Origins of the American Revolution* (Cambridge, Massachusetts, 1979); B.G. Smith, 'The material lives of laboring Philadelphians, 1750–1800', *William and Mary Quarterly*, 3rd ser., 38 (1981), 163–202.

66   B. McConville, *The King's Three Faces. The Rise and Fall of Royal America, 1688–1776* (Chapel Hill, North Carolina), p. 206.

67   NA. SP. 78/291 fols 184–5.

68   Porter to Weston, 12 Aug. 1768, BL. Add. 57928.

69   D. Ammermann, *In the Common Cause: American Response to the Coercive Acts of 1774* (Charlottesville, Virginia, 1974).

70   G.S. Wood, 'The American Revolution', in M. Goldie and R. Wokler (eds), *The Cambridge History of Eighteenth Century Political Thought* (Cambridge, 2006), p. 613.

71   P. Lawson, *The Imperial Challenge: Quebec and Britain in the Age of the American Revolution* (Montréal, 1989).

72   T. Bickham, *Savages within the Empire. Representations of American Indians in Eighteenth-Century Britain* (Oxford, 2005), p. 167.

73   M. Egnal, *A Mighty Empire: the Origins of the American Revolution* (Ithaca, New York, 1988).

74   B. Baack, 'British versus American interests in land and the War of American Independence', *Journal of European Economic History*, 33 (2004), 533–7.

75   C. Mulford (ed.), *John Leacock's 'The First Book of the American Chronicles of the Times, 1774–1775'* (Newark, Delaware, 1987).

76   R. Bloch, *Visionary Republic: Millenial Themes in American Thought, 1756–1800* (Cambridge, 1985).

77   B. Bailyn, *Voyagers to the West: A Passage in the Peopling of America on the Eve of the Revolution* (New York, 1986).

78   *The Diplomatic Correspondence of the United States* II (1889), pp. 11–13, 31–3.

79   F.P. Lock, *Edmund Burke.* I, *1730–1784* (Oxford, 1998), pp. 349–97.

80   R.R. Rea, 'Anglo-American parliamentary reporting: a case study in historical bibliography', *Bibliographical Society of America, Papers*, 49 (1955), 224–8; L.D. Campbell (ed.), *Jonathan Williams and William Pitt: A Letter of January 21, 1775* (Bloomington, 1949).

81 A.G. Olson, 'Eighteenth-century colonial legislatures and their constituents', *Journal of American History*, 79 (1992), 543–67; C.A. Desan, 'The constitutional commitment to legislative Adjudication in the early American tradition', *Harvard Law Review*, 111 (1998), 1381–503.

82 M. Jensen (ed.), *Tracts of the American Revolution* (2nd edn, Indianapolis, Indiana, 2003), pp. 274–5.

83 R.A. Ryerson, 'John Adams, Republican Monarchist', in E.H. Gould and P.S. Onuf (eds), *Empire and Nation. The Atlantic Revolution in the Atlantic World* (Baltimore, Maryland, 2005), pp. 76–7.

84 J.G.A. Pocock, 'Empire, State and Confederation: the War of American Independence as a crisis in multiple monarchy', in J. Robertson (ed.), *A Union for Empire; Political Thought and the Union of 1707* (Cambridge, 1995), pp. 318–48.

85 N. York, 'Federalism and the failure of imperial reform, 1774–1775', *History*, 86 (2001), 155–79.

86 J.E. Bradley, *Popular Politics and the American Revolution in England: Petitions, the Crown and Public Opinion* (Macon, Georgia, 1986).

87 Lindsey to William Turner, 26 Jan. 1775, in G.M. Ditchfield (ed.), *The Letters of Theophilus Lindsey: I, 1747–1788* (Woodbridge, 2007), p. 206.

88 W.S. Taylor and J.H. Pringle (eds), *The Correspondence of William Pitt, Earl of Chatham* (4 vols, London, 1838–40); *The Diplomatic Correspondence of the United States*, II, 355; I.R. Christie, 'The Earl of Chatham and American taxation, 1774–5', *The Eighteenth Century*, 20 (1979), 258–9.

89 F. Anderson and A. Cayton, *The Dominion of War. Empire and Liberty in North America, 1500–2000* (London, 2005), p. 158.

Notes to Chapter 5: Civil War, 1775–8

1 After writing this, I noted the similar cover of Jimmy Carter's novel *The Hornet's Nest* (New York, 2003).

2 C. Royster, *A Revolutionary People at War. The Continental Army and American Character, 1775–1783* (Chapel Hill, North Carolina, 1996), p. 327.

3 J.E. Bradley, *Popular Politics and the American Revolution in England. Petitions, the Crown, and Public Opinion* (Macon, Georgia, 1986).

4 J. Sainsbury, *Disaffected Patriots: London Supporters of Revolutionary America, 1769–1782* (Kingston, Ontario, 1987).

5 George to William, 2nd Earl of Dartmouth, 10 June 1775, Historical Manuscripts Commission, *Dartmouth Manuscripts, Supplementary*, p. 502.

6 J. Fleigelman, *Prodigals and Pilgrims: The American Revolution against Patriarchal Authority, 1750–1800* (Cambridge, 1982).

7 *Parliamentary Register*, III, 42–3.

8 M. Barone, *Our First Revolution. The Remarkable British Upheaval That Inspired America's Founding Fathers* (New York, 2007).

9 A. Ortiz, *Eighteenth-Century Reforms in the Caribbean. Miguel de Muesas, Governor of Puerto Rico, 1769–76* (Toronto, 1983).

10 M.P. McKinley, *Pre-Revolutionary Caracas: Politics, Economy and Society 1777–1811* (Cambridge, 1985).

11 J.R. Fisher, A.J. Kuethe and A. McFarlane (eds), *Reform and Insurrection in Bourbon New Granada and Peru* (Baton Rouge, Louisiana, 1990).

12 A.C. Metcalf, *Family and Frontier in Colonial Brazil. Santa de Parnaiba 1580–1822* (Berkeley, California, 1992).

13 A.S. Marks, 'The statue of King George III in New York and the iconology of regicide', *The American Art Journal*, 13 (1981), 61–82.

14 N.L. York, *Turning the World Upside Down. The War of American Independence and the Problem of Empire* (Westport, Connecticut, 2003), p. 89.

15 J.G. Marston, *King and Congress. The Transfer of Political Legitimacy, 1774–1776* (Princeton, New Jersey, 1987).

16 P. Langford, *A Polite and Commercial People: England, 1727–1783* (Oxford, 1989).

17 J. Black, *Eighteenth-Century Britain, 1688–1783* (2nd edn, Basingstoke, 2008).

18 S.G. Fisher, 'The twenty-eight charges against the King in the Declaration of Independence', *Pennsylvania Magazine of History and Biography*, 31 (1907), 257–303; W.L. Hedges, 'Telling off the King: Jefferson's summary view as American fantasy', *Early American Literature*, 22 (1987), 166–74; S.E. Lucas, 'The stylistic artistry of the Declaration of Independence', *US National Archives and Records Administration*, 30 Jan. 2005, www.archives. gov.

19 T. Hutchinson, *Strictures upon the Declaration of the Congress at Philadelphia* (London, 1776), p. 16.

20 A.J. O'Shaughnessy, '"If others will not be active, I must drive." George III and the American revolution', *Early American Studies*, 2, 1 (Spring 2004), 1.

21 L.W. Labaree et al. (eds), *The Papers of Benjamin Franklin* (New Haven, Connecticut, 1959), XXII, 520–1.

22 W.T. Hutchinson et al. (eds), *The Papers of James Madison* (Chicago, Illinois, 1962), pp. 129–30, 153.

23 G.S. McCowen, *The British Occupation of Charleston, 1780–1782* (Columbia, South Carolina, 1972), p. 99.

24 D.W. Galenson, 'The settlement and growth of the Colonies: population, labour and economic development', in S.L. Engerman and R.E. Gallman (eds), *The Cambridge Economic History of the United States* (Cambridge, 1996), pp. 171–3.

25 M. Rose, *Washington's War: From Independence to Iraq* (London, 2007).

26 Evelyn to Sir Frederick Evelyn, 23 Apr., 19 Aug. 1775, BL. Evelyn papers LE1.

27 Gage to Viscount Barrington, 26 June 1775, BL. Add. 73550.

28 C. Cox, *A Proper Sense of Honor: Service and Sacrifice in George Washington's Army* (Chapel Hill, North Carolina, 2004).

29 R. Middlekauff, 'Why men fought in the American revolution', *Huntington Library Quarterly*, 43 (1980), 147.

30 A.H. Tillson Jr., 'The localist roots of backcountry loyalism: an examination of popular political culture in Virginia's New River Valley', *Journal of Southern History*, 54 (1988), 403–4.

31 *Annual Register*, 19 (1776), p. 2.

32 The Articles of Confederation were designed specifically to avoid the creation of a new state.

33 H. Ward, *The War for Independence and the Transformation of American Society* (London, 1999) and, less successfully, C.P. Niemeyer, *America Goes to War: A Social History of the Continental Army* (New York, 1996).

34 Jenkinson to Amherst, 24 Oct. 1780, NA, War Office papers 34/127 fol. 155.

35 J. Huston, *Logistics of Liberty. American Services of Supply in the Revolutionary War and After* (Newark, New Jersey, 1991); J. Shy, 'Logistical crisis and the American Revolution', in J. Lynn (ed.), *Feeding Mars. Logistics in Western Warfare from the Middle Ages to the Present* (Boulder, Colorado, 1993).

36 A.M. Becker, 'Smallpox in Washington's army: strategic implications of the disease during the American revolutionary war', *Journal of Military History*, 68 (2004), 429.

37 E. Venn, *Pox Americana: The Great Smallpox Epidemic of 1775* (New York, 2001).

38 Congreve to Reverend Richard Congreve, 4 Sept. 1776, Stafford, County Record Office, D1057/M/F/30.

39 D. Twohig, *The Papers of George Washington: Revolutionary War Series*, VIII (Charlottesville, Virginia, 1998), pp. 182, 238, IX (1999), pp. 317, 561.

40 Twohig, *Papers of George Washington*, VIII, p. 454.

41 J. Dull, *A Diplomatic History of the American Revolution* (New Haven, Connecticut, 1985).

42 P. Ang. 522 fols 50, 117–22, 134, 162–, 401.

43 Na. SP., 78/291 fol. 181.

44 Clinton's notes, BL. Add. 3441 fols 155–6.

45 S. Frey, *The British Soldier in America* (Austin, Texas, 1981).

46 George to Robinson, 24 May 1777, BL. Add. 37833 fol. 200.

47 George to Robinson, 6 Mar. 1777, BL. Add. 38733 fol. 143.

48 J.M. Price, *France and the Chesapeake: A History of the French Tobacco Monopoly, 1674–1791, and of its Relationship to the British and American Tobacco Trades* (2 vols, Ann Arbor, Michigan, 1973), II, 681–3.

Notes to Chapter 6: France and America Win, 1778–83

1 S. Conway, 'From fellow-nations to foreigners: British perceptions of the Americans, *circa* 1739–1783', *William and Mary Quarterly*, 3rd ser., 59 (Jan. 2002).

2 Cobbett, XIX, 740.

3 J. Bradley, *Religion, Revolution and English Radicalism. Nonconformity in Eighteenth-Century Politics and Society* (Cambridge, 1990), pp. 378–9; S. Lutnick, *The American Revolution and the British Press, 1775–1783* (Columbia, Missouri, 1967); J. Sainsbury, *Disaffected Patriots: London Supporters of Revolutionary America, 1769–1782* (Kingston, Ontario, 1987).

4 S. Bradford, 'Hunger menaces the Revolution, December 1789–January 1780', *Maryland Historical Magazine*, 61 (1966), 5–23.

5 BL. Add. 35517 fol. 170.

6 J.R. Fischer, *A Well-Executed Failure: The Sullivan Campaign against the Iroquois* (Columbia, South Carolina, 1997); M.M. Mintz, *Seeds of Empire: The American Revolutionary Conquest of the Iroquois* (New York, 1999).

7   Greene to General Thomas Sumter, 30 Mar. 1781, Library of Congress, Washington, Sumter papers.

8   J.S. Tiedermann, 'Patriots by default: Queens County, New York, and the British Army, 1776-1783', *William and Mary Quarterly*, 3rd ser., 43 (1986), 63.

9   Report by Dreyer, Danish envoy, 31 Dec. 1781, Copenhagen, Danske Rigsarkivet, Department of Foreign Affairs, vol. 1965.

10 George to Lord Chancellor Thurlow, 28 Feb. 1782, R. Gore-Browne, *Chancellor Thurlow* (London, 1953), p. 173.

11 B. Franklin, *Two Letters from Dr Franklin, to the Earl of Shelburne* (London, 1782), p. 21.

12 G. Lanctot, *Canada and the American Revolution, 1774-1783* (London, 1967), p. 208.

13 A. Stockley, *Britain and France at the Birth of America. The European Powers and the Peace Negotiations of 1782-1783* (Exeter, 2001), pp. 52-73.

14 M.J. Crawford (ed.), *Naval Documents of the American Revolution*, XI (Washington, 2005), pp. 696-9.

15 A.A. Lawrence, *Storm over Savannah* (Athens, Georgia, 1951), p. 73.

16 B. Quarles, *The Negro in the American Revolution* (Chapel Hill, North Carolina, 1961).

17 J. Black, *Using History* (London, 2005) and *The Curse of History* (London, 2008).

Notes to Chapter 7: After the Revolution

1   H.H. Peckham (ed.), *The Toll of Independence. Engagements and Battle Casualties of the American Revolution* (Chicago, Illinois, 1974), pp. 130-3.

2   J.P. Greene, *Peripheries and Center: Constitutional Development in the Extended Polities of the British Empire and the United States, 1607-1788* (Athens, Georgia, 1986).

3   S.J. Hornsby, *British Atlantic, American Frontier. Spaces of Power in Early Modern British America* (Hanover, New Hampshire, 2005), p. 223.

4   J. Black, *Flames and Water: The War of 1812* (Norman, Oklahoma, 2009).

5   E.H. Gould, *The Persistence of Empire. British Political Culture in the Age of the American Revolution* (Chapel Hill, North Carolina, 2000), pp. 198-9, 208.

6   W. Holton, *Unruly Americans and the Origins of the Constitution* (New York, 2007), p. 140.

7   Miles to Pitt, Oct. 1785, New Haven, Connecticut, Beinecke Library, Miles file.

8   Hammond to William, Lord Grenville, Foreign Secretary, 1 Nov. 1791, BL. Add. 58939.

9   Edward Thornton, British Secretary of Legation, to Sir James Bland Burges, 25 Apr. 1796, Oxford, Bodleian Library, Bland Burges papers, vol. 21.

10 G.S. Rowe and A.W. Knott, 'The Longchamps affair (1784-1786). The law of nations, and the shaping of early American foreign policy', *Diplomatic History*, 10 (1986), 199-220.

11 John Adams to John Jay, Secretary of State, 2 June 1785, C.F. Adams (ed.), *The Works of John Adams* (10 vols, Boston, Massachusetts, 1853), VIII, 255-7.

12 P.L. Ford (ed.), *The Autobiography of Thomas Jefferson 1743-1790* (New York, 1914), p. 94; C.R. Ritcheson, 'The fragile memory: Thomas Jefferson at the court of George III', *Eighteenth-Century Life*, 6, pts 2-3 (1981), 1-16.

13 P. and N. Onuf, *Federal Union, Modern World: The Law of Nations in an Age of Revolutions, 1776-1814* (Madison, Wisconsin, 1993).

14 J. Klaits and M. Haltzel (eds), *The Global Ramifications of the French Revolution* (Cambridge, 1994), p. 53.

15 A.G. Condon, *The Envy of the American States: The Loyalist Dream for New Brunswick* (Frederickton, New Brunswick, 1984); N. MacKinnon, *This Unfriendly Soil: The Loyalist Experience in Nova Scotia, 1783–1791* (Kingston, Ontario, 1986).

16 P. Langford, 'Manners and character in Anglo-American perceptions, 1750–1850' in F.M. Leventhal and R. Quinault (eds), *Anglo-American Attitudes: From Revolution to Partnership* (Aldershot, 2000), p. 85.

17 R.A. Burchell, *The End of Anglo-America. Historical Essays in the Study of Cultural Divergence* (Manchester, 1991); Jay to Webster, 31 May 1813, H.P. Johnston (ed.), *The Correspondence and Public Papers of John Jay*, IV (New York, 1893), p. 373. There has also been an emphasis on continuities, e.g. debate in *Historically Speaking*, 6, 4 (Mar.–Apr. 2005), pp. 19–22.

18 P.P. Hill, *French Perceptions of the Early American Republic 1783–1793* (Philadelphia, Pennsylvania, 1988); J. Meyer, 'Les difficultés du commerce franco-american vues de Nantes, 1776–1790', *French Historical Studies*, 11 (1979), 159–83; Fohlem, 'The commercial failure of France in America', in N.L. Roelker and C.K. Warner (eds), *Two Hundred Years of Franco–American Relations* (Worcester, Massachusetts, 1983), pp. 93–119.

19 AE. CP. Etats Unis 35, fol 135.

20 Hawkesbury to William, Lord Grenville, Foreign Secretary, 17 Oct. 1794, BL. Add. 38310 fol. 122.

21 Hawkesbury to Charles Bond, 4 Jan. 1790, BL. Add. 38310 fol. 148.

22 Liverpool to William Ludlam, 17 June 1797, BL. Add. 38310 fol. 197.

23 C. Williamson, *Vermont in Quandary: 1763-1825* (Montpelier, Vermont, 1949), pp. 151–64.

24 C.G. Calloway, *Crown and Calumet: British-Indian Relations, 1783–1815* (Norman, Oklahoma, 1987).

25 R.J. Miller, *Native America, Discovered and Conquered: Thomas Jefferson, Lewis and Clark, and Manifest Destiny* (Westport, Connecticut, 2006).

26 Jefferson to Adams, 11 June 1812, L.J. Cappon (ed.), *The Adams-Jefferson Letters* (Chapel Hill, North Carolina, 1959), pp. 307–8.

27 A. DeConde, *The Quasi-War: The Politics and Diplomacy of the Undeclared War with France, 1797–1801* (New York, 1966).

28 Liverpool to Phenias Bond, 23 May 1798, BL. Add. 38310 fol. 221.

29 B. Perkins, *The Cambridge History of American Foreign Relations. I. The Creation of a Republican Empire, 1776–1865* (Cambridge, 1993), p. 84.

Notes to Chapter 8: Conclusions

1 K. Burk, *Old World, New World. The Story of Britain and America* (London, 2007).

Selected Further Reading

This introductory list concentrates on recent works. Further guidance to the extensive and excellent scholarship on the subject can be found in their bibliographies.

Altman, I. and Horn, J. (eds), 'To Make America': European Emigration in the Early Modern Period (Berkeley, California, 1991).

Anderson, F., Crucible of War: The Seven Years' War and the Fate of Empire in British North America, 1754–1766 (New York, 2000).

Armitage, D., The Ideological Origins of the British Empire (Cambridge, 2000).

Bailyn, B., The Ideological Origins of the American Revolution (Cambridge, Massachusetts, 1967).

Bailyn, B., The Peopling of British North America (New York, 1986).

Bailyn, B., Voyagers to the West: A Passage in the Peopling of America on the Eve of the Revolution (New York, 1986).

Bailyn, B. and Morgan, P.D. (eds), Strangers within the Realm: Cultural Margins of the First British Empire (Chapel Hill, North Carolina, 1991).

Bliss, R., Revolution and Empire: English Politics and the American Colonies in the Seventeenth Century (Manchester, 1990).

Bonomi, P.U., Under the Cope of Heaven: Religion, Society, and Politics in Colonial America (Oxford, 1986).

Brown, R.D., Knowledge Is Power: The Diffusion of Information in Early America, 1700–1865 (New York, 1989).

Calloway, C.G., New Worlds for All: Indians, Europeans, and the Remaking of Early America (Baltimore, Maryland, 1997).

Canny, N. (ed.), Europeans on the Move: Studies on European Migration, 1500–1800 (Oxford, 1994).

Ekirch, A.R., 'Poor Carolina': Politics and Society in Colonial North Carolina, 1729–1776 (Chapel Hill, North Carolina, 1981).

Ekirch, A.R., Bound for America: The Transportation of British Convicts to the Colonies, 1718–1775 (Oxford, 1987).

Ferlin, J., Almost a Miracle: The American Victory in the War of Independence (Oxford, 2007).

Fischer, D.H., Albion's Seed: Four British Folkways in America (New York, 1989).

Games, A., *Migration and the Origins of the English Atlantic World* (Cambridge, Massachusetts, 1999).

Gould, E.H., *The Persistence of Empire: British Political Culture in the Age of the American Revolution* (Chapel Hill, North Carolina, 2000).

Greene, J.P. and Pole, J.R. (eds), *Colonial British America: Essays in the New History of the Early Modern Era* (Baltimore, Maryland, 1984).

Greene, J.P., *Pursuits of Happiness: The Social Development of Early Modern British Colonies and the Formation of American Culture* (Chapel Hill, North Carolina, 1988).

Hancock, D., *Citizens of the World: London Merchants and the Integration of the British Atlantic Economy, 1735–1785* (Cambridge, 1995).

Hatley, T., *The Dividing Paths: Cherokees and South Carolinians through the Revolutionary Era* (New York, 1995).

Henretta, J.A., *'Salutary Neglect': Colonial Administration under the Duke of Newcastle* (Princeton, New Jersey, 1972).

Horn, J., *Adapting to a New World: English Society in the Seventeenth-Century Chesapeake* (Chapel Hill, North Carolina, 1994).

Hornsby, S.J., *British Atlantic, American Frontier. Spaces of Power in Early Modern British America* (Hanover, New Hampshire, 2005).

Isaac, R., *The Transformation of Virginia, 1740–1790* (Chapel Hill, North Carolina, 1982).

Jennings, F., *The Invasion of America: Indians, Colonialism, and the Cant of Conquest* (Chapel Hill, North Carolina, 1975).

Jones, A.H., *Wealth of a Nation to Be: The American Colonies on the Eve of the Revolution* (New York, 1980).

Kars, M., *Breaking Loose Together: The Regulator Rebellion in Pre-Revolutionary North Carolina* (Chapel Hill, North Carolina, 2002).

Katz, S.N., *Newcastle's New York: Anglo-American Politics, 1732–1753* (Cambridge, Massachusetts, 1968).

Landsman, N.C., *Scotland and its First American Colony, 1683–1765* (Princeton, New Jersey, 1985).

McCusker, J.J. and Menard, R.R., *The Economy of British America, 1607–1789* (Chapel Hill, North Carolina, 1991).

Marshall, P.J. (ed.), *The Oxford History of the British Empire*, II. *The Eighteenth Century* (Oxford, 1998).

Meinig, D.W., *The Shaping of America: A Geographical Perspective on Five Hundred Years of History*, I. *Atlantic America, 1492–1800* (New Haven, Connecticut, 1986).

Merrell, J.H., *The Indians' New World: Catawbas and their Neighbors from European Contact Through the Era of Removal* (Chapel Hill, North Carolina, 1989).

Middleton, R. *Pontiac's War. Its Causes, Course and Consequences* (New York, 2007).

Morgan, P.D., *Slave Counterpoint: Black Culture in the Eighteenth-Century Chesapeake and Lowcountry* (Chapel Hill, North Carolina, 1998).

Nash, G.B., *The Urban Crucible: Social Change, Political Consciousness, and the Origins of the American Revolution* (Cambridge, Massachusetts, 1979).

Olson, A.G., *Making the Empire Work: London and American Interest Groups, 1690–1790* (Cambridge, Massachusetts, 1992).

Olwell, R. and A Tully (eds), *Cultures and Identities in Colonial British America* (Baltimore, Maryland, 2006).

Pagden, A., *Lords of all the World: Ideologies of Empire in Spain, Britain, and France, c. 1500 to c. 1800* (New Haven, Connecticut, 1995).

Ragsdale, B.A., *A Planters' Republic. The Search for Economic Independence in Revolutionary Virginia* (Madison, Wisconsin, 1996).

Rediker, M., *Between the Devil and the Deep Blue Sea: Merchant Seamen, Pirates, and the Anglo-American Maritime World, 1700–1750* (New York, 1987).

Richter, D., *Facing East from Indian Country: A Native History of Early America* (Cambridge, Massachusetts, 2001).

Shammas, C., *The Pre-industrial Consumer in England and America* (Oxford, 1990).

Sher, R. and Smitten, J.R. (eds), *Scotland and America in the Age of the Enlightenment* (Princeton, New Jersey, 1990).

Sosin, J.M., *Whitehall and the Wilderness: The Middle West in British Colonial Policy, 1760–1775* (Lincoln, Nebraska, 1961).

Steele, I.K., *Politics of Colonial Policy: The Board of Trade in Colonial Administration, 1696–1720* (Oxford, 1968).

Steele, I.K., *The English Atlantic, 1675–1740: An Exploration of Communication and Community* (New York, 1986).

Usner, D.H., *Indians, Settlers, and Slaves in a Frontier Exchange Economy: The Lower Mississippi Valley before 1783* (Chapel Hill, North Carolina, 1992).

Vickers, D. (ed.), *A Companion to Colonial America* (Oxford, 2003).

Ward, H., *The War for Independence and the Transformation of American Society* (London, 1999).

White, R., *The Middle Ground: Indians, Empires, and Republics in the Great Lakes Region, 1650–1815* (Cambridge, 1991).

Wilson, K., *The Sense of the People: Politics, Culture, and Imperialism in England, 1715–1785* (Cambridge, 1995).

Wood, G.S., *The American Revolution. A History* (London, 2003).

Index

(whole chapter or section references in **bold**)

Abenaki tribe 4, 25, 34, 39, 55, 70, 90, 93
Abercromby, General James 76–7
Abe rdeen 23
Acadia 18, 34–5, 75, 77 *see also* New Scotland *and* Nova Scotia
Acadians 18, 36, 71 *see also* Cajuns
Act against importation of slaves (Georgia) 29
Adams, John 118, 123–4, 132, 171, 176, 180
Adams, Samuel 111, 131
Administration of Justice Act (1774) 113
Admiralty 54, 70, 96
Adolphustown 177
African Americans 18, 24, 28, 31–2, 64, 83, 90, 97, 100, 102, 184
and American Revolution/ War of Independence 132–4, 137, 169–71
African culture 31
African slaves *see* slavery
Africanization process (in North America) 31
Aix-la-Chapelle (1748), Peace of 57–8, 61
Alabama River 39, 90
Alamance 98
Albany 5, 18, 35, 55–6, 69–70, 73, 147
Alexander, Sir William 5
Alexander Jr, Sir William 5
Alexandria (Virginia) 130
Algonquian tribe 4
Ali, Haidar 159
Allegheny Mountains 77, 95, 102
Allegheny River 62
Altamaha River 51, 53
Amazon region 128
Amherst, General Jeffrey 76, 79–81, 86, 90, 94
The American Atlas or, a Geographical Description of the Whole Continent of America (1776) 133

American Constitution *see* Constitution, American
American culture 63, 86, 137 *see also* American identity
American Department (of British government) 168
American Dictionary of the English Language (1828) 177
American identity 58 *see also* American culture
American Post Office Act (1711) 17
American Rangers 90
American Revolution 17, 92, 99, **123–72**, 183–4
American War of Independence 70, 73, 95, **123–72**
An Appeal to the Unprejudiced; or, a Vindication of the Measures of Government, with Respect to America (1776) 171
Andros, Sir Edmund 15, 17
Anglicanism 45, 100 *see also* Anglicans *and* Church of England
Anglicans 17, 83, 100 *see also* Anglicanism *and* Church of England
Anglicization process (in North America) 27, 41, 45, 67–8
Anglo-Dutch Wars (seventeenth century) 7–8
Anglo-Irish establishment 47
Anglo-Spanish treaty (1670) 51
Angolans 97 *see also* African slaves
Annapolis (Royal) 25, 35
Ansbach-Bayreuth forces (in War of Independence) 166
Anse au Foulon 79
Apalachee tribe 13, 33
Appalachian Mountains 11, 71, 78, 92, 101, 113, 169
Arnold, Benedict 139
Articles of Confederation 159
Arkansas River 33
Asia 1
Assiniboine River 39

Atlantic Ocean (navigation of) 1
see also trans-Atlantic links (commercial and political)
Atlantic slave trade *see* slave trade
Augusta (Georgia) 51, 67
Augusta (St Lawrence Valley) 177
Augusta Conference 91
Austria 55, 149, 183
Austrian Succession, War of the 51

Bacon, Nathaniel 14
Bacon's Rebellion 9, 14
Baker, William 60–1
Baltic 60
Baltimore 25, 148
Baltimore, Cecil, Lord 2, 10, 14
Bambara tribe (Africa) 97
Barbados 13
Barnstaple 30
Beauport 78
Bedford, John, 4th Duke of 104
Belgium 56
Bengal 110
Bethesda (orphanage) 84
Berkeley, Sir William 14
Bermuda 7, 177
Bernadotte, General 182
Berwick 134
Bideford 30
Bight of Biafra 97
Bill of Rights (US) 119
Biloxi Bay 32
Bismarck (North Dakota) 39
'Blackbeard' (Edward Teach) 37–8
blacks 128 *see also* slavery
Bladen, Martin 42
Bloody Marsh, Battle of 52
Blue Ridge Mountains 36, 64
Board of Customs Commissioners 108
Board of Ordnance 35
Board of Trade 38, 42, 44, 47, 59–60, 69, 86
Board of War and Ordnance 143
Bordeaux 153
Boscawen, Admiral 74, 76

Boston 4, 5, 15, 31, 34–5, 41–2, 57, 72, 84, 86, 108–9, 111–12, 116–17, 121, 127, 130, 134–6, 142, 146
Boston Gazette 134
'Boston Massacre' 109
Boston News Letter 41
Boston Port Act (1774) 112–13
Boston Tea Party 99, 111
Bouquet, Lieutenant-Colonel Henry 93
Bourbons 16, 47, 58–9, 61–2, 89, 114, 134, 145, 166–7, 169–70
boycott of British imports by Americans 110
Braddock, Major-General Edward 72–4, 77, 117
Bradstreet, Lieutenant-Colonel John 77
Brandywine, Battle of 145
Brazil 13, 128
Breda (1667), Treaty of 8
Breed's Hill (Charlestown peninsula) 135
Brest 75, 81, 158
Bristol 1, 5, 10, 23, 30, 60, 153
British Army 72, 74–6, 81, 93, 123, 136–7, 139, 145 *see also* individual commanders, battles and engagements
British Columbia 179
British–Creek treaty (1733) 32
British Empire 26–7, 56, 58, 66–7, 80, 87, 89, 100, 103, 114, 118, 120, 123–4, 129, 132–3, 150, 158, 172–3, 178 *see also* English Empire
British government 16–17, 19, 24, 30, 35, 39, 42, 44–5, 47, 51–2, 56–8, 60–3, 65–6, 71, 73–4, 77–8, 82, 86, 89, 95, 99–101, 103–5, 108–12, 114–16, 118–19, 121, 124, 127–30, 140, 148, 157, 164, 167–8, 173, 176, 184
British identity 58, 184
British Isles 6–7, 14–16, 25, 27–8, 41, 47, 49, 65, 85, 105, 119, 131, 140, 164
British Journal 39
British navy *see* Royal Navy
British North America
    in seventeenth century **1–21**
    in eighteenth century **23–121**
British Parliament 16–18, 28, 46–9, 58, 67, 70, 100, 106–11, 113–14, 117–21, 125–6, 131, 138, 147, 157, 170, 177, 179
British West Indies 5, 13–14, 19, 29–31, 36, 40, 44–5, 51, 57, 59, 80, 83, 108, 128–9, 138, 140, 155, 158, 161, 165–8, 170, 179 *see also* English West Indies
Briton, the 97

Brooklyn 144
Bull, William 91
Bunker Hill, Battle of 135–6, 145, 151
Burgoyne, General 150–3
Burke, Edmund 116, 124
Bushy Run 93
Bute, John, 3rd Earl of 104

'Cabbage Planting Expedition' 75
Cabot, John 1
Cajuns 71 *see also* Acadians
California 11
Calvert, Leonard 3, 15
Calvinistic revivalism 83–4, 100
Cambridge Chronicle 157
Camden, Battle of 162, 164
Camden, Charles, 1st Earl of 157
Canada 5, 10–11, 18–19, 24, 29, 35–6, 39, 49, 53–8, 62, 70, 74, 78, 80–2, 86–7, 89–90, 93, 104, 113, 115, 138–9, 140, 142–4, 151–2, 164, 168, 177 *see also* New France
Canada, Viscount *see* Alexander Jr, Sir William
Canada River 63
Canadian militia 82
Candid Inquiry into the Causes of the Late and Intended Migrations from Scotland (1771) 102
Cape Breton Island (Ile Royale) 5, 38, 53, 55–6, 59, 75–6, 78, 139
Cape Cod 3
Cape Fear 3
Cape Fear River 64
Cape Finisterre 57
Caracas 128
Caribbean 40, 51–3, 56, 158–9, 167 *see also* British West Indies, French West Indies *and* Spanish West Indies
Carleton, Guy 139
Carlisle, Frederick, 5th Earl of 157
Carlisle Commission 119, 158
Carolina 8, 11, 13, 25, 33, 46
Carolina militia 33
Carolina Rangers 91
Cartagena (Colombia) 52–3
Castine 34, 139
Catawba tribe 37, 72
Catesby, Mark 41
Catholic Church 139
Catholics
    in America 16, 101
    in England 2, 10
    in France 10
    in French Canada 24, 101, 113
    in Ireland 21, 47, 126
Chambly 80

Champlain, Lake 35, 55, 74, 78–9, 139
Charles I, King 2, 5–6, 101, 112
Charles II, King 7–8, 11, 14
Charles III of Spain, King 128
Charleston (Charles Town) 13, 26, 30, 33, 37–8, 42, 67, 84, 143, 145–6, 148, 151, 161–4, 167–8, 170
Charles Town *see* Charleston (Charles Town)
Charlestown Peninsula 135
Charlotte (New Brunswick) 177
Charlotte (North Carolina) 64, 164
Charlottesburg 177
Charlottesville 64
Charter of Liberties and Privileges (New York) 15
Charter of Privileges (Pennsylvania and Delaware) 17
Chatham, William Pitt the Elder, Earl of 107–8, 115–16, 118–21, 134 *see also* Pitt the Elder, William
Chatham ministry 107–8
Cherokee tribe 36–7, 62–3, 72, 77, 90–1, 93, 95, 133
Chesapeake Bay/area 2–5, 8, 12–13, 23, 25, 28–9, 31, 44–5, 60, 64, 85, 97–9, 114, 133, 153, 162, 164–6, 170
Chesterfield Inlet (Hudson Bay) 54
Chickasaw tribe 33, 39, 62, 91
China 110
Choctaw tribe 13, 57, 62
Church, Benjamin 20
Church of England 10, 15, 27, 83–5, 173, 177 *see also* Anglicanism *and* Anglicans
Church of Ireland 21
Clinton, Brigadier-General George 147
Clinton, Sir Henry 151, 157, 162, 165
'Coercive Acts' *see* 'Intolerable Acts' ('Coercive Acts') (1774)
colonial militia 37, 55, 65, 73, 74–5, 81, 93–4, 117, 128, 140–3, 146–8, 152, 156, 160, 163, 171
Comanche tribe 38
Common Sense 125, 130
Committee of Public Safety (Massachusetts) 117
Concord 4, 117, 121, 134
Congregationalism 15, 17, 26, 83
Congress of Aix-la Chapelle *see* Aix-la-Chapelle (1748), Peace of
Congreve, Captain William 144

Connecticut 4, 8, 13, 17–18, 35, 105
Connecticut militia 35
Connecticut River 7
Connecticut River Valley 4, 6
Continental Army 137–8, 140–4, 146–9, 151–3, 156–9, 165–6, 171
Continental Association 118
Continental Congress 101, 105, 115–16, 118–19, 121, 124, 130, 137, 140–3, 147–9, 159, 165
Cook, Captain James 54, 78, 115
Cornell, Ezekiel 162
Cornwallis, Charles, 2nd Earl of 146, 151, 162–6
Coulange, Pierre Petit de33
Council for New England 3
Courier de Boston 178
Courier de l'Amérique 178
Covenant Chain (between Iroquois and New York) 19
Cree tribe 11
Creek tribe 13, 23, 32–3, 37, 39, 52, 62–3, 91, 95
Creek–Cherokee conflict 62–3
Cromwellian regime 7
Crown, British/English 2–4, 8, 14–15, 18, 24, 45, 47, 49, 67, 95, 101, 109, 117–19, 126, 130, 146, 152, 162
Crown Fort 79
Crown Point 55, 80, 139
Cruden, John 170
Cuba 33
Culloden, Battle of 48, 117, 136
Cumberland, William, Duke of 71, 74
Cumberland Pacquet 133–4
Currency Act (1764) 105–6

d'Aiguillon, Emmanuel, Duke 112, 150
Dartmouth 30
Day, Thomas 134
De Brahm, William 96
Declaration of Independence, American 119, 129–31, 147
Declaration of Rights, English 119
Declaratory Act (1720) 47, 126
Declaratory Act (1766) 48, 107, 116, 120
Deerfield 34
Delamotte, Charles 83
DeLancey, James 73
DeLancey, Susannah 56
Delaware 8, 27
Delaware tribe 37, 72, 90, 92–4
Delaware River 7, 105, 146, 148, 167
Delaware Valley 5–6, 8
Denmark 179

Description of New England (1616) 3
The Desolation of America (1777) 134
Detroit 33, 93, 175
'Devil's Hole Massacre' 93
Devon 30
The Devoted Legions (1776) 134
d'Iberville, Pierre Le Moyne, Sieur 32
Dieskau, Baron 73
Dinwiddie, Robert 24, 63, 70, 86
Discovery, HMS 54
Dismal Swamp 97
Dissenters 56, 84–5, 100, 118, 127
Dixon, Jeremiah 105
Dobbs, Arthur 54
Döhla, Johann Conrad 166
Drake, Francis 11
Dudley, Colonel Joseph 34, 43, 46
Dummer, William 39
Dummer's War 39
Dunmore, John, 4th Earl of 132–3, 146, 170
Durand, François-Marie 62
Durham 30
Dutch (in America) 5–8, 27, 55
Dutch Crisis (1787) 178
Dutch Republic 56 *see also* Netherlands
    in American War of Independence 159, 169, 178
The Dying Negro (1773) 134

East Anglia 45
East Florida 96, 98, 158, 169, 180, 183
East India Company 57–60, 110, 112–13
East Jersey 148
Easton Conference 77
East River (New York) 144
Echard, Laurence 41
Edict of Nantes (1685) 10
Edinburgh 109
Edwardsburg 177
Elizabeth I, Queen 1–2, 11
Ellis, John 96
emigration to North America
    from England 2–11, 20, 24, 45–6, 51, 62–3, 102, 114
    from English West Indies 13
    from Europe (continent) 25, 27
    from France 20, 24, 71
    from Germany 24, 26, 36, 63–4
    from Holland 27
    Jewish 26
    from Scotland 24, 102, 114
    from Sweden 5–6, 27
    Swiss 26

from Ulster/Ireland 63–4, 99, 102
English/British Civil Wars 6–7, 45, 48, 101, 184
English Empire 7, 23 *see also* British Empire
English navy *see* Royal Navy
English West Indies 13 *see also* British West Indies
Erie, Lake 62, 93
Evelyn, William 134–5
European expansion into North America 1–11, 19–20, 23–4, 27, 29, 37–8, 90, 96
European rivalry in North America **51–87**
Excise Act (1660) 110
Exeter (England) 30
Exeter (New England) 4

Falkirk, Battle of 136
Fallen Timbers, Battle of 180
Felix Farley's Bristol Journal 57
Ferrar, John 11
The First Book of the American Chronicle of the Times, 1774–1775 114
Flanders 56
Florida 2, 26, 33, 36, 40, 51–3, 67, 89, 96, 104
Forbes, Brigadier-General John 76–7
Fort Beauséjour 71
Fort Bedford 93–4
Fort Bourbon 54
Fort Bull 74
Fort Carillon (Ticonderoga) 74, 76, 78–9
Fort Carlisle 94
Fort Christina 5
Fort Cumberland 71–2
Fort Dauphin 54
Fort de la Presque Isle 62
Fort Detroit 175
Fort Dobbs 73
Fort d'Orléans 38
Fort Duquesne 62, 72–3, 76–7, 117
Fort Edward Augusta 93
Fort Frederica 84
Fort Frontenac 77
Fort Gaspereau 71
Fort George 74, 89
Fort King George 51
Fort la Corne 54
Fort Lancaster 94
Fort La Reine 39
Fort Le Boeuf 62
Fort Lévis 80
Fort Ligonier 93–4
Fort London 94
Fort Loudon 63, 91
Fort Louis 33

Fort Lyttleton 93
Fort Mackinac 175
Fort Massachusetts 55
Fort Maurepas 32–3, 39
Fort Miami 57, 92
Fort Michilimackinac 92
Fort Mississippi 33
Fort Montgomery 147
Fort Mose 53
Fort Necessity 69–70
Fort Niagara 38, 93, 175
Fort Ontario 74
Fort Oswego 38, 74, 77, 93, 175
Fort Ouiatenon 92
Fort Pitt 77, 93–4
Fort Prince George 63, 69, 90–1
Fort Sandusky 92
Fort St Charles 39
Fort St Frédéric 55, 73
Fort St Johns 139
Fort Ticonderoga 74, 139, 147,
 152 see also Fort Carillon
 (Ticonderoga)
Fort Toulouse 39, 90
Fort Venango 92–3
Fort Vincennes 57
Fort Washington 145–6, 148
Fort William Henry 75
Fort York 11
Fox tribe 39
Fox, Charles James 126
Fox, Henry 71
France
 alliance with America in War
  of Independence 155–72
 empire in North America
  5, 10, 17–19, 24–5, 32–4,
  38–40, 54, 57, 61–3, 65–6,
  81, 91, 127–8, 139, 181, 184
 relations with USA after War
  of Independence 177–8,
  181–2
 wars with Britain/England
  5, 18, 21, 27, 32–4, 51–7,
  69–87, 89–90, 135, 141, 146,
  150, 176, 179–80, 182
Franklin, Benjamin 28, 63–4,
 69–70, 84, 105, 115, 119–20,
 132, 147, 175
Frederick II of Hesse-Cassel,
 Landgrave 141
Fredericksburg 177
Fredericton 177
Freeman's Farm 152
Freemasonry 84
French and Indian War see Seven
 Years' War
French-Canadian militia 34, 82
French National Assembly 175
French navy 32, 149, 162
French Revolution 178
French West Indies 38, 44, 53, 60,
 83, 106, 178

Fundy, Bay of 3, 5
Furnace, HMS 54

Gabarus Bay 47
Gage, Lieutenant-Colonel/
 General Thomas 72, 109,
 116–17, 135–6, 140, 145
Gaspé Peninsula 77
Gaspée, the
Gates, Major-General Horatio
 147, 162, 164
Gauld, George 96
The Gazeteer's or Newsman's
 Interpreter … a Geographical
 Index … in Europe 41
General Post Office 17
A General Topography of North
 America and the West Indies
 (1768) 133
George I, King 47
George II, King 23, 74, 100
George III, King 89, 100, 104,
 106–7, 109–10, 117–19, 124–8,
 130–2, 138–40, 143, 153, 155,
 157, 168, 176–7
George, Lake 73, 75
Georgetown 25, 130, 162
Georgia 23, 26–30, 32, 51–2, 60,
 64–5, 67, 83–4, 89, 91, 95, 97,
 118, 130, 133, 158, 162,
 164–5
Georgia Trustees 26, 29–30, 51,
 58, 67
Germain, Lord George 73, 167 see
 also Sackville, Lord George
Germantown 152–3, 156
Germany 81
German emigration see
 emigration to North America
Gibraltar 155
Gilbert, Humphrey 1
Glasgow 23, 30, 98
Glen, James 57, 63
Glorious Revolution 15–17, 21,
 27, 48, 48–9, 101, 119, 126, 129,
 138, 156, 184
Gnadenhütten 26
Gommans, Jos 99
Gooch, William 53
Gordon Riots 164
Gosnold, Bartholomew 3
Gosport 133
Grand Banks (Newfoundland) 1
Grant, Lieutenant-Colonel James
 91
Grasse, François-Joseph, Count
 of 167
Gray, Edward 67
Great Awakening 27, 83–4, 92,
 98, 101–1
Great Bridge 133, 146
Great Island 46
Great Lakes 11, 55, 92, 96, 113

Great Philadelphia Wagon Road
 30, 64
Great Swamp Fight 20
Greene, Nathaniel 147, 160, 165
Greenville (1795), Treaty of 180
Grenville, George 104, 107
Grenville ministry 107
Grey Lock (Abenake leader) 39
Guadeloupe 167, 178
Guerchy, Charles, Count of 24
Guilford Court House, Battle of
 145, 151, 165
Gulf of Mexico/coast 32, 96, 155,
 180

Halifax (Nova Scotia) 42, 61,
 74–5, 78
Halifax, George, 2nd Earl of 71
Hamburg 45, 110
Hamilton, Charles 41
Hammond, George 175
Hanover 81
Hanover, Elector of 130
Hariot, Thomas 2
Harris, Howell 83
Harris, Sir James 175
Hartford 4
Harvard 84
Havana 89, 128, 146
Haverhill 34
Haviland, Colonel William 80
Hawkesbury, Charles, Lord
 see Liverpool, Charles, Lord
 Hawkesbury, 1st Earl of
Hazen, Moses 143
Herald 75
Herbert, Lord 159
Hessians 130, 148, 169
Hillsborough, Wills, Viscount 95
Holdernesse, Robert, 4th Earl
 of 61
Hopkey, Sophy 84
Horton, Lieutenant William 52
House of Commons 43, 106–7,
 113, 124, 126, 167
House of Lords 116, 134
House of Representatives (US)
 175
Howe, Admiral 147
Howe, Major-General William
 135, 141, 144–5, 149–51, 153,
 156–7
Hudson Bay 11, 36, 54, 57, 62
Hudson's Bay Company 11, 54,
 60–1
Hudson River 3, 75, 151–3, 160
Hudson valley 55, 78–9, 150, 152
Huguenots 10, 24
Hume, David 86
Humphrys, Richard 76, 79–81
Hungary 126
Huntington, Ebenezer 137
Huron tribe 57

Hutchinson, Thomas 101, 132
'Huy and Crye' rebellion
  (Maryland) 14

Ibo tribe (Africa) 97
Icy Cape (Alaska) 54
Ile aux Oeufs 35
Ile Royale see Cape Breton Island
  (Ile Royale)
Iles des Saintes 167
Illinois Country 62
Illinois Grand Prairie 39
immigration see emigration to
  North America
India 57, 110–11, 159
Indians see Native Americans
'Intolerable Acts' ('Coercive
  Acts') (1774) 112
Ireland 16, 47–8, 101–2, 108, 119,
  124, 126, 135, 164, 171
Irish emigration see emigration
  to North America
Irish Parliament 21, 47, 119, 129
Irish Woollen Export Prohibition
  Act (1699) 47
Iron Act (1750) 45
Iroquois tribe 19, 21, 34, 36–8,
  55, 64, 159

Jacobitism 16, 35, 117, 135–6, 156
Jamaica 53, 60, 138
James II (Duke of York), King
  7–8, 15–18, 127, 184
James, Duke of York see James II
  (Duke of York), King
James River 11, 64
Jamestown 2, 12, 14
Jay, John 177
Jay's Treaty 180
Jefferson, Thomas 29, 67, 117–18,
  175–6, 180–1
Jefferys, Thomas 133
Jeffreys, Sir Hubert 14
Jenkins, Captain Robert 51
Jenkins' Ear, War of 51
Jenkinson, Charles 141
Jesuits 34, 39
Jewish emigration see emigration
  to North America
Jews 17, 24, 26
Johnson, Sir Nathaniel 46
Johnson, William 55, 73
Johnstone, George 96

Kalm, Peter 27
Kansas 38
Kelsey, Henry 11
Kent Island 3
Kentucky 159, 169
Keswick 30
Kettle Creek 160
King George's War see Austrian
  Succession, War of the

King Philip's War 12–13, 19–20
King's Mountain, Battle of 163
Kingston (St Lawrence Valley)
  177
Knight, James 53–4

Labrador 54
La Harpe, Bénard de 38
Lake of the Woods 39
Lancaster 30
Latin America 20, 128
Laud, Archbishop of Canterbury/
  Bishop of London, William
  4, 101
La Vérendrye, Pierre Gaultier de
  38–9, 54
Law, John 40
Leacock, John 114
Lee, Charles 137, 145
Lee, Richard Henry 130, 148
Leeds Mercury 134, 157
Legge, Henry 104
Leiden 3
Leisler's Rebellion 15, 27
Leland, John 91
Leopold II of Hungary, King
  126
Léry, Chaussegros de 39
Lewis and Clarke expedition 180
Lexington 121, 134
Lincoln, Benjamin 161
Lindsey, Theophilus 118
Liverpool 23, 30, 153
Liverpool, Charles, Lord
  Hawkesbury, 1st Earl of 179,
  181
Liverpool, 2nd Earl of 179
Livingstones 55
Livorno 45
London 5, 7, 10, 19, 23, 30, 41, 54,
  60, 104, 109, 114, 164, 176, 179
London Chronicle 89
London Evening Post 70, 89
London Magazine 113
London press 133, 157
Longchamps affair 175
Long Island 144–5
Lorient 57
Loudoun, John, 4th Earl of 74–5
Louis XIV of France, King 16
Louis XV of France, King 127,
  150
Louis XVI of France, King 150
Louisbourg 38, 51, 55–9, 61, 71,
  74–8, 86
Louisiana 24, 33, 36, 38–40, 51,
  53, 62, 71, 89, 96, 127, 176,
  180–2
Louisiana Purchase 180, 182
Louisiana Superior Council 127
Lowndes, William 42
Loyalists, American 124–5, 133,
  138, 140, 142–3, 146, 148–9,

156–8, 160–1, 163, 165, 167–71,
  175, 177
Low Countries 35, 56–7 see also
  Belgium and Dutch Republic
Lutheran Church 26
Lyttleton, William 90

Madison, James 132
Madras 57
Maine 3, 34, 39, 55, 139
Malimke tribe (Africa) 97
Manhattan Island 148
The Map of Virginia (1651) 11
Marathas 92, 159
Marlborough, John Churchill, 1st
  Duke of 34
Maritime Provinces (Canada) 5
Martin, Josiah 146
Martinique 178
Maryland 2–3, 7–10, 14–15, 17,
  25, 28, 45, 64, 101, 105, 114
Maryland Assembly 6, 10
Massachusetts 4, 6, 8, 14–19,
  28, 34–5, 38–9, 44, 55–6, 58,
  70, 85–6, 99, 101, 106, 108–9,
  115–16, 121, 128, 139
Massachusetts Assembly 108
Massachusetts Bay Company 4
Massachusetts Council 46
Massachusetts, Court of 18
Massachusetts Gazette 134
Massachusetts militia 35
Matthew, the 1
Mayflower, the 3
Mediterranean 9, 44, 159
Menstrie 5
Merchant Adventurers 3
Metacom (Sachem of Pokanoket
  tribe) 20
Methodism 84, 173
Mexico 1, 20
Miami tribe 57, 62, 92
Micmac tribe 36
Middle Colonies/states 13–14, 24,
  27, 31, 85, 111, 120, 130, 142,
  146, 150, 157–8, 160–3, 166
Middleton, Christopher 54
Miles, William 175
militia see colonial militia and
  individual colonies/states
Miller, Thomas 96
Monorca 74, 169
Mississauga tribe 92
Mississippi Company 40
Mississippi River 32, 38–9, 55, 63,
  96, 113, 169, 180, 182
Missouri River 38–9
Mobile 32–3, 40, 96
Mobile, Bay of 96
Mohawk tribe 6, 12, 55
Molasses Act (1733) 45
Moll, Senex and Bowen (atlas
  publishers) 41

Monckton, Lieutenant-Colonel
    Robert 71
Monitor 78
Monmouth Court House, Battle
    of 144, 158
Monongahela River 62
Montcalm, Louis Joseph, Marquis
    de 74–82
Montgomery, Colonel Archibald
    90
Montgomery, Richard 139
Montmorency 78
Montréal 35, 70, 80–1, 139
Moor, William 54
Moore, James 33
Moore's Creek Bridge, Battle of
    143, 146
Moravians 26, 90
Morris, Robert 142
Morristown 147
Mount Venture 53
Murray, Brigadier James 80
Muskingum Valley 94
Mysore 92, 141, 159

Nairne, Thomas 33, 46
Nantes 153
Napoleon 182
Napoleonic wars 179
Narragansett tribe 6, 20
Narragansett Bay 30
Natchez 169
Natchez tribe 40
Native Americans 3, 5, 13, 17–18,
    26, 28, 31, 53, 75, 81–2, 97–8,
    100–2, 128, 132, 137, 140–1,
    145, 160, 171–4, 183–4
    and colonial Americans 101,
        132, 137, 159, 169, 180
    and Christianity 20, 83–5
    and economy 2, 36, 38, 46,
        54, 57
    and English/British 2, 4, 6,
        11–12, 14, 16, 19–20, 23–5,
        32–4, 36–40, 46, 52, 55, 57,
        62, 64–7, 69–73, 77, 89–96,
        103, 113–14, 152, 159, 169,
        175, 180
    and European disease 4, 12
    and French 6, 17, 25, 34, 38,
        40, 51, 54, 57, 62, 69–73, 75,
        77, 81–2, 91, 93
    as slaves 13
The Natural History of Carolina,
Florida, and the Bahama Islands
    (1731) 41
Naturalization Act (1740) 17
Navigation Acts (1650/1651) 7,
    15, 23, 45, 106
Navigation Act (1660) 7, 15, 23,
    44–5, 106
Navigation Act (1696) 17, 23, 43,
    45, 106

Nebraska 38
Neoheroka fortress 36
Neolin 85, 92
Netherlands 3, 27, 57 *see also*
    Dutch Republic
New Albion 11
New Amsterdam 5, 7–8
Newark and Nottingham Journal
    157
New Bern 26
New Brunswick 177
Newcastle, Thomas, Duke of
    70–1, 75, 104
Newcastle Chronicle 157
Newcastle Courant 157
New England 3–5, 7–8, 12–15,
    17–20, 25–6, 28–31, 34–5, 44–5,
    49, 53, 55, 58–9, 82–6, 90, 97–8,
    100–2, 106, 111–14, 117, 120–1,
    124, 137, 139, 142, 144, 150,
    152, 169, 174
New England militia 56, 71, 121
Newfoundland 1, 30, 36, 38, 44,
    120, 140, 169
New France 18, 24 38–9, 56, 76,
    79–82, 86 *see also* Canada
New Hampshire 8, 35, 39, 46, 55,
    70, 86
New Hampshire militia 35
New Haven 4, 8
New Jersey 8, 15, 25, 27, 148–9, 158
New Jersey militia 148
New Netherland 8, 15
New Orleans 32, 127–8, 169,
    180–1
Newport (Rhode Island) 148,
    155, 161
Newport (Wales) 30
New River Valley 64
New Scotland 5, 57 *see also*
    Acadia *and* Nova Scotia
New Sweden 8
New World 1, 5, 10, 15–16, 19–20,
    25, 27, 32, 40, 51, 56–7, 60, 111,
    129, 150, 179
New York (city) 5, 7–8, 26, 28, 31,
    42, 86, 129–30, 136, 141–2, 144,
    146, 149, 151, 158, 161, 164–5,
    167–9, 178, 180–1
New York (colony/state) 8, 15, 17,
    27, 35, 39, 43, 55, 70, 77, 114,
    130, 143, 159, 169
New York Assembly 8, 108, 129
Nicholls, Colonel Richard 7
Nine Years' War 18
Nootka Sound Crisis 179
Norfolk 133
Norridgewock Jesuit mission 39
North, Frederick, Lord 110, 113,
    121, 126, 164, 168
North Carolina 2–3, 17, 25–7,
    36–9, 51, 55, 64, 73, 90–1, 97–9,
    114, 143, 146, 162–3, 165, 167

North Carolina militia 143
North Dakota 39
North-West (American) 175, 180
North-West Committee 54
North-West Passage 53–4
Nottingham Gazette 157
Nova Scotia 18, 35–6, 38, 49, 53,
    55, 61–2, 71, 74–5, 77, 106, 114,
    139–40 *see also* Acadia *and* New
    Scotland

Oconostota 90
Oglethorpe, Colonel James 23,
    26, 29, 51–2, 83
Ohio Company 62–3, 92, 113
Ohio region 69, 72, 77, 92
Ohio River 62, 72, 75, 113, 169
Ohio Valley 39, 62–4, 69, 72,
    75, 95
Oklahoma 38
Olive Branch Petition 124
Ontario 177
Ontario, Lake 74–5, 77, 80, 93
Oracle 173
Osnabruck 177
Otis, James 106
Ottawa tribe 92
Otto, Louis-Guillaume 178
Overhill Cherokee Towns 63
Oxford University 84

Pacific Ocean 11, 39, 53–4, 78,
    115
Padouca tribe 38
Paine, Tom 125, 130
Painshill 41
Palatinate (Germany) 26, 36
Palmer, John 40
Papacy 59
Paris 152, 169, 176
Paris (1763), Peace of 89–90, 91
Parliament *see* British Parliament
Parliamentary Union (England
    and Scotland) 16, 23, 49
Pawnee tribe 38
'Paxton Boys' 95
Peace Commissioners (1778) 157
Peace of Aix-la-Chapelle *see* Aix-
    la-Chapelle (1748), Peace of
Peace of Paris *see* Paris (1763),
    Peace of
Peace of Utrecht *see* Utrecht
    (1713), Peace of
Peace of Versailles *see* Versailles
    (1783), Peace of
Peace of Westminster *see*
    Westminster, Peace of
Penn, William 8, 17
Penn Jr, William 37
Pennant, Thomas 30
Pennsylvania 8, 17, 26–8, 62,
    64–5, 69, 73, 76–7, 90, 94–5, 99,
    101, 112, 114, 143, 153, 156, 159

Pennsylvania Council of Safety 147
Pennsylvania Gazette 69
Pennsylvania Journal 134
Pennsylvania militia 76, 148
Penobscot 39
Pensacola 33, 40, 96–7
Pepperrell, William 56
Pequot tribe 4, 20
Pequot War 6, 20
Peru 1
Philadelphia 8, 26–7, 31, 41,
  57, 60, 65, 105, 111, 115, 118,
  148–9, 152–3, 156, 158, 175,
  178, 181
Philadelphia Associators 148
Philip II of Spain, King 1
Phips, Sir William 18–19
Piedmont 29, 64, 98
Pilgrim Fathers 3
Pitt the Elder, William 74–6, 80,
  104 *see also* Chatham, William
  Pitt the Elder, Earl of
Pittsburgh 69, 169
Plains of Abraham 79–80
Platte River 54
Plymley, Joesph 171
Plymouth (England) 3, 30
Plymouth (New England) 3, 8, 18
Plymouth Company 3
Point Pelée 93
Point Pleasant, Battle of 96
Pontiac 92
Pontiac's War 92, 95–6, 100
Pokanoket tribe 20
Polish Succession, War of the 38
Pombal, Sebastiáo, Marques of
  128
Port aux Balemes 5
Porter, Sir James 112
Port Royal 5, 18, 34–6, 56
Portuguese Empire 128–9
Presbyterians
  colonial 24
  Ulster 21, 63
press (American) 41
Prestonpans, Battle of 136
Prevost, General Augustine 161,
  170
Prince Edward Island 77
Princeton, Battle of 148–9
privateers
  American 138, 153
  French 60
  Spanish 60
Privy Council 6, 8
Protestant Ascendancy (in
  Ireland) 126
Protestant Association
  (Maryland) 15
Protestants *see also* Dissenters
  Canadian 24, 56
  colonial/American 15, 17,
  85, 101

Dutch 1, 15
English 3–4, 10, 14–15 *see also*
  Puritans
French *see* Huguenots
German 26
Providence (Rhode Island) 30
Provincial Congress (Concord)
  117, 121
'Provisional Act for Settling the
  Troubles in America' (1775)
  119
Prussia 78, 81, 141, 149
The Public Advertiser 177
*Public Occurrences Foreign and
  Domestic* (1690) 41
Puritans 4, 7, 10, 13, 45, 85, 101
  see also Protestants/English
Purrysburg 26
Puysieulx, Brûlart, Marquis de 62

Quadruple Alliance, War of the
  40
Quakers 8, 143
Quartering Act (1774) 113
Quasi War 181
Québec 5, 18–19, 35, 38, 52, 76,
  78–82, 86–7, 101, 113, 121,
  138–40, 143, 146, 155, 177
Québec Act (1774) 101, 113–14,
  121, 128
Quiberon Bay 81
Quincy, Josiah 101

Râle, Sebastian 39
Randolph, Peyton 86
*Reflections on the Present State of
  England and the Independence
  of America* (1782) 134
Regulators (North Carolina)
  98–9
Repulse Bay 54
Revenue Act (1766) 107–8
Rhineland 26
Rhode Island 4, 30, 35, 112, 148,
  155, 167
Rhode Island militia 35
Richelieu River 139
Richmond (Virginia) 25
The Rights of the Colonies Asserted
  (1764) 106
Rio de la Plata 128
Rittenhouse, David 105
Roanoke Gap 64
Roanoke Island 2, 4
Roanoke River 165
Robinson, John 153, 161
Rochambeau, Jean, Count of 167
Rockingham, Charles, 2nd
  Marquess of 107, 134, 168–9
Rockingham ministry 107, 168
Rockingham Whigs (in
  opposition) 116, 134
Rocky Mountains 182

Rodney, Admiral George 167
Rogers, Major Robert 90
Rouillé, Antoine-Louis 71
Royal African Company 29–30
Royalists 16, 45
Royal Navy 7, 56, 60, 78, 140–1,
  144, 150, 166, 181
Royal Proclamation (1763) 94–5
Rush, Richard 78
Russia 142, 145, 149, 176
Rutledge, Edward 147

Sackville, Lord George 73 *see also*
  Germain, Lord George
Sagadahoc River 3
Saint Dominique 178
Sainte-Foy, Battle of 80
Salem witch trials 17–19, 28
Salzburg 26
San Ildefonso (1800), Treaty of 181
San Miguel de los Adaes 33
Saratoga 55
Saratoga, Battle of152, 156, 161
Sardinia 55
Saskatchewan River 11, 54
Sauk tribe 92
Saulteaux tribe 92
Savannah 26, 42, 51, 84, 146,
  158–62, 167–8, 170
Savannah River 36, 89, 95
Scotland 6, 16, 23–4, 30, 35, 98,
  100, 102, 114, 124, 135–6, 141,
  171
Scots-Irish 63–4, 95, 99
Sedgwick, Edward 106–8
Seneca tribe 38, 92–4
Senegal 169
Senegambia 97
Seven Years' War 63, 68, **69–87**,
  89–90, 92, 99–100, 102, 104–5,
  111, 119, 127–8, 133, 136–7,
  139, 144, 146, 149–50
Sharp, Horatio 73
Shawnee tribe 73, 92, 94, 96
Shay's Rebellion 99
Shelburne, William, 2nd Earl of
  168–9
Shenandoah Valley 64
Shingas (Delaware chief) 72
Shirley, William 61
slavery 6, 8–10, 12–14, 24, 26–33,
  36–7, 42, 51–3, 64, 66–7, 84,
  96–8, 132–4, 169–70
slave trade 13–14, 28–30, 33, 54,
  66–7, 97–8, 170
Smith, Adam 95
Smith, Captain John 3
smugglers (American) 83
Society for the Propagation of the
  Gospel in Foreign Parts 83
*Some Reflections on the Trade
  Between Great Britain and
  Sweden* (1756) 61

Sons of Liberty 111, 140
South (colonial/American) 13, 27–9, 32, 36, 53, 60, 91, 111, 120, 130, 133, 142–5, 150, 155, 158–66, 170
South Asia 10, 20
South Carolina 17, 25–7, 29, 31–3, 36–7, 39, 44, 46–7, 51–2, 55, 57, 60, 63–4, 67, 77, 90–1, 97–8, 132–3, 147, 161–5
South Carolina Continentals 161
South Carolina General Assembly 39, 52, 67
South Carolina militia 47, 67
South Sea Bubble 44
Spain 6, 10, 32–3, 35–8, 40, 51–2, 58, 67, 86, 89, 96, 102, 114, 133, 149–50, 155, 158–9, 164–5, 169, 176, 178–81, 183
Spanish Empire 1–2, 17, 20, 23, 26, 33, 40–1, 44, 51–3, 62, 89, 96–7, 104, 127–9, 180
Spanish navy 32, 149
Spanish Succession, War of the 27, 32
Spanish West Indies 44, 51, 53
Stamp Act (1766) 61, 99, 104–8, 117
Stamp Act crisis (1765–6) 47–8, 99, 104, 106–7, 109
Staple Act (1663) 7
Staten Island 136
St Augustine 2, 33, 40, 51–3, 97
St Catherine's Island 40
St Croix River 3
Steuben, Baron von 156
Stewart, Colonel John 53
St François 90
St James's Chronicle 96
St Lawrence River 35, 55–7, 71, 76, 78–80, 139, 143
St Lawrence Valley 177
St Lucia 169
Stono Rebellion 66–7
Stony Point 160
Stormont, David, Viscount 112, 150
St Simon's Island 52, 84
Stuarts 7, 15–16, 48
Sugar Act (1764) 106–7
Sullivan, John 159
A Summary View of the Rights of British America (1774) 117
Supreme Court (US) 175–6
Susquehannock tribe 6
Sweden 42, 59–61

Tallahassee 33
Tea Act (1773) 110–11
Teach, Edward see 'Blackbeard' (Edward Teach)
Tennessee 63, 90

Third Anglo-Dutch War see Anglo-Dutch War (1672–4), Third
Thomas, Jeremiah 132
tobacco cultivation/trade 2, 7–9, 13, 23, 31, 40, 43–5, 60, 96–8, 102, 153, 179
Tobago 169
Toleration Act (1689) 17, 127
Tomochichi (representative of Lower Creeks) 23
Topsham 30
Toulmin, Joshua 127
Toulon 158
Tour of Scotland (1771) 30
Townsend, Charles 70, 72, 108, 110–11
Townsend Duties 108–10
trans-Atlantic links (commercial and political) 7, 10, 14–16, 19, 41–2, 48–9, 57–8, 60–1, 64, 66, 68, 83–4, 87, 89, 98, 105–6, 109, 184
Transportation Act (1718) 28
Transportation Acts (1720–63) 28
Trenton, Battle of 147–9
Trustees of Georgia see Georgia trustees
Tuscarora tribe 13, 36

Ulster Presbyterians see Presbyterians/Ulster
Ulster-Scots see Scots-Irish
Union (England and Scotland) see Parliamentary Union (England and Scotland)
Unitarians 118, 127
United States see USA
Universal Spectator 56
USA 67, 78, 98, 133, 138, 155, 169, 175–83
Utrecht (1713), Peace of 36, 40

Valley Forge 156
Vauban plan 56
Vaudreuil, Marquis de 81
Vergennes, Charles Gravier, Count of 149–50, 155
Vermont 34, 55, 179
Vernon, Admiral Edward 53, 59
Versailles (1783), Peace of 169
Virginia 1–3, 5–15, 17, 25–6, 28, 30–2, 37, 43, 45, 53, 63–4, 86, 90, 97, 113–14, 129–30, 133–4, 146, 153, 156, 165–6
Virginia Company 2–3
Virginia Gazette 134
Virginia House of Assembly 62
Virginia House of Burgesses 86
Virginia militia 69, 72, 76, 96, 146

Wabash River 180
Wadgaon 159
Wadsworth, Jeremiah 147
Wager Bay 54
'Walking Purchase' 37
Walpole, Horatio 63
Walpole, Sir Robert 49
Walpole ministry 47, 49
War of 1812 92, 174, 179, 182
War of American Independence see American War of Independence
Warren, Commodore Peter 56
Washington, George 63, 69, 130, 137, 141–9, 151–3, 156–8, 160–1, 165–8, 173
Waterford (Pennsylvania) 62
Wayne, Anthony 180
Webster, Noah 177
Weekly Medley 40
Weekly Packet 40
Wesley, Charles 83–4
Wesley, John 183–4
West Africa 10, 21
West Florida 33, 40, 89, 96–7, 140, 158, 169, 180
West Indies see British West Indies, French West Indies and Spanish West Indies
Westminster Parliament see British Parliament
Westminster, Peace of 8
Weston, Thomas 3
Whigs 43, 49, 115–16, 183
Whiskey Rebellion 99
Whitefield, George 84–5, 92
Whitehall 43, 126
Whitehaven 30, 153
Wilkes, John 109–10
William III, King 18, 48
Williams, Roger 4
Williamsburg (Virginia) 25
Williamsburg (St Lawrence Valley) 177
Willing, Captain James 169
Wilmington 167
Winnipeg, Lake 39, 54
Winnipegosis, Lake 54
Wolfe, General James 76, 78–9, 86
Wood, William 47, 108
Wool Act (1699) 45
Wright, James 95
Wyandot tribe 92
Wythe, George 130

Yamasee tribe 36–7, 40, 53
Yorke, Joseph 61, 100
Yorkshire Association 164
Yorktown 146, 164–8